FACT OR FICTION?

YOU DECIDE!

M ARCELLA B OWLEN

BALBOA.
PRESS
A DIVISION OF HAY HOUSE

Balboa Press books may be ordered through booksellers or by contacting:

Balboa Press
A Division of Hay House
1663 Liberty Drive
Bloomington, IN 47403
www.balboapress.com
1 (877) 407-4847

Because of the dynamic nature of the Internet, any web addresses or links contained in this book may have changed since publication and may no longer be valid. The views expressed in this work are solely those of the author and do not necessarily reflect the views of the publisher, and the publisher hereby disclaims any responsibility for them.

The author of this book does not dispense medical advice or prescribe the use of any technique as a form of treatment for physical, emotional, or medical problems without the advice of a physician, either directly or indirectly. The intent of the author is only to offer information of a general nature to help you in your quest for emotional and spiritual well-being. In the event you use any of the information in this book for yourself, which is your constitutional right, the author and the publisher assume no responsibility for your actions.

Any people depicted in stock imagery provided by Thinkstock are models, and such images are being used for illustrative purposes only. Certain stock imagery © Thinkstock.

Print information available on the last page.

ISBN: 978-1-5043-3173-9 (sc)
ISBN: 978-1-5043-3174-6 (e)

Balboa Press rev. date: 07/11/2016

Introduction

To the readers of *"Fact or Fiction? ~ You decide!"* I would like to introduce myself and prepare you for the substance of this book. My name is Marcella Bowlen and I believe God inspired me to write this book to reach others who have lived in a *"Sea of great sorrow."* The stories you will read in this book are those of real people I have known and Loved throughout my life. This book is about people who have suffered from alcohol and drug addiction and my inability to help them despite the desire in my heart to do so, due to my own afflictions. This book is about finding the answers to not only help me, but to also help those whom I love. Without a doubt, *"Fact or Fiction? ~You Decide!"* was inspired to provide hope and a way out of what God called the *"Sea of great sorrow"* for all who are seeking to obtain a better life or a closer walk with Him.

The main character in this book is a woman named Molly who is very dear to my heart. Molly and I are so close you could actually say this book is as much about my life experiences as it is Molly's. Several years ago, I was trying to find my way back to the Lord after many years of disobedience and found myself sitting in front of the computer one night writing about the people who made an impact on my life. The thought came across my mind to write a book and call it *"Fact or Fiction? ~ You Decide!"* because some of the things I have seen in my life seem more like fiction than something that could actually be real. That was about 5 years ago when I failed yet another attempt to become the person God created me to be. It took Molly's worst experience ever to bring me to my knees and finally find my way back to my Father in Heaven.

For about a year after her phenomenal experience, Molly and I went through what I like to call "Spiritual boot camp".

It took every bit of that year for me to realize, the thoughts in my head to write a book weren't my own. The Holy Spirit had been leading me to write this book for years but I kept ignoring it because I wasn't educated to be a writer and thought it was some silly fantasy in my own mind. Once I finally realized how to communicate with my Father in Heaven I realized there was no getting out of it. He wanted me to write this book and I had to be obedient if I wanted Him to do anything I asked. After months of arguing with God that I wasn't capable of doing what He asked, I finally gave in when He told me, **"I am the great teacher, let me teach you"**.

This is a book about real life Spiritual Warfare and to my surprise it turned out to be more about Molly instead of me, *"Marci"*. Once I allowed God to lead me to write the book, He led me back to Molly whom I had not spent time with in many months. Molly's days on this earth have been numbered and she may only see the rewards of what God has planned for this book in spirit. However, she will forever be with us in ***"Fact or Fiction? ~ You Decide!"***

Foreword

It was the first week of July 2008 but Molly couldn't remember the exact day. She was driving in her car when the spirit of God hit her in the gut like a piercing sword that went all the way to her heart. She had a very strong feeling to pray for her 19 year old Son Nick. As she began to pray she knew in her heart something was very wrong. Without knowing why, she began to rebuke the enemy and demand him to get away from her Son.

"He is my Son", she declared. *"He is mine and he belongs to my Lord and Savior Jesus Christ! You can't have him and I will fight you tooth and nail if you think you can!"*

She drove for miles declaring her Son unto God. Molly couldn't remember how long this battle against darkness went on; she only said it seemed to have been a long while. When the spirit of God left her that day she went on with life as usual. Finishing her work, going home and doing whatever came next; as if it was just an average day of the week. The weekend to come was the 4th of July holiday and she had plans to go to a party on Friday the 4th and fireworks Saturday the 5th. Molly went home and was preparing to go on with her plans. She never thought about what she might say to Nick because she usually only saw him in passing.

She saw him briefly that day after her experience in the car and casually asked him if there was anything going on that she should know about.

Of course his reply was, **"No, is there supposed to be something going on?"**

Molly replied with her usual *"You tell me, is there something going on? Have you been doing things you're not supposed to be doing?"*

Nick replied, **"No, have you been doing things you're not supposed to be doing?"**

Molly just dropped the subject right there, for fear he might nail her to the wall about all the things she had done wrong in her life. Besides, Nick never thought she needed to know about anything that was going on in his life and Molly thought it was too late to change things now. Nicholas was always very quiet and secretive. He rarely told his Mom or anyone else that she knew of, what was going on in his life or in his head. Nick had battled with drug addiction since he was 15 but Molly didn't find out until he was 17 and got in trouble at school. Not long before that, Molly got one of those same gut feelings that Nick was slipping away and prayed for God to help her get closer to her Son. Nick had always been a loner and Molly didn't know how to get him to come out of his shell. She was convinced he was just a quiet person like his Dad and there was nothing she could do about it. Molly expressed regrets that she didn't do allot of things different while Nick was growing up.

Molly said, *"Looking back now I realize, I was sleeping while the enemy invaded my camp and stole my son".*

CHAPTER 1

Keeping us in the darkness by keeping us undercover

Molly wasn't sure what generation of her family the curse had started with but she knew it had gone back as far as her Mother's parents.

Molly's mother was a beautiful woman inside and out. However, the dark spirits that controlled her life only allowed her beauty to shine in the darkness. Sue was the baby of six children born to Robert and Marie Reid. Robert was an alcoholic in his younger years and was known to take his paycheck to the bar before bringing it home for Marie to buy food for the children. They never lived in anything better than a shack, nor did they have anything better than hand me downs to wear. Marie did her best to find a way to feed the children even if it meant making them some gravy from borrowed lard and flour. There was six years difference in Sue and her older brother so the older kids did see harder times than Sue. Never the less, her life was as bone chilling cold as the January wind in the arctic. Sue told Molly she didn't know what it was like to have someone hug and kiss her good night before she went to bed until she met Molly's Dad Ray. She didn't know what it was like to go to the refrigerator and get what she wanted to eat when she wanted it. She didn't know what it was like to have new clothes or new shoes. She didn't know what it was like to depend on someone who was actually going to make sure everything was going to be alright until she met Ray.

Molly said, *"I didn't really understand my Mother until the Lord revealed the power of the spirit realm to me; now I understand why she was the way she was and it breaks my heart."*

Sue told Molly how Ray had taught her how to hug and say I love you. She told Molly of how cold it was in her house growing up and how she thought there was something wrong with Ray when they first got together because he gave her so much love. Sue didn't know how to love like that and often found herself running away because she felt smothered. Sue had married her first husband Leland when she was 15 because she got pregnant at 14. They stayed married long enough for Sue to have 2 children; but Sue ran from Leland like a wild cat would run from a cage. Their first child was a son they named Leon then came little Marie "named after Sue's mother" less than 2 years later. Sue was a rebellious child having children and her rebellion later showed up in them, especially Marie.

Molly said, *"Marie followed in our Mother's footsteps even though our Mother didn't raise her."*

Sue was as wild as a deer and everyone knew it; but instead of teaching her how to be a Mother her older sister took Leon when he was a year old. Sue didn't want to let him go because she loved him very much; but Sue's Mother convinced her to let Lorene and Roy adopt Leon because she was too young and didn't want to stay with Leland. At that time Sue was already pregnant again with Marie and feeling like her life was over. She knew she didn't want to stay with Leland and didn't want the responsibility of a child but didn't want to let another one go to her Sister. She couldn't handle the pain of loving a child and losing it again. So Sue tried everything she could think of to have a miscarriage. She jumped off of high places and she drank things she thought would make her lose the baby but nothing worked. In her mind it would be easier to not have the child at all, than to have it and then go through the pain of losing it.

Sue was oppressed with spirits of depression, confusion and rebellion that later opened the door for the spirit of addiction. The Lord had given Sue a beautiful spirit of love and charity when she was born and the enemy knew it. He knew Sue would be greatly loved by many people and he also knew he could use that love to destroy many lives. All he had to do was put the thought in her mind she was just another burden on her Mother who already had more kids than she could feed. Satan had already afflicted Sue's parents with a spirit of addiction and poverty so it was easy to use the love she had to destroy her. When Sue met Leland there is no doubt she must have thought this could be her only way out of that unhappy home. She most likely thought she would have complete control of her life once she left home as the spirit of rebellion controlled her thoughts. However, Sue had no idea her destructive thoughts were controlled by tormenting spirits or that those same spirits that controlled her parent's house would follow her wherever she went.

In less than a year after Lorene and Roy adopted Leon, Sue had Marie. By this time the spirit of addiction had attached itself to Sue and she was wilder than she had ever been; so Leland did most of the caring for Marie. Marie was only about two when Sue had moved on to someone else and took off to Florida where she got pregnant with her third child. While she was gone Lorene had Marie and took her to the doctor to find out she was malnourished. The Doctor told Lorene she needed to get a court order to take Marie away from Sue and Leland. Since Lorene and Roy already had Leon they felt it would only be right to take his sister so they could be raised together in a stable home. Leland agreed to sign the adoption papers because he was so broken over Sue he knew he couldn't take care of Marie anymore. Sue came back from Florida to find out Lorene had gotten a court order to take Marie from her.

Within no time, Sue found out she was pregnant with baby #3 and wasn't sure if it belonged to Leland or the man she ran away with to Florida. Still to this day no one really knows why the third baby girl was given up at birth. All Sue ever said was that she had no way to care for her and thought the people she gave her to would let her be in her life. Sue always hoped that child would hunt her down some day but her adoptive parents had taken her very far away when they heard Sue was looking for her and that day never came until Sue was long in her grave. Sue had found out that Robin was going to the same school with a little blonde haired girl named Frannie, so she went to the school during recess to see if it could be her long lost daughter. She took one look at her and knew she was her child so later that night Sue put Robin up to asking Frannie to spend the night with her. When Frannie went home and asked her adoptive parents if she could spend the night with a friend from school named Robin, they figured out Sue had found her and moved to another state. Sue never found Frannie again but Frannie eventually found her siblings in 2005 when her daughter decided to find her biological Grandmother. Frannie's relationship with her siblings was brief and Molly wonders if she is even still alive. Frannie kept in touch for a few years but then suddenly stopped calling and has not been heard from since 2008.

Marie had a really hard time after she was taken from Sue & Leland. Leon didn't like having Marie around getting his attention and Marie cried for Leland whom she called Mommy all of the time.

Lorene said, ***"Marie would sit in her little rocking chair for hours rocking her dolls and crying for her Mommy, which was really Leland."***

No one really understood how bad the adoption had affected Marie until she got older and started asking Sue why she didn't want her. Leland died of a drug over dose after Sue married Ray, some said he never got over Sue and just took too many pills to dull the pain.

That is when things started getting really bad for the kids. Leon was about 14 and Marie was about 12. Although Lorene and Roy were known as their parents the kids always knew who their biological parents were. By this time things had started going bad with Lorene and Roy's marriage and the kids were drawing closer to Sue. For the first time in her life Sue had a stable home with money to buy clothes and food for her children. Sue had already had 5 kids by the time she married Ray but Robin was the only child she still had to call her own. Lorene and Roy had adopted Leon and Marie, Frannie was adopted out to an acquaintance that hid her from Sue; so when Robin was born, Sue was determined no one would take her away. So finally Sue's mother Marie decided to help her raise one of these children and did most of the caring for Robin until Sue met Ray.

However, there was yet another child before Sue met Ray that she had by the only man Sue had truly ever loved named Cal. Cal was a very talented musician and Sue loved to sing and dance, so he stole her heart away like no one ever had a chance before. By this time Sue was in her early twenties and was a very beautiful woman that didn't know her potential because her soul was tormented with shame. Both Sue and Cal were very shy and backward until they got a little liquid courage in them; but they were both the center of attention when they did. Needless to say, they were too much alike to make things work and there were far too many jealous fights that destroyed their love. Sue got into trouble for writing bad checks to survive and was sentenced to two years in prison when she was 8 months pregnant with her fourth child. Sue and Cal's sister were the best of friends, so Sue trusted her to adopt the baby boy Daelee and let her be a part of his life when she got out of prison. To Sue's surprise, Cal's sister wouldn't allow her to be a part of his life so Sue only got to see Daelee a few times when he was a little tot and Cal snuck her into his mother's house to see him.

Molly said, *"I will never forget the love and the pain in my mother's eyes when she would talk about Daelee. He was her love child that she thought about all the time. She often told the story of the last time she ever got to see him. He was somewhere between 2 & 3 years old when Cal took her to his mother's house to see him. She said Daelee was*

5

already carrying around a guitar, so she knew he would be able to play as good as his daddy one day. She always wondered if he would come and find her when he got 18 and prayed every day that he would. She wondered if anyone ever told him who she was and if they did, what did they tell him about her? She wondered if he knew how much she loved him and how bad she wanted to keep him or at least be a part of his life. I remember hating Cal when I was a little girl because he would use my Mother's love for Daelee to lure her away from my dad. She would often run away with Cal for a few days in hopes she could see Daelee but she never got to see him again. Daelee never came looking for her before she died because he never really knew anything about her. His cousin who was his sister by adoption told him he was adopted when he was young. I'm not really sure who it was that told him about her but he later told me all he knew was she was a worthless woman so he had no desire to ever find her. He grew up knowing Cal was his real dad and I think it was really sad Cal never even bothered to tell him about our mother. Now I'm sure Cal loved our mother in his own selfish way but if he couldn't have mom, he wasn't about to let her have anything to do with Daelee. I remember seeing her cry when she would come back after running off with Cal to see Daelee because she knew how much she had hurt me, my sisters and our dad for nothing! Cal would keep her away from us for days promising to let her see Daelee but never did. Mom knew Cal could have found a way to let her see Daelee if he really wanted to so she fell for his promises to let her see him every time. Eventually the love she had for Cal grew to hate because she blamed him that she lost Daelee. If only he had been the man my dad was, she would have never went to prison in the first place because she wouldn't have had to write bad checks to survive. After Daelee turned 18, Cal told mom Daelee didn't want anything to do with her so she stopped running off with him. It was about 1998 when our sister Lynn found Daelee's adopted mother and we got to finally meet him. Mom had been gone for several years by the time we found him. Daelee didn't seem to have much interest in being a part of our life but he told us not to take it personal. Shortly after we met him, he got married and invited us to his wedding reception. That was when we got to meet his adoptive mother for the first time. She was a beautiful lady that was full of remorse for keeping him away from us. She told me that day how much she loved our mother and how bad she felt for doing her wrong with Daelee. She said mom was so beautiful and gracious that she was afraid Daelee would love mom more than her if she allowed him to be in her life. She said she would give anything if she could turn back time; because our mom didn't deserve to be treated like that and she realized that Daelee would always resent her for what she had done. I pray someday Daelee will see how blessed he was to be loved so much by two beautiful women and he will find a way to forgive them for all of their mistakes. It breaks my heart that our mother never got to be a part of his life or see him play his guitar; but I know she can see him now and I know how happy she is he finally got to meet his siblings. He never got to meet Robin but he did come when we met Franny; which was an amazing moment I know our mother was smiling down on.

Robin was the only child Sue had to care for when she married Ray and then they had Molly and the youngest child Lynn together. Leon was 13 years older than Molly, Marie was 11 years older and Robin was 7 years older than Molly.

Molly said, *"I can't remember a time when Leon and Marie weren't in our life; we always knew they were our siblings and they were always around. We always wished Franny and Daelee could have been there too and wondered if they would have loved us as much as we loved them even though they weren't even there. It is so strange to love someone you have never even met but we all just did. Franny & Daelee didn't grow up always having that love for us because they didn't know we existed until we found each other; so I don't know if their love could have possibly been as strong for us when we met as our love was for them. We all grew up loving them. Even Leon and Marie who were older than them and were also adopted, grew up wishing they were a part of our life and just longing for the day they would come and find us. Daelee got to meet Marie but not Robin because Robin wasn't around when we found Daelee. Franny got to meet Robin but not Marie because Marie had already passed away when Franny found us. I would have given anything if I could have had just one photo with all of us in it!"*

Molly didn't remember Leland although he had been to her house when she was a toddler but she remembered people talking about him.

Molly said, *"I remember people talking about Leland so much it felt like I knew him, I always just loved him and didn't know why."*

Within a few years after Leland's death Marie and Leon were on their way to being parents their selves and repeating the patterns of their parents. First Marie got pregnant with Tammy and married at 15 just like Sue. Then Leon got married when he was 18 and had a baby girl named Kara in the same month Marie had her second child Jimmy.

Molly said, *"I was a week shy of being 5 when Marie had Tammy; 8 months later before I turned 6 my Mom had my younger sister Lynn; 3 months after I turned 6, along came Kara and Jimmy in the same month, I was surrounded by babies."*

Although Leon had married a good girl who took good care of Kara, Marie wasn't even close to being ready to care for her two children. Lorene had moved in with Sue and Ray when her marriage ended with Roy. Every day Marie brought her two children to the house where her two Moms lived because she was still a child herself at only 17. Molly remembered carrying all of the babies around on her hip because she didn't like to hear them cry.

Molly said, *"Things started getting really bad when we lived in that house; I think that is when the spirits of darkness really started to take over my loved ones. I remember that house always being dark because my Mother put up foam back curtains to keep the sun light from coming in. Now I know it was a spirit of depression that controlled my Mother because dark spirits don't like the sun light. People who are depressed often keep the curtains closed so it will be dark in the house. Now I understand why my Mother always wanted the house to be dark and didn't like to be awake in the day time. The spirits of darkness don't like the sun light because the sun light is the light of the Lord. I remember my little sister crying in the bedroom while my Mom was in bed. The bedroom would be so dark when I went in there that I had to feel my way to the crib to give her a bottle. I was too little to get her out of the crib and I always felt scared when I went in that room. The spirits of darkness were controlling the adults in the house and trying to attach themselves to the children I'm sure. Marie lived a couple of blocks down the street from our house and when she didn't show up with the kids I knew I better go check on them. I remember going to her apartment and finding the children unattended many times while we lived in that house. I remember one day little Jimmy was in his crib crying, in a dirty diaper that had his whole body soaking wet. Little Tammy, only a little over a year old herself, was trying to feed him a bottle of spoiled milk. Marie went to a party upstairs the night before and left them with their Dad who was still passed out drunk when I went to check on them. I wasn't tall enough to get little Jimmy out of the crib so I tried to clean him up through the bars. I remember little Tammy staring at me while I tried to clean Jimmy up and calm him down. It was so hot in there and flies were blowing all over those kids, I knew I had to get them out! Tammy was old enough to walk so I took her back to my house and got my Aunt Lorene to come help me get Jimmy out of the crib. Aunt Lorene got him out of the crib and went looking for Marie while I cleaned him up."*

Things like that happened quite a bit so Molly just knew she had to watch out for the little ones. Sue always said Molly was born old; because she somehow instinctively knew how to take care of things when she was only a child herself. Most of us can't even imagine depending on a 5 year old to take care of the little babies and toddlers; but the adults in Molly's family somehow knew they could trust her to take care of things. It didn't take long before the children were taken to a foster home which cost Ray and Roy allot of money to get them back.

Molly said, "*I remember the day the kids got to come home, the whole family went to see them and they were all dressed up in nice clothes, sitting on the couch like little angels. I remember thinking to myself it looked like they were better off where they were at. Everyone was so worried they had been mistreated at the foster home because they were being so quiet and good, like they were afraid to move. I remember thinking, I bet they are afraid to be back here and I wondered if they remembered how bad it was before they were taken. The sad part is; no one in the family thought there was anything wrong with the way things were because we all loved each other so much. When a person is oppressed by spirits of darkness they don't even realize how screwed up things are and my whole family was oppressed with unclean spirits of addiction, tormenting spirits of depression, confusion and poverty.*"

It didn't take long before Marie was divorced and living with Sue and Ray off and on from there on out until the kids went to live with their Dad. Little Jimmy went to live with his Dad at about 4 years old but Tammy continued to stay with Marie and was raised mostly at Sue and Ray's house until she was about 12. Once the kids went to live with their Dad they didn't look back. They never wanted to come to visit or have anything to do with their Mom's side of the family again.

Molly said, "*I remember how much it hurt the family that the kids just acted like we didn't exist once they went to their Dad's. Everyone could sort of understand why little Jimmy didn't come around because he was so young when he went to live with his Dad, but no one understood what happened with Tammy. I mean, I know it was hard on her that she had to live at our house most of the time because Marie couldn't keep a stable home for her; but she was always loved at our house.*"

Tammy and Lynn were only 8 months a part so everyone treated them like twins. Whatever Lynn got, Tammy got also; and they were always treated the same. However, no matter how much love they tried to give to Tammy she never seemed to receive it.

Molly said, *"Tammy always seemed like she hated being at our house no matter what we did for her. When she went to live with her Dad she walked out on our family as if someone had done her wrong and never looked back. We never understood why she didn't love us enough to ever want to come and spend the night or even call to say hi, she barely even kept in touch with Marie. Now that I understand the spirit realm I understand Tammy was being tormented with the same spirits that tormented Marie. The adversary speaks to us in our thoughts; he is the master of confusion and the father of lies. He sends tormenting spirits to speak to our children from the time they are old enough to understand anything. As a matter of fact, whatever spirits are tormenting a Mother while she is pregnant will also oppress her child in the womb. Marie felt un-loved, un-wanted and insecure from the time she was in the womb because of the spirits that controlled our Mother while she was pregnant with Marie. When Marie was taken from Leland and Sue she was attacked by spirits of control and felt abandoned, those spirits then opened the door for a spirit of rebellion that eventually destroyed her life. Tammy was so oppressed by all those spirits from the time she was born she couldn't receive the love that was given to her in our house. Those lying, tormenting spirits of darkness made her think she was un-loved, un-wanted and abandoned by everyone just like they did her Mother. I only wish I had known then what I know now so I could have cast those spirits out of our home in the name of Jesus."*

Tammy met a good man when she was young. He came from a good Christian family and had a good support system unlike Tammy had ever known. She fell in love with Darren and although she admired his parents she was afraid to let them know who she really was or where she came from for fear they wouldn't want her to be with their son. Tammy spent years hiding from her past, avoiding her family and wishing the love she had for her Mother would just go away. Although she loved Marie she had so much resentment for her that she just couldn't forgive her for the childhood she tried so hard to forget. Tammy swore she would never abandon her children the way Marie had abandoned her. She wanted so badly to forgive Marie but her forgiveness would only come when Marie had changed. Tammy built up so many walls around the part of her heart that loved Marie she could never see anything good in Marie no matter how hard Marie tried.

When Tammy started having children Marie tried the best she could to reach out to Tammy and be a Grandma to the kids; but Tammy was too afraid to let her be a real Grandma. She was afraid to leave Marie alone with the kids because she didn't trust her to keep a good eye on them. Over the years they had many fights over Tammy not trusting Marie to watch the kids. Tammy would of course blame it on Darren that the kids could only stay the night with his Mother; but Marie still felt like she wasn't good enough to be in their life. Their relationship had always been up and down like a roller coaster ride. Tammy would get mad at Marie and say things to Darren about what a bad mother Marie was. Darren had no understanding of any Mother behaving the way Marie had behaved and would then say bad things about Marie when Tammy was getting along with her. Then Tammy would get mad at Darren for what he had said about her Mother because she didn't understand she had formed his bad opinion of Marie. Tammy didn't understand how she could forgive Marie long enough to let her back in until she got hurt again but Darren couldn't. Darren couldn't understand why Tammy would even want to let Marie back in after all the times she had hurt her. Then Tammy would get mad at Marie again because she felt Darren was right and Marie wasn't worth giving her the time of day. Then Marie would get hurt because Tammy was pushing her away and say something to hurt Tammy back. The adversary must have really been getting his kicks from all that division he had created for all those years.

Tammy and Marie had been in a fight and not speaking for a couple of weeks before Marie passed away.

Molly said, *"I'll never forget the pain in Tammy's eyes when she saw her Mom laying in that hospital bed, brain dead from a drug over dose. I knew her pain because I had been in a fight with my Mom for a couple of weeks before she died. Thank God, me and my Mom had made up a few days before she died but I still couldn't get over the fact that I wasn't speaking to my Mother the last 2 weeks of her life, Although my Mother didn't die of a drug over dose she might have survived the pneumonia had she have not destroyed her liver with alcohol and drugs. I could relate to Tammy's pain and knew exactly how she felt. All of their fights were because Tammy loved Marie so much and just wanted to change her; but now she would never have the chance to tell her how she really felt."*

Although Molly knew Tammy's pain and knew it would have a negative impact on her life, Darren didn't understand. When Marie first passed away Molly tried to reach out to Tammy because she knew Tammy would need someone to talk to that understood what she was going through; but Tammy pushed Molly away and pretended to be o.k. It took a while before the grief began to destroy Tammy's life but once it got a hold of her she was on a HWY to hell. Tammy had 3 young children when Marie passed away with one who would be on her way to being born shortly after Marie had been laid to rest. Molly also knew how hard it would be for Tammy to give birth to a child her Mother would never see because she had been there too. Tammy tried her best to cover up her pain. She went on with her everyday life of being a house wife, taking the older kids to school, staying home and taking care of the house with the younger ones. But night after night she couldn't sleep from the grief. When the house got quiet the grief set in and Tammy would stay awake with her grief while her family slept.

As the days went by Tammy became more and more tired from the depression. She couldn't wait for the weekend to come so she could get a break from the kids when they went to Darren's parent's house on Saturday. She tried to fill the empty spot in her heart with material things and when that didn't work she turned to alcohol and drugs. It didn't take long before she found a pick me up drug that helped her to get through the day; but that kept her up even more at night. She became unhappy with being a wife and a mother. There was something brewing inside of her that was turning her into the woman she tried so hard to forget.

Molly said, *"If Tammy was anything like I was when my parents died; I'm sure she wanted to be like Marie so she could show Marie how much she loved her. Those tormenting spirits told me if I were like them, they would see how much I loved them and I believed that crap. For years I thought I was going to show my parents I was better than them and when they died all I could think about was being just like them. In a way I think that is what happened with Marie. I think being adopted made Marie feel like she had lost her parents. Therefore, if she acted just like them they would see how much she loved them and they would love her back. Those thoughts we have when we lose someone are nothing but a trick from the adversary to get us to look for something to ease our pain in hopes of bringing back the one we lost."*

Just as he always does, the adversary uses the love we have for someone against us. He used the love Tammy had for Marie to destroy the love she had for Darren. It was no wonder Darren didn't understand what Tammy was going through because she had hid the pain of her childhood from everyone. Sure, she told Darren what a worthless Mom she had and how bad her childhood was; but instead of expressing her pain with tears that showed her love for her Mom, she expressed it with harsh words against Marie. The spirit of rebellion that was on Marie had attached itself to Tammy when she was a child. Therefore, when Tammy felt pain it made her angry and she rebelled against it. It is hard for another person who has never experienced that same kind of pain to see beyond the anger and callused exterior. Darren didn't understand Tammy's pain so he couldn't help her with it or understand when she began to change. Their relationship began to suffer and was slowly but surely destroyed just as the enemy planned it to be when he stole the life of Marie from her family.

Molly said, *"The enemy stole my Sisters life from her and all of us who loved her and now I must find a way to destroy his cohorts before they destroy Tammy. I know if I could get Tammy to listen to me it is not too late for her to get her husband and her children back. I know the enemy is trying his best to take her out just like he took Marie so this same curse will be passed on to her children; and there is no way I will let that happen. I believe where there is still life there is still hope and we can do all things through Christ who strengthens us. I will not stop praying or trying to get that message through to Tammy because she is my niece and I love her! More importantly she has 4 children who love and need her as much as we loved and needed our Moms who left us too young."*

Molly always knew she had to do something to change the way things were in her family, she just didn't know what to do until it was too late for her parents and siblings.

Molly said, *"I may not have had time to change things for my parents or siblings when I was young but I darn sure plan on changing things for my children and what family I have left from now on. My parents died young and so did Marie because of the spirits that controlled their life; I will fight to my death before they will take out another one of my family members before their time."*

Just as Molly said, tormenting spirits attach themselves to our children in the womb. If a Mother is under attack of a tormenting spirit so shall their unborn child be. There are 3 kinds of spirits; unclean spirits, tormenting spirits and evil spirits. These spirits rarely work alone. Once they have attached themselves to a person they have the power to open the door for others to come in. Most often it starts with tormenting spirits that put thoughts in our mind about our desires to be loved and accepted......"No one loves me"...... "I'm not good enough for that"...... "I'm not pretty enough for him"....... "If she knew about my family, she wouldn't like me"....... "If I want any friends I better not let them know where I live"......... "I'm always going to be poor, if I want to have anything I'm going to have to steal it".......... "If I smoke this pot I will feel better and have more friends"....... "I'm so much funnier when I drink"...... "I'm so much more attractive when I drink and I get more attention."...... "If there was really a God why would he let this happen?"......... "God doesn't love me, I'm not good enough for him to love"........... "There is no such thing as going to hell, we already live in hell here on earth"........ "There is no heaven or hell, when you die that is it, just like sleeping without waking up"........ "Who cares if I die? I would rather be asleep than awake anyway."

When a spirit of depression gets a hold of a person it will invite the spirit of good time Charlie to make them feel better......FOR A WHILE!!! The spirits of depression, control, lies and confusion are all tormenting spirits. The spirit of addiction that I like to call "good time Charlie" is an un-clean spirit who will eventually open the door to your soul, "which is where your thoughts come from in your mind" to evil spirits who are out to take your life and the lives of others. Evil spirits are those that tell you it doesn't matter if you live or die because no one loves you anyway so you might as well do what you want and live until you die. Eventually they put thoughts in your mind of suicide because your life has got so bad it isn't worth living anymore. They often put thoughts in your mind to kill the people who have hurt you; and that is why people murder other people and kill themselves. Depending on the person, it can sometimes take years before their soul gets so weak that the evil spirits can talk them into doing something terrible. It can also depend on the family history. All dark spirits invite other dark spirits to come when they can't get a job done. They attach themselves to families and they are passed down from generation to generation "this is known as a generational curse in the bible"; but otherwise known as "heredity". The only way to stop these spirits of darkness is for someone in that family to seek the power of the Holy Spirit to break the strong holds of darkness afflicting that family.

Since the adversary knows the heart of all mankind is to love and to be loved, he uses our love to break us down. If we feel un-loved or un-wanted we build walls around our heart so we don't get hurt. When a person has walls built up around their heart they won't let love in because if they don't feel it, they can't get hurt by it. No one likes to feel pain and our body is designed to go into shock and shut down if we are experiencing too much pain. Therefore, our emotions are designed the same way and Satan knows that. This is why he uses the people we love the most to bring us down; because if we didn't love a person, what they do would have no effect on our emotions. However, the spirit that keeps us alive came from our Father in Heaven. That spirit desires to enjoy the presence of Love as it did when it were in heaven with our Father of Love. Therefore, we cannot be complete or happy without love in our lives.

When the adversary sends the unclean spirits of addiction to attach themselves to a person, he knows the addicted person will eventually crush the heart of all who love them. Now even more doors are open for tormenting spirits to come in and destroy the souls of many more. It is a vicious and repetitive cycle that can only be broken through prayer and fasting.

Molly said, "The bible teaches us, when a curse is put on a family it will pass down to the third or fourth generation; I'm sure our family has suffered through 4 generations of this curse and it is time for it to be broken. We have been cursed with spirits of addiction and depression that have opened the doors for countless other spirits to torment the *souls of our family. I lost my parents, I lost Marie and many others whom I have loved because there was no one there to teach them that their destructive thoughts are not their own. No one in our family ever taught me about the power of the spirit realm or how to control those destructive thoughts in my mind. It took the Love I had for my Son to give me the desire to fight the spirits that oppressed him. But you can't fight what you can't see and if you don't know it is there, you can't see it. It took me many hours of prayer and studying the word of God to understand the spirit realm and how it destroys our lives. The word of God say's we can do all things through Christ who strengthens us; and if we cast our burdens upon the Lord He will sustain us. The bible also say's the word of God is as powerful as a two edged sword against the enemy. I feel the Lord has called me to learn His word to fight this battle of freedom for my family. I feel in my spirit that one by one they will be set free of this generational curse and live life more abundantly. Praise be to the Lord that curse shall be broken from our future generations through the Power in the Blood of the Lamb! For all those who believe in Christ our Lord, let not only they believe in their heart but also confess with their lips, that they will overcome the forces of darkness and be set free!"*

CHAPTER 2

The Sea of Great Sorrow

Molly got saved when she was a very small child. She couldn't remember a time when she didn't know about God or believe He was real. He was always very real to her and her daughter Sara inherited her same faith, but that wasn't always the case with her son Nick.

Although Molly had been filled with the Holy Spirit when she was 10 years old and had received spiritual gifts from God; she strayed away at age 13 when her parents moved her away from the church she dearly loved. As most teenagers do, Molly rebelled and thought she would show her parents just what a mistake they had made. Molly's parents were alcoholics, so she blamed their alcohol problems for the reason she had to move from her little small town church and friends.

Molly said, "I thought if I couldn't beat them, I would join them!"

She thought, they would see what they had done to her and move her back home. But Molly was as good at hiding her habits as her Son later became. Her parents thought she was far too good of a kid to ever do the things they were doing, just like Molly thought about Nick.

Molly understood everything that Nick was going through because she had been there herself. How could she protect Nick from the demons that tormented his mind, when she was still struggling to understand and deal with her own demons? Molly wondered if Nick would someday be like her and believe in the Lord to keep him from being the addict her parents and siblings all were; or would he continue to follow the road of his natural father who was trapped inside his own head like a fish in a net. Molly couldn't stand the thoughts of Nick not believing or having any faith because she knew that was the only thing that had helped her to overcome the struggles she had been through. Molly was the one who had raised Nick and Sarah all alone, so she couldn't help but wonder where she went wrong with sharing her gift of faith with Nick.

Molly said, *"Looking back I wasn't raising my children alone because God was always there with me. However, I regret not making it perfectly clear that they really did have a Father at home; their Father in heaven who was always there anytime they called upon His name. If only I had stayed close to the Lord and never strayed from Him I would have been a better Mother."*

Then she smiled and said, *"The only good thing that came from me straying from God is my two kids. If I hadn't strayed away from Him, I would have never wound up with Joey and then I might not have my two kids. I just wish I would have gone back to serving the Lord allot sooner than I did so I would have had a better chance of none of this stuff ever happening to my Son."*

Molly never stopped believing or talking to God but her relationship with Him was weak to say the least.

Molly said, *"All my prayers were selfish, asking God to take care of me and the kids but never waiting to hear his voice or asking Him what I could do for Him. But to God I give the glory for taking care of Nick and Sarah when I wasn't able to. It was like the foot prints in the sand, because it was then that he carried us."*

Nicholas was the oldest child, he was 6 when Molly and Joey parted ways; Sarah had just turned 2. By the grace and mercy of God Molly and Joey never married.

Molly said, *"It didn't take long after Nick was born before I realized I had made a terrible mistake; but before I knew it there was Sarah and 8 years of my life had gone by."*

Molly remembered how she prayed for the Lord to remove Joey from her life. She knew it wasn't the will of God for a believer to enter into marriage with an unbeliever because the word of God tells us to not be unequally yoked. She had spent over 8 years of her life trying to convince this man to believe in God, if not for his self, at least for the sake of the children.

Molly said, *"As the old saying goes, if you lay with dogs you're going to get fleas, I got fleas."*

The longer she stayed with him the weaker she got in her faith. The harder she tried to convince him God was real, the more his doubt got in her head. She knew she was growing to hate him and that wasn't a good thing; but she didn't know how to get away without feeling the guilt over her children. He brought her down in so many ways she didn't even realize how low she had gotten until several years after she had gotten away from him.

Molly said, *"I just remember being so miserable that I prayed every night for a year for the Lord to either change him or remove him from my life; needless to say, he didn't change."*

Looking back on the years she spent running away from the word of God, Molly realized she had brought all of this pain upon herself.

Molly said, *"Thank God, for the forgiveness and mercy that came from the shedding of the innocent blood of Christ on the cross. I can't imagine spending a year in bondage for every day I was disobedient like the children of Israel did. The years I spent in sin and disobedience were bondage enough to my soul and spirit; God knows I don't ever want to go back to that. I can't help but wonder if this is what the bible is talking about when it lists all of the people who will have their part in the lake of fire. Adulterers, drunkards, liars, fornicators etc.... I've often heard people say the bible contradicts itself because in some parts it condemns us all to hell but in other parts it says all those who believe in Christ shall be forgiven. I've even heard people say, "It sounds like those who believe in Christ have a free ticket to sin". But I don't believe that is true, nor do I believe some of the scriptures are fully understood by most people. Anyone who has ever lived in a life of sin knows what it is like to live in hell on earth. If you look at the life of a drunk it is easy to understand how their life on earth can be interpreted as being a living hell. Regardless of whether they turn their life over to Christ and get redeemed of their sins at the last minute; they have still had their part in hell on this earth. The bible tells us that hell or the "lake of fire" as it is otherwise known, is a place of torment that was actually created for Satan and the angels he took with him when he fell from grace. This place of torment can only be avoided by accepting Christ as your savior and accepting the gift of pardon He suffered and died to give. However, even those who believe are often known to stray away from the path of righteousness and I believe if there was no misery or torment that followed our sin, many of us would never make it back to the right path. The bible says, "God chastises those whom He loves" and I Praise Him for that chastisement that never allows me to get too far astray."*

Molly went on to say, *"My life reminds me of a song we used to sing in that little country church when I was a child. "I don't know why Jesus loves me; I don't know why He cares. I don't know why he sacrificed his life! Oh, but I'm glad, I'm so glad he did". Jesus was with me through it all! When I was good, when I was bad, when I was sick and when I was sad, He was always there. I guess when the scripture said he would never leave us or forsake us that must have meant the sinners too."*

Molly realized it wasn't only that God had carried her through the sand and brought her through the darkness, but there was also Nick and Sarah He carried too. As she looked back on all those years when she was too low to lift them up, tears filled her eyes.

Molly said, "When I worked 3 jobs to pay the bills, it was Him who kept my kids safe from day light till dark. When I was leaving my kids with teenagers while I went out at midnight with my friends to party on the weekends, it was Him who took care of them. When I was too tired or too sick to play with them, it was Him who brought them joy. When I was too broke to buy food or clothes, it was him that made a way for me to find an extra cash paying job or get another credit card. When their school work became too complicated for me to figure out, it was Him who blessed them with the intelligence to get it right and make good grades. It was Him who delivered my son out of the hands of the enemy, when the enemy tried to take his life and it was Him who gave me the strength and the courage to fight the good fight".

Molly's eyes were filled with tears but her heart was filled with joy when she talked about all the Good Lord had done for her and her children.

Molly always knew the Lord was there for her. She remembered back when she was a child herself and all the times He had been her shelter and her safety. Molly's parents were very kind and loving people who taught her to be kind and loving to others, but still they suffered from alcohol and drug addiction. There were many times she could recall being afraid they wouldn't make it home. She couldn't remember a time when she didn't pray for their safety and salvation.

Molly remembered first going to church with her aunt & uncle when she was about 2 or maybe 3. She remembered her Mom and Dad taking her to Sunday school a few times when she was 3 or 4 but that was never consistent.

Molly said, "There was this really nice preacher who tried his best to get them in church; but he only got them to go a few times when the church was having an Easter contest. My Dad really loved to gamble and he loved winning contest so they stopped going after the Easter contest was over".

Molly's Mom taught her a lot about the Lord but her Dad never said too much one way or the other. He always told her she would need to ask her Mom about that kind of stuff because she knew more about it than he did. When Molly was 7 her Grandma was diagnosed with cancer and her mother almost lost her mind. At first her mom thought she could run to the church and make everything alright. She took Molly to church and insisted she be baptized right away.

Molly said, "*looking back, I think my Mom must have thought she had to make up for lost time and do all the things she knew she should have been doing before, if she wanted God to heal her Mother. Not only that, but of course in the 1970's it seemed like every Preacher in every church was preaching the Lord was coming soon and the world was going to end any day. Now I know from experience when you are about to lose one of your parents it feels like the world is coming to an end. Or at least you wish it would come to an end for you before it does for them. I think my Mom was just doing the best she could to make sure we would all be saved when Jesus came. I'm sure she didn't really want to live without her mom and she knew enough about the bible to know she had to teach us all she could in the little time she thought she had. She wanted her mother to be healed so desperately bad she must have felt if she did all the right things she would have a much better chance of God answering her prayers. Never the less, Mom made sure she found someone who was willing to baptize me immediately and I will never forget how happy she was that night".*

Molly's Grandma didn't make it long after they found out she had cancer. She passed away in only 3 months after her diagnosis and that is when Molly's nightmare began. That was when her mostly happy little childhood turned into a mostly miserable life. Her mom was so grief stricken, she only came to life when she was drowning her sorrows in alcohol. Most of the time she stayed in bed knocked out on sleeping pills that were so strong, one could sedate a horse. Molly remembers thinking those pills were little green and red devils. The family called them "Big Reds" or "Big Greens". It started with the "Big Reds" and then moved up to the "Big Greens" when her body got immune to the lesser strength.

Molly remembered her mother would take a whole month supply within a few days and it would take her an entire week to fully recover. She remembered all the tears she and her older sister had shed when they couldn't get their mom to wake up.

Molly said, *"We used to get pitchers of water and pour them over her head to get her to open her eyes for just a moment, so we would know she was still alive. Mom always had a problem with the sleeping pills for as long as I could remember but it got 100 times worse after Grandma died."*

Not long after Molly's Grandma passed away her parents moved them to a small country town where she met a lady who took her to church.

Molly said, *"I don't know what would have happened to me if we hadn't moved to Stilesville and I hadn't found that church."*

When her parents first moved to Stilesville her Mother tried to find her way back to God, she called it "getting on the wagon". She took Molly to that little country church where she met the lady who lived over the hill that continued to take her to church. It didn't take long before her mom "fell off the wagon" and got even worse than she was before. It seemed like after they moved to Stilesville everything got worse. Her Dads drinking and gambling got worse. Her mom's drinking and taking pills got worse. Their fighting got worse and her older Sister Robin whom she depended so much upon went completely wild at the age of 15. Now it was just Molly and all the younger kids that she had to take care of at 8 years old. She had a younger Sister Lynn who was 3, a niece who was 4 and a nephew who was 2 when they moved to Stilesville.

Her niece and nephew moved in with them because her older Sister Marie was getting a divorce at the time. They went from having nice things to having no things! Molly's Grandpa came to stay with them after he had a stroke but her mom was usually too messed up to take care of him either. Needless to say, that left Molly to do that job as well.

Molly said, *"My best memories in that house were when Grandpa came to stay. He would always ask me to sing church songs and read him the bible. He would always say thank you when I made him something to eat and he thought I made the best lumpy cream of wheat in the world. He would play the harmonica while I sang and tell me what a good kid I was when I brushed his hair. Yes, those were some of the best days of my life in Stilesville."*

Molly didn't remember playing much as a kid because there was too many things to do and way too much to worry about to feel like playing. Her Dad taught her to write checks when she was in 3rd grade because her mom couldn't stay in her right mind long enough to pay the bills and he got tired of paying reconnect fees. The younger kids weren't old enough to wash their own clothes. So Molly usually had to wash them in the sink and hang them on the line because they couldn't keep the washer or dryer working for long. Their lawn mower never seemed to work for long either so the yard would get too high with weeds to go outside and play in the summer time. Although her Dad installed heating and air conditioning for a living, he never seemed to get too hot in the summer or too cold in the winter so they didn't have a furnace or A.C. either. In the winter Molly had to chop the wood and build the fires when her Dad wasn't home because her Mom only knew how to start fires with shoes.

Molly laughed when she told the story of her mom starting the fires with shoes. She said, *"Mom found it much easier to start a fire with shoes because she could light the shoe strings and then the rubber would melt to the wood and get it going. Dad taught me how to chop the wood and make it small enough to start the fire so we could keep warm without losing our shoes to the wood stove when he wasn't home. The really sad part is both my parents were far too good and way too smart to live that kind of life but they were so afflicted with the addiction it seemed to be the best they could do. Looking back on my life I realize now, how very hard Satan tried to destroy my entire family. I guess God had another plan because no matter how hard he tried, he never got the job done!"*

When Molly was ten years old the Lord filled her with the Holy Spirit and she said, *"The Holy Spirit knows how to pray even when we don't."*

Molly never stopped praying for her family even though she rebelled against them and against God when she was 13.

Molly said, *"Most back slid Christians don't talk to God as much as I did because they don't think he will listen. Religion will teach us that God doesn't want to hear from us unless we are perfect and I'm glad I rebelled against that idea and kept right on talking. Believe me, there were times I didn't feel worthy to say His name but He was the only one I had that I knew beyond the shadow of a doubt I could trust to help me."*

Molly spent 26 years of her life running away from God; and then running back to Him at the end of the day for fear she would get too far away from the only thing she ever had to count on.

CHAPTER 3

Love Lessons

As Molly took a stroll down memory lane she said, *"It would take all day for me to tell you all the crazy things I have done. When my parents moved me away from my church I actually thought I would make them sorry for doing the things they were doing if I started doing it too. The funny thing was, as soon as I started doing bad stuff I felt so ashamed of myself I didn't want them to find out. Since I was a little church kid in Stilesville it took them a while to figure out what I was doing. By the time they figured it out, I was having too much fun to stop. Not that they tried real hard to stop me, but I would imagine they were disappointed to say the least. In case people don't know, it is always fun when you first start using drugs and alcohol to come out of your shell. Suddenly Clark Kent becomes Super Man with some liquid courage."*

Molly was always quiet and shy before she discovered drugs and alcohol. Then suddenly she was bold and brave. When she was in her right mind she felt ugly and thought no one liked her. But when she was under the influence she felt attractive and confident that she could speak her mind.

Molly said, *"It was like I transformed into someone I wasn't when I was under the influence of drugs or alcohol. I wasn't afraid of anything, I wasn't insecure and that felt really good! I got a lot more attention from men when I was out drinking than when I was sober. Maybe I was more approachable then because I was more outgoing; or maybe they could tell I was drunk and they were a little insecure themselves. Maybe they needed some liquid courage to get their nerve to talk as well. All I know is when I went out sober it wasn't near as much fun. Thank God, since my life has changed I can actually enjoy myself in public without being under the influence of something, for the first time in my life. Now I care more about what God thinks of me than what other people think of me and that feels really good."*

As a child Molly remembered being too afraid to try and make friends because she feared they would find out her parents were alcoholics and make even more fun of her than they already did. She didn't really have any friends at school until she moved to Stilesville in the third grade. In fourth grade she found her best friend for life, Beth. Molly and Beth went to the same country church and Beth wasn't allowed to spend the night with anyone very often so it worked out great. Molly spent the night with Beth most of the time and no one really knew how bad it was at Molly's house. Beth and Molly became such good friends that Beth eventually found out how bad things were at Molly's house with the alcohol and drugs. By then Beth had already met Molly's parents when they were sober and to know them was to love them. Beth never really understood people who were addicted to anything but she loved Molly and her family enough that it didn't seem to bother her.

Molly said, *"After 30 years, Beth is my best friend still to this day and I would imagine she always will be! We are truly what some would call soul Sisters."*

Beth was a big part of what happened that day in July because of her prayers for Molly and the kids. Although Beth also strayed away from the Lord in her younger years she didn't stray too far or for too long. Beth never dabbled in drugs and barely ever drank alcohol; so she wasn't really around for that part of Molly's life. There was a period of time when the two of them had drifted apart but they still remained close in each other's heart.

When Molly moved away and then went wild at 14, Beth was still going to their little country church. By the time Molly was 18 she had settled down with Joey and then Beth went a little wild. Then Molly's Dad passed away when she was 22 and Molly began to fall into her old habits again. By that time Beth had started making her way back to the arms of the Lord and tried to get Molly to go to church with her; but Molly was angry and bitter over losing her Dad. Over the years they each had their ups and downs and tried to help each other when one was up and the other was down; but their different life styles had robbed them of so much time. They were so distant when Molly's Dad passed away that Beth didn't even know he had passed for a few weeks. Then Molly's Mother passed away when she was 25, just as she was starting to heal from the loss of her Dad.

Molly said, *"I remember the day Beth came to my house after my Mom had passed away. She had tears in her eyes and told me she would have been there for me if she had known when my Dad had passed away. I remember feeling numb and wondering why she even cared."*

It wasn't long after Molly lost her Mom that she and Joey split up for good. Molly was all alone with Nick & Sarah and turned to the only comfort she knew to ease her pain. She cried out to the Lord every day to take the pain away but ran to the bars every weekend to take it away herself.

Molly said, *"Looking back on that time in my life, I realize, I never gave the Lord time to take away my pain before I took matters into my own hands."*

The more Molly went out to the bars on the weekends and made allot of friends. The more friends she got, the less she needed the Lord.

Molly said, *"For years I felt like my friends were all I had, they became my family, because they didn't need me for anything but to have fun. Maybe that is why I tried to avoid spending time with Beth, she needed me to do what was right and I just couldn't at that time."*

Not long after Molly became single Beth got married because she was so determined to do what was right and Beth always thought her life couldn't be right without a husband. Molly had still never married, but this was Beth's second marriage. Beth married the first time when they were 18 and Molly was her maid of honor. Molly really liked Beth's first husband because she could see inside his heart and knew he had a sweet spirit. But Rick had an alcohol and drug problem that Beth just didn't relate to and couldn't understand. Molly on the other hand understood him well, because she had lived with those problems her entire life. There were very few people in Molly's life that wasn't addicted to one or both and Beth's life didn't look so bad compared to what Molly was used to. When Beth married Rick Molly had just got with Joey a few months before and Joey got drunk every night after work. Molly just couldn't understand what Beth had to complain about because Rick never seemed to be that bad.

Molly said, *"I know Beth loved Rick with all her heart, it was sad that she just couldn't change him into the man she needed him to be. Beth needed a strong man of God who loved to have fun and could act like a clown in his right mind. She loved to go dancing, but Rick didn't dance. She loved to talk, but Rick was pretty quiet. She needed to be in church, but Rick wasn't a church kind of guy. Needless to say their marriage didn't last very long and Beth went a little wild when it ended. I think Beth must have been playing her hand when she left Rick, betting everything she had he would call but instead he folded. Beth tried for years to get back in the game with Rick, but Rick seemed to fold every time she called his bluff."*

Molly was with Joey most of the bad time in Beth's life with Rick. By the time Molly and Joey split up, Beth was desperate to find a new husband and father for her kids. Beth had been going back to church for several years but hadn't found that perfect man of God just yet. It wasn't long after Molly became single again that Beth was on her way down the isle. Molly didn't like the man she was about to marry and was very glad Beth didn't ask her to stand up with her at this wedding.

Molly said, *"If she hadn't been my best friend for so many years I wouldn't have even gone to that wedding, I was so opposed to it. Never the less, I went because I knew how desperate Beth was to get over Rick and how very hard she had tried at convincing herself and everyone else that he was the one. She may have convinced herself, him and everyone else, but she never convinced me he was the right one; or even that she really loved him because I knew her too well. Looking back, I should have put duct tape over her mouth, tied her up and hid her in a cave until she came to her senses! Now I realize I wasn't being a very good friend when I let her make that mistake! Needless to say, it didn't take long before Beth was calling me crying; and I felt like a real looser for letting my best friend get herself into such a mess without even trying to have her committed."*

Molly and Beth stayed pretty close while Beth was going through her very difficult second marriage. Beth finally felt O.K. to leave after several months of Molly coaching her as well as, constant prayer and seeking her release of this marriage from God. Beth kept telling Molly she didn't want to be a "two times loser" and he was at least good to her kids. She was so miserable and Molly knew he wasn't the man God had planned for her.

Molly said, *"I remember the day Beth came to me and said God had released her of the marriage and told her it was time to go. She asked me if her and the girls could come and stay with us for a while until she got back on her feet and I was so glad to have her stay. Beth never really knew how much light she brought into my life or even how dark my life had been. Beth always looked at me as the strong one because I was reserved and conservative; but she had no idea what a strong influence she had in my life in such a good way".*

During that time Molly too had been in a difficult relationship that had broken her heart as well; and she needed Beth as much as Beth needed her! Within a few months of her break up with Joey, Molly met the man she thought she was destined to spend the rest of her life with, Johnny.

Molly said, *"The first night we met, we were talking about when we get married stuff; and I had never felt anything like that in my life! It had been one of those on again, off again things for a few years but when Beth and the girls came to stay it was off for a good long while".*

Beth and the girls didn't stay too long before they got a place and moved on; but Beth sure lifted Molly's spirit while she was there. It wasn't long after Beth and the girls moved out that Molly got a call with the good news. Beth and Rick had finally got back together after all of those years apart. Molly was so happy for her but a little jealous because she longed to be back with Johnny. Molly thought Rick and Beth would live happily ever after and eventually her and Johnny would work everything out and live happily ever after too. She thought of how great it would be when she and Johnny got back together and she could introduce him to Rick.

Molly said, *"In my heart I prayed we would all be in church together one day and every Sunday they would bring the kids to our house for dinner."*

Molly secretly wished for happier days but didn't dare tell anyone of her hopes and dreams for fear of looking like a fool when they didn't come true. She never really believed that anything good could happen in her life. The only thing good in her life that she knew would last forever was her love for Nick and Sarah.

Molly said, *"I prayed every day God would keep them safe and let me die first because I couldn't stand to lose one of them."*

Molly had lost her parents, all of her Grandparents, uncles, friends, and just recently had lost her first love that had always had a special place in her heart. She knew all about heart ache and pain but didn't know much about forever. To Molly forever was another word for pain because she thought her heart would be broken forever.

Before she could get over the loss of one person she loved another would leave. Molly didn't know how to love a little, when she loved someone she loved them allot.

Molly said, *"I know this sounds really bad but I got to the point I couldn't cry anymore unless I was drunk or someone died and sometimes I didn't cry then. When I met Johnny, I was so broken down I had walls built up around my heart I thought no one could tear apart. It took him quite a while to tear my walls down and when he did my broken heart began to heal. I don't know if he ever knew how bad it hurt when he ripped it apart again. It didn't make any sense to me; it was like a surgeon going in and slicing up the new heart he had just transplanted with a scalpel so he could see if it would still bleed. It was like a sick joke, like someone said, oops, sorry, you weren't supposed to get that heart filled with love you are supposed to have this broken one that has scars all over it. It was like, this can't be real, am I on let's make a Deal and just got Zonked? I mean really, I didn't trade that new heart for the one that was behind door number three, I said I wanted to keep the new one! Somebody PLEASE, stop this Johnny be good roller coaster ride I'm on!"*

You could see the pain in Molly's eyes when she talked about her love for Johnny. She still doesn't know why it didn't work because she got to see the Love Johnny had in his eyes for Jesus and she really thought he had that same perfect love for her. After Molly made the mistake of wasting so many years of her life with a man who professed to be an atheist when he was drunk and dared not talk about it when he was sober; she made herself a promise that she would never commit herself to anyone ever again who didn't love the Lord.

She also made herself a promise she would never let anyone in her heart again who didn't love her enough to be the kind of man God wanted him to be; but she thought Johnny could be that man because she knew he knew God, so she let him in her heart.

Molly said, *"I knew in my gut he would break my heart but he made everything that felt so wrong, feel so right."*

Molly was six years older than Johnny and she truly believed that was the problem. They were on again; off again for three years and then it was off for the next six. Soon after Beth and Rick got back together, Beth got bored with Rick and took her girls to Florida to visit her Sister. About 2 weeks after Beth got back from vacation she called Molly and said, **"I'm moving to Florida"**. Molly thought Beth had really flipped her lid this time.

Molly said, *"After all those years she had cried and tried to get Rick back, now she has him back and she is leaving him! I truly thought she had lost her mind! She was running off to Florida to be with some man she had met on vacation, that she had only known for a couple of weeks and leaving the Love of Her Life! I tried my best to talk her out of that one! It was insane to take those girls that far away from home to be with a stranger, what if he was a serial killer or a pedophile?"*

Beth was very head strong and when she wanted to do something there was no stopping her. Rick found the e-mails she had been sharing with Mike and away she went.

Molly said, *"Just like that, my best friend was gone!"*

Molly wasn't living the kind of life she knew the Lord wanted her to live but she still talked to Jesus every day and she had a lot to say about Beth. She prayed and prayed He would keep her and the girls safe. She told the Lord how Beth was the only friend she had that she knew truly loved Him and wanted to do the right things too. She told the Lord, Beth knew not what she was doing, just like He said about the people who crucified Him. She pleaded with God to put some sense in Beth's head and bring her back safe.

It didn't take long until Beth was calling, sounding as happy as a lark. Molly didn't believe her at first. She thought Beth was living in fantasy land and pretending everything was grand like she always did. Beth was great at pretending and that was one of the things Molly loved about her; but this time Molly feared Beth had gone a little too far. Beth left in the winter so Molly went down to see her for Spring Break. To Molly's surprise Beth really was living the good life. She had met a wonderful man and Molly greatly approved of him. He was a kind and gentle giant of a man with a heart of gold. Not at all what Molly expected would steal Beth away from Rick, but a wonderful man none the less. Molly left Florida feeling very happy for Beth, she had met her Knight in Shining Armor and her struggles were over.

However, for Molly the struggles got bigger and the wounds got deeper. In the year and a half since Johnny had been completely out of Molly's life she had already been through two disappointing relationships and was on her third. The third was the result of revenge on the girl who stole the first one's heart away from her. Molly had very strong feelings for Kline for many years, long before she met Johnny. Kline was a teenage flame that had rekindled several times over the past 15 years. He was the one who managed to give her the strength to get rid of Joey, but then broke her heart when he married the girl he said he wanted rid of 3 months after Joey left. Kline continued to call about every three months the whole time he was married and tell her how miserable he was and how much he missed her. He was one of the reasons Molly's heart was so broken when she met Johnny. Kline only stayed married for three years and then he was calling Molly telling her he was getting a divorce. Molly was with Johnny and loved him very much but their relationship was more off than it was on by that time.

Molly said, *"I'll never forget what he said to me when I told him he had waited a little too late to call because I was back with Johnny."*

Kline said, ***"Molly I can't believe after all this time it has been my fault we haven't been together, now I'm single and you're with him, now it's your fault!"***

Molly said, *"I remember saying God, is this a sign? I know I love Johnny so much more than I ever loved Kline because Johnny is in my soul but why is this happening now when there are so many problems with me and Johnny?"*

Johnny had been doing allot of drugs and couldn't hold down a job. Nick and Johnny couldn't get along and Molly was struggling just to hold things together.

Molly said, *"There were times when I didn't think I could handle all the stress. I was in Love with an insanely jealous drug addict who couldn't keep a job and didn't help me financially. I was trying to start a new business and that wasn't going well, so I was living off credit that was about to run out. Sarah was only 5 and so very much needed and wanted my attention. Nick was a very angry nine year old who resented me because his Dad wouldn't come around and he hated my boyfriend. I was an emotional wreck who couldn't cry unless I was drunk, so I drank every weekend hoping to get rid of some frustration! When Kline called all I could think about were all the good times we had. He always made me laugh and we shared allot of the same friends. Unlike Johnny, who didn't want to be around any of my friends at all. I knew it was probably only a matter of time before Johnny would get mad and leave again. I wondered what I would do if Johnny had another fit and left again. Would I try to make something work out with Kline after all these years of playing cat and mouse, or did Johnny have his name engraved so deep in my heart that I couldn't get over it?"*

Sure enough it didn't take a week before Johnny got mad and left again. Joey had managed to talk Nick and Sarah into living with him so he wouldn't have to pay child support. It wasn't that hard to talk Nick into leaving after he filled his head full of horrible things about

Johnny. Sarah just enjoyed being at Grandma's house and getting to spend time with her Dad. Joey couldn't stand it because he knew how much Molly loved Johnny and after several failed attempts to get her back he decided to get her where he knew it would hurt the most, by taking the kids away. Joey managed to convince his Mother that Molly wasn't taking care of the kids and got her to push Molly into letting the kids stay at her house for a while.

Molly said, *"I was so broken over what was going on with Johnny and I was drowning in debt. When I was faced with losing my kids too, I thought, I would rather die."*

When Johnny got mad and left Molly was totally alone because the kids had moved in with their Dad at Grandma's. She was crying to her Sister on the phone and Lynn knew Molly was about to lose it. Lynn told Molly to call Kline and ask him to come over and stay with her since she was alone. Molly knew above all else she could trust Kline to just be there with her as a friend and let her cry on his shoulder but still wondered if it was the right thing to do in this situation. Lynn kept insisting she call Kline and she finally did; but that was a big mistake. Kline came over and stayed with her all night, letting her cry on his shoulder over Johnny. Kline knew how broken Molly was over Johnny and just held her all night like she asked him to. The next day was the end of Molly and Johnny for the next six years.

CHAPTER 4

Spirits of darkness unleashed

Johnny decided to do a drive by sometime late in the night. When he saw the strange car in Molly's drive he decided to sneak in the house and check things out. Somehow, Johnny always managed to get in the house without making a sound.

Molly said, *"He must have snuck in the back door and went through the house looking for something to tell him whose car was in the drive. I'm sure he must have sat up all night thinking of how he was going to kill me when he found Kline's shoes and wallet in the living room. You would think he would have just confronted us right then and there but no, he left and came back the next day when Kline was gone. I will never forget that day. It was back when people had to carry a pager for work. I was sitting in my chase lounge chair when I got the page that read 666. At first I thought it might be Kline trying to page me but all the numbers didn't go through. Then, my pager went off again; it was the same thing, 666 and then again a third time. Chills went up my spine like the sound of church bells in Transylvania. Then my phone rings and it is Johnny. He told me he had his daughter and she wanted to see us. He asked me if he could bring her over to see us so we could talk about things. Of course I said yes, even though I was a little freaked out about him calling me right after the 666 pages. I had a feeling in my gut those pages were either Johnny trying to scare me or a divine warning from God something bad was about to happen.*

I told him the kids were with their Dad but they would be home soon and I would love to see his daughter."

It didn't take long before Johnny was at the door but his daughter wasn't with him. The first thing Molly thought of was the 666 messages and wondered why he lied about having his daughter with him. Even though Molly had a scared feeling in her gut she was glad to see Johnny and hoped they could work things out so he would come back home. They talked and things seemed to be going really good until she saw that dreadful look in his eyes.

Molly said, "*I will never forget the way his facial features would change when he was about to get violent. It was like his whole countenance changed and I was suddenly talking to a demon.*"

Just minutes before the kids got home from being with their Dad, Johnny got that look in his eyes and Molly knew things were about to get ugly. He began to question her about the strange car in her drive the night before. Doing the only thing she thought she could do without taking a chance on him killing her for having her ex-boyfriend spend the night, she lied!

Molly said, "*This wasn't the first time I had seen that look in Johnny's eyes and I knew what was coming if he got mad. Looking back, I know it was stupid of me to lie; I should have just stood up to him and told him the truth! Yes, Kline did stay at my house and yes, we did sleep in the same bed, but that is all we did besides talk about you all night! I don't know why I let fear get a hold of me like that. I loved him so much, I was scared to death if I told him the truth he wouldn't believe me and I would lose him forever all because I was weak enough to have Kline spend the night. It was so stupid anyway, he had walked out on me, how did he think he had the right to go through my house while I was asleep?*"

Molly lied but it didn't do her any good because Johnny already knew it was Kline in the house the night before. The crazier that look got in Johnny's eyes the more Molly tried to change the subject but he wasn't about to let that happen. Johnny grabbed a knife from the knife rack and held it to Molly's throat demanding she tell him the truth about who was really in the house. About that time the kids got home and Sarah came running in the kitchen where they were. When Molly heard the door open she quietly begged Johnny to put the knife down and not let them see him like this. When Sarah ran in the kitchen Molly told her to hurry up and go upstairs. Johnny was standing in front of Molly so Sarah couldn't see the knife to her throat and went on upstairs like she was told. Molly begged Johnny to not kill her in front of her children.

Molly said, *"I begged him to please not kill me in front of my little girl because I knew he loved Sarah. I begged him, please Johnny, don't do this with the kids in the house, do you want Sarah to find me like that?"*

About that time while Molly was pleading for her life she heard a noise in the side yard. Her eyes looked toward the kitchen window and to her surprise the good Lord had sent the Calvary and they didn't even know what was going on. When Molly looked out the window she saw her sister and brother in-law in her yard. Johnny looked back to see what Molly was looking at and then threw the knife at the wall and ran out the front door. Molly really thought he was going to kill her that time and knew this had to end. Johnny knew it had to end as well, before he did something he would later on regret. They spent the next 6 years apart but not a day went by that Molly didn't think about Johnny and pray for things to change so they could be back together and happy again.

Molly said, *"Looking back, I know now exactly what demons I was fighting, I just wish I would have known it then. Johnny and I both dealt with un-clean and tormenting spirits. There were the un-clean spirits of drugs, alcohol, and lust. Then there were the tormenting spirits of depression, confusion, rebellion, doubt, anger, vanity, jealousy and control! One seemed to open the door for the other until finally they all took control and opened the door for that evil spirit of murder that wanted Johnny to kill me. Thank God, Johnny and I both had been filled with the Holy Spirit when we were young. If it hadn't been for the spirit inside us that gave our soul the strength to fight off the forces of darkness, I'm sure we would have wound up being another statistic."*

After 6 long years of begging God to bring Johnny back Molly finally got her wish. Johnny had gotten back into church for a while and was preaching at a little country church again. Molly was at the lowest part of her life spiritually because she was drinking more than she had ever drunk before. Although she talked to the Lord every day she hadn't yet learned to hear His voice and He seemed so very far away. As soon as Molly heard Johnny was back in church, she prayed God would bring him back to save her from this pit she had fallen into. She made several attempt to reach out to him by asking him to pray for certain people but he always blew her off. She saw him a couple of times at his family gatherings but he never showed any interest in talking to her. Then one night in a drunken state she got the nerve to call him and ask for a ride. He came to get her at a bar but turned her down when she asked him to stay with her after he got her home.

Molly said, *"I still remember the pain I felt that night when Johnny pulled out of my driveway. I wanted to die and decided if God wouldn't let me die, I would just kill myself. I got in my car with intentions to drive down the road to a friend's quarry and drive my car into the water to end it once and for all. I remember screaming at God, why didn't you just let Johnny kill me 6 years ago if you're not going to ever let me get over him? I don't want to live like this anymore! Just as I was backing my car out of the garage my roommate came out of the house and stopped me; I guess God wasn't finished with me yet! Ironically the roommate I had at the time was arrested a few months later for child pornography; once again, it looks like God really does use all things for the good of those who love him! When I woke the next day I felt even more hopeless than I ever did before. I knew I had gone over the edge the night before but didn't know how long it would be before I did it again if Johnny didn't come back soon".*

This wasn't the first time Molly had wanted to kill herself when she was drunk. She had made several attempts in her drunken states in the past, after her parents died and before she met Johnny. Always before she would just get in her car and drive as fast as she could go, begging God to put something in her path that would take her out so she didn't have to do it herself. Death was something Molly fantasized about quite often since she was a child; it seemed to be her only escape. However, she was always taught that suicide was an unforgiveable sin, so she felt it would have to be an accident for God to forgive her. In her drunken state of mind the enemy could easily convince her if it happened in her car, it was an accident.

Molly said, *"I'll always remember the remorse I would feel the next day when I woke up after one of my suicidal drunks. I remember begging God to forgive me for being so selfish and wanting to end my life when I had 2 children who needed a mother; but at the time I felt they would be better off without me. I never felt worthy to be their mother. I always felt like such a failure that it made sense to me if I was out of the picture, God could find them a good mom that had a good dad to love them; and I trusted Him to do so! I had gotten really good at hiding my pain until I got drunk and then it was like someone turned on a water hose full blast. Looking back on that time in my life, I wonder if the times I was able to release my emotions through alcohol is what kept me from completely losing my mind? I wonder if it was another one of those times God used something bad for my good. The bible tells us what Satan meant for our harm, God will use for our good and I'm sure Satan intended every single one of those drunks for my harm; but it was probably a good thing I was able to cry sometimes".*

Not long after the night Molly wanted to drive her car into the quarry she went to a Jimmy Buffet concert with a bunch of friends. Buffet was famous for the Margaritaville song so it was a tradition they would drink Margarita's all the way to the concert every year. Since it took them over an hour to get to the concert, they had plenty of time to get good and drunk before they got there. Molly had asked Johnny's sister to be their D.D. but she left the concert with some friends once they got there. Margarita's just happened to be Molly's drink of choice at that time, so she was able to drink more than her fair share on the way up to the concert. No more than 30 minutes into the trip Molly had already consumed all but 2 glasses out of a ½ gallon of Margarita's. They stopped at the next town to buy another ½ gallon and she consumed almost half of that one by the time they got to the concert. She was dancing and having the time of her life, until she had to wake up and face herself the next day.

One of Molly's best friends called the next day to let her know he would never go to another concert with her or Lynn again. It wasn't that either one of them did anything bad, but that they got so drunk he felt like he had to stay sober to babysit them so they didn't get hurt. As if Molly wasn't feeling bad enough from the horrible hangover, that phone call really sent her into depression and then repentance. She lay in bed most of the day begging God for forgiveness once again and pleading with him to just bring Johnny back one more time so she could stop living this life. After several hours of the blues and repentance, she got the nerve to send Johnny a text and ask if he would like to go to dinner with her. To her surprise he said yes! Molly jumped out of her bed and got ready as fast as she could, praying the whole time that Johnny was finally ready to come back. Molly promised God if He would let Johnny come back she would do her very best to make it work and if it didn't she would never ask Him to bring Johnny back again.

Molly said, *"Looking back I realize now, that was the biggest mistake I ever made by making God that promise. Satan knew I wouldn't go back on my word to God and he knew I wasn't strong enough to help Johnny, any more than Johnny was strong enough to help me!"*

A little while later Johnny came to pick Molly up and told her he wanted to get out of town for the night. Molly didn't think much about it at first until they got to the restaurant and Johnny ordered a glass of wine.

He told her, ***"I hope you don't think badly of me for drinking this wine, but I don't see anything wrong with having a glass of wine every now and then".***

At that point Molly would have probably let Johnny feed her broken glass and tell her it was crushed ice; so she told him she had no right to think badly of him and she would have one with him if she weren't so hung over. Never the less, Molly had a feeling in her gut something just wasn't right even though all the pieces to the puzzle seemed to be falling into place.

Molly said, *"I remember getting a sick feeling in my gut when Johnny ordered that glass of wine but I told myself it must be the hangover and didn't bother to talk to the Lord about it. I remember thinking the Johnny I once knew would have never had a glass of wine when he was going to church. He was preaching at a Pentecostal church and that was totally against their religion, but I was too happy to be in his presence to question his beliefs at the time."*

As the days went by Johnny and Molly spent more and more time together. Sarah had a beauty pageant the following weekend in a nearby town and Johnny went with them to her pageant. Molly was the happiest she had been in her life but every now and again that sick feeling would come to her gut again that something just wasn't right. When they were out of town Johnny would always have some wine at dinner and Molly knew that wasn't accepted by his church. When they were behind closed doors his love felt more like lust to her but she thought it was because they had been apart for so many years and in time he would trust her enough to love her the way he once did again. When it was time to go to church they had to drive in separate cars and pretend they were just friends because Johnny said the people at his church wouldn't accept him being with her.

Marcella Bowlen

Molly said, "*I remember one day I noticed what was left of the second ½ gallon bottle of Margarita's I had at the Jimmy Buffet concert in my garage. I thought about throwing it away and then the thought came to my mind, why would you do that? Johnny still drinks wine you might need that someday. Looking back, I realize that was Satan putting that thought in my head so I would feel I had to have that bottle for security just in case things went wrong again. I would give anything if I had just thrown it away! I remember one night Johnny came over and I was really nervous about him being there. He still hadn't committed to us being back together and I was tired of pretending I was just his friend in public. I was starting to feel he wasn't ever going to love me like he did before. The Johnny I fell in love with was happy to let the whole world know I was his girl, but the new Johnny seemed to be ashamed of me. I can't begin to tell you how much it hurt to think he was ashamed of me when I had stopped drinking, given up all of my friends and barely spent any time at all with my family to be with him. We were supposed to watch a movie that night but I was going to take a shower first. Johnny was in the family room sitting in the recliner chair watching TV. when I went upstairs to take a shower. When I started up the stairs I remembered that bottle of Margarita's in the garage and thought I could really use a drink right now to calm my nerves. I got all the way upstairs before the urge got so strong I couldn't deny it and came up with what I thought was a master plan that no one would ever know about. I decided to go to the kitchen and let Johnny hear me getting a drink and then tell him I had to get something out of the garage and take my cup outside and fill it up with Margarita. I thought it was the perfect plan; I could slam that drink in the shower and then brush my teeth and he would never know. But Johnny always knew everything! Sure I knew if I asked him if he wanted to have a drink with me he would; but I couldn't stand the thought of offering him a drink because I didn't want us to go back to the way things were before. I justified me having the drink because he had been drinking wine and I hadn't, but I knew in my heart if he saw*

46

me drinking, it would be a green light for disaster. I still don't know for sure if the man could just read my mind or if Johnny had seen the bottle in the garage and intended on drinking it himself when I went to take a shower. Or maybe Satan just made sure he knew every move I made to keep him mad at me all the time; but somehow, he always knew if I tried to pull anything over on him. It had been a good while since I had a drink so that one glass had me a little buzzed. When I came back down to the family room Johnny was still sitting in the recliner so I sat down on the sofa for fear he could still smell the booze on my breath if I got too close. Maybe he could just tell by the look on my face that I had a buzz but I was making sure I didn't say too much and give it away.

Within a few minutes of me sitting on the sofa Johnny looked at me and said, **"Hey red, don't ever try to pull a stunt like that again or I will leave you and never come back."**

"My heart fell to my feet and all I could say was what?"

He said, **"I know what you did! I know you went out to the garage and poured your cup full of Margarita and drank it in the shower so don't even try to lie to me! I'm telling you right now, if you ever pull another stunt like that again, I will leave you and I'll never be back!"**

"I don't even remember what I said back to him, I was so scared to death I had just blown any chance I may have had over a drink! When Johnny left that night I thought I would never see him again. Suddenly I began to feel hopeless, worthless and destined to be alone again; the enemy must have really enjoyed his time with me that night and all the next day!"

The next day Johnny showed up when he got off work and Lynn happened to be there listening to Molly whine about how bad she had screwed up. Lynn was never the type to hold anything back so she point blank asked Johnny when he walked in if he still loved her sister or not! She told him she was sick and tired of hearing her sister whine over him and he needed to make his mind up if he still loved her enough to give her another chance and if he didn't he needed to let her know and let her go! Johnny stood there telling Lynn he loved Molly but he wasn't going to put up with her drinking and Lynn told him if he loved her he needed to start acting like it. She told him it was wrong off him to expect Molly to be his secret girlfriend and take her to a church where everyone could see how much she loved him and was shunning her like she was some harlot trying to get him to backslide! She told him Molly drinking a margarita was no different than him drinking a glass of wine and he couldn't expect her to be perfect when he wasn't! Johnny just stood there with his head down looking at the floor while Lynn chewed him out. He knew she was right and that he hadn't been fair to Molly but Molly was so upset at Lynn for calling him out she ran into the bathroom in tears.

Johnny opened the bathroom door, looked her straight in the eyes and said, ***"You know if we're going to make this work you can't hide anything from me."***

So Molly promised she had learned her lesson and she would never try to drink away her anxiety again. She promised she would talk to him the next time she started feeling insecure. Then Johnny finally admitted that he did want her back and agreed to let her go to another church because he knew the members at his church were shunning her. He told Molly he couldn't let them know he loved her because they would never accept their Pastor being with her. You see this was a Pentecostal church that didn't believe in wearing makeup, jeans or jewelry and God had not yet convicted Molly about her attire. Johnny didn't really want a woman who looked the way the women did in the Pentecostal church but he knew he could never be with one who didn't look like the others if he wanted to be accepted as a Pastor in the church.

Molly said, *"I remember when I was about 12 and I went to the Pentecostal church in Stilesville where I received the gift of the Holy Spirit. I was getting at the age where I wanted to fit in with the other kids but knew it was against the church doctrine to dress like the other kids at school. So I went to the mother of my church who was the closest person I had ever known to God. She had the gifts of tongues and interpretation of tongues. She had the gift of prophecy and the gifts of wisdom & knowledge, among other gifts. There was no one in this world I respected more than her and if she would have told me I had to dress like the church wanted me to dress to get to heaven, I think I would have. But instead of telling me I had to do as the church wanted me to do, she simply said,* **"Sister Molly, if Jesus came back today and you had on makeup, jewelry & jeans would you gladly greet him or would you run and hide?"**

I said, "I don't know."

Then she said, **"Well I suggest you pray about that and if you feel convicted in your heart about dressing that way, you shouldn't do it. But if you feel like you would gladly run and greet the Lord in the clothes and makeup you want to wear, go ahead. If God doesn't want you to do something, He will let you know."**

"She had the sweetest smile on her face and looked at me with so much love in her eyes, in my eyes, that woman was a saint! So I did what she said and asked the Lord to prick my heart when I was wearing something the church said He didn't want me to wear. I prayed about it daily until I came to the conclusion if I was supposed to be the bride of Christ I should look my very best for my groom. Since I felt I looked much better with makeup than I did without it, I felt God would like me better with it too! I won't tell you I never wore anything I felt convicted about when I was living in rebellion because that would be a lie; but that wasn't the issue at this time in my life."

"I had told Johnny that story and he agreed but he also knew if he wanted to be a Pastor of a Pentecostal church he would have to go along with their doctrine and that would mean he had to hide how he really felt. I knew Johnny found me a lot more attractive when I wore makeup & jeans and the truth was he didn't really want me to look like the women in his church. Johnny fell in love with me because I

was a Pentecostal girl at heart that didn't look Pentecostal. However, he was torn because he knew if he wanted to Pastor that Pentecostal church he had to have a wife who obeyed their doctrine at church; and I wasn't about to be caught dead without makeup on. Although I only wore long dresses to church because I felt that is what God would want me to wear in his house; I didn't feel it would be right to take off my jewelry in church when God knew I wore it everywhere else. Besides, I wasn't about to lie if anyone ask me anything and Johnny knew that. Johnny was much better at hiding things from people than I was. I saved my lies for when I needed them to keep from getting into trouble. I felt there was no need in trying to hide anything because God could see everything and He was the only person I cared to please. It was clear the only way we could make this work is if we went to different churches so Johnny could keep me a secret from the flock."

For a few minutes Molly was on cloud nine and then as soon as Lynn left she got that uneasy feeling in her gut again. Within a short period of time after Lynn left Johnny looked at Molly and said, **"I know you have xanax, you always do, now give me one of them so I can put up with you!"**

Molly said, *"I immediately got that sick feeling in my gut as soon as Johnny asked me for a xanax; but instead of saying no or calling him out on it like I should have, I gave him one to keep him from getting mad at me again."*

The doctor had been giving Molly xanax for anxiety since she and Joey split up but she rarely ever took them and Johnny knew that. He knew she most likely had a stash but didn't know where they were until that day when he saw Molly get in the closet to get him one out. From that day forward Johnny just got in the closet and took what he wanted because he knew Molly would never miss them because she rarely got in them. Molly had been letting Johnny call all the shots. When it was time to go to church he let Molly take Sarah to her old church and he went to his church. That way the people at his church wouldn't figure out he was with Molly and Molly wouldn't have anxiety about him keeping her a secret. When he wanted to drink wine, it was o.k. if Molly wanted to but she rarely did because Molly wasn't a social drinker. When Molly wanted to buy the house she was living in Johnny told her it was too expensive and she needed to find something cheaper to live in until she could get back in her old house. So Molly let one of her friends buy the house on a short sale and make all the money she knew her and Johnny could have made; which once again started her resentment towards Johnny for holding her back from having a better life. In her mind she thought if they were going to get married he should start working on helping her financially and wanting a better life together. When Molly sold that house and moved a few weeks later, Johnny brought his things to move in too.

When Molly asked him what he was doing he said, **"I love you and I can't stand being without you any longer."**

After they moved in together Molly started noticing she was the only one going to church and when she questioned Johnny about why he hadn't been going he said,

"I can't go to church and live in sin! When we get married, I'll go back to church."

It didn't take long until Molly started seeing him slip back into his old ways when he quit going to church. So she went out one day and bought some wedding rings and told Johnny they better set a date fast or they wouldn't make it much longer.

It was October of 2004 and they set a date for New Year's Eve. Within a few days they went out to buy a dress and start making plans to pull a wedding off in 2 months. All the way to the bridal shop Molly kept thinking she must be crazy to think getting married was going to solve their problems. She was stressed out about how she would come up with the money to pay for a wedding and pay all of their bills. She had already bought the rings and that didn't settle well with her that he didn't even have the money to buy her a ring if he wanted to marry her. Johnny had already quit his job not long after he stopped going to church and she had recently found out he had been sneaking in her Xanax. His drinking had become more and more frequent and she had caught him smoking pot several times. She wanted to believe he would go back to church and start working again if they got married but something in her gut told her he would only get worse! So she held in all of her fears and proceeded to plan the wedding she so desperately wanted. They went to the bridal shop and Johnny never looked so happy as he helped her pick out a dress. She tried one on and his face lit up with joy. He stood there in awe as she walked out to show him the dress.

Molly said, *"I'll never forget the way he looked at me and how he grabbed me and kissed me."*

Johnny said, ***"This is the one! You look so beautiful I can't wait to marry you, can we go get married today?"***

Molly laughed and said, *"Don't you want me to try on a few more?"*

Johnny said, ***"No! I want you to wear this one and I want to marry you today!"***

For the next few minutes they were the happiest they had been in years. For the first time since they got back together Molly felt like Johnny was really in love with her again. Then she went in to change back into her clothes so she could buy the dress and along came that spirit of fear. By the time she got to the counter with the dress she was so overwhelmed with fear of all the "What If's" that were flooding her mind, she was shaking so much she could barely write the check. Molly knew all sales were final and if she walked out that door with the dress she would be out a lot of money she really couldn't afford to spend if this all went bad. She tried so hard to fight off the fear because there was nothing in the world she wanted more than to spend the rest of her life with Johnny. However, she knew her expectations of how she wanted their life together to be may be more than Johnny was capable of if he didn't go back to church and learn how to be the man God created him to be. Molly wanted Johnny to be willing to do whatever he had to do to make things work, even if he didn't want to. Thoughts kept flooding her mind of how she was willing to give up spending time with her family and friends to make him happy. How she was willing to give up going to the same church so he could keep her hidden. How she was willing to do whatever he wanted to do even if she didn't want to do it just to make him happy; but he wouldn't do the same for her. How she was willing to go out and clean toilets to get the money to pay for the things they needed, but he quit a good job because he didn't like what he had to do. She was still upset that she had to give up a nice house because he thought it was too expensive and wasn't willing to help her do what they needed to do to flip the house and make the profit. By the time they walked out of the bridal shop Molly was about to throw up from anxiety. Johnny was still walking on cloud nine and kept talking to her about how beautiful she looked in that dress but she wasn't able to respond and he soon caught on.

Johnny said, ***"What is wrong with you?"***

Molly said, *"Nothing!"*

Another mile down the road he asked her again and again she said, *"nothing!"*

A few minutes later he asked her again and she said, *"nothing"* but he said he knew her better than that and she better let him know what was wrong.

Molly was at the point of tears and immediately blurted out, *"WE CAN"T DO THIS!"*

Molly said, *"I will never forget the look on Johnny's face. He looked like someone had just killed his best friend and I wanted to die because I knew how much I had just hurt him!"*

Molly began to explain to Johnny how much she wanted to be his wife but she feared there is no way she could afford to pull off a wedding by herself and she felt they needed to wait until he got another job and could help her with some of the bills. She tried to explain herself all the way home but Johnny just kept quiet and all he said was, ***"I understand"*** when he said anything at all.

Molly said, *"I can remember once I started telling him about my fears it was like a water hose I couldn't shut off. I told him my fears about him not working and me not being able to afford it all.*

Johnny just said, ***"I understand."***

I told him my fears of him not going to church until we got married; because I was afraid if he waited that long the addiction would get a hold of him again.

Johnny only said, ***"I understand."***

I told him I was afraid if he started drinking and drugging like he did before it would destroy us again and I couldn't stand the thoughts of divorce.

Johnny only said, ***"I understand."***

"By the time we got home I remember feeling like such a fool for spending all that money on a dress I didn't know if I would ever wear. All I wanted was to hear him say he loved me so much he would go to my church until we got married. I just wanted him to look me straight in the eyes and say I had nothing to worry about because he was never going to go down that road with drugs and alcohol again. I just wanted to hear him say he would go out and get any job he could, even if he didn't like it so he could help me pay for this wedding; but he never said any of the things I needed to hear. Instead he just got silent and went to his dad's as soon as we got home. Looking back, I realize Satan was tormenting Johnny's mind with fears of being inadequate as much as he was mine, but I didn't know that at the time. His silence only made me feel he didn't care enough to make sure we wouldn't wind up in a divorce. I'm sure Satan was having the time of his life tormenting our minds with fear that day and I would give anything if I had known then how to rebuke those spirits of fear like I do know. If only I had stood up in faith and told the enemy he was a liar; and I had faith in the Lord to empower Johnny with the strength to overcome temptation. I can't

help but wonder if I had rebuked those spirits of fear and trusted in God to help me find a way to pay for the wedding, if Johnny would have had more of a desire to stay sober. Would he have went back to church and been the man I knew he was capable of being when he was walking the path of righteousness? Would he have finally felt confident in our love once we got married? All Johnny ever wanted was me to love him enough to take a risk and be willing to live in a tent if we had to. All I wanted was him to love me enough to be willing to work as hard as I did to have a better quality of life together. Now I realize it wasn't that we lacked in loving each other but that we lacked in trusting ourselves and having faith in God to help us overcome our own demons!"

Satan knows when two people who are equally yoked of the Holy Spirit get together they can really mess up his plans. Molly spent years trying to figure out if Satan had sent Johnny to her to mess up her life; or if God had sent Johnny to her to save her life. Molly knew it was the Holy Spirit in Johnny that had broken down her walls and repaired her heart but it was the spirits that oppressed him that tore her world apart again. When Molly met Johnny he was married, but he wanted her so bad he lied and said he was divorced. By the time Molly found out Johnny was still married she had already fallen in love with him. She tried her best to push him away so he would go back to his wife and daughter; but no matter what she said or did he wouldn't leave her alone. Night after night he would climb on her roof to knock on her bedroom window and beg to come in. She would let him in, they would make up and then the guilt would set in with Molly again. Marriage was one of the most important things in the world to Molly. She never married because she promised herself she would only marry once and if it didn't work she would be alone forever.

Molly said, *"I always did everything backwards; I screwed up the plans I had for my life when I was young, but I wasn't about to screw up marriage! To me, there was a difference in sinning and breaking a* commandment. *Breaking Commandments are breaking the Laws of God. When we break the law we go to jail, God's jail is Hell, but you can't ever get out and I don't want to go there."*

No matter how hard Molly tried she couldn't get her heart and her head to agree on Johnny. She loved him with all of her heart but her head couldn't accept the way he handled things; or the things he did. It was crazy to think they could ever be happy when their relationship was based on lies and adultery. Johnny didn't just break one commandment when he met Molly, he broke two and Molly felt like it was her fault. All she ever wanted was for Johnny to get down on his knees and ask God to forgive him, take her in his arms and say, *"We have to go ask my wife to forgive us and release me of this marriage."*

Molly thought if Johnny truly loved the Lord the way he should he would feel as bad over what they had done as she did. Molly never looked at the other stuff in their life as much of an obstacle to overcome as Johnny's lies and the adultery.

Molly said, *"Johnny had such a lying spirit on him that I couldn't believe a word he said, but he always managed to make me feel like it was my fault when he lied. He lied about his age and being married the night we met and told me it was because he fell in love at first sight. Johnny said he knew I would never give him a chance if I knew he was married and he wasn't old enough to be in the bar I met him in, so he lied."*

Johnny always had a good excuse for his lies and his good excuses always had something to do with Molly. Molly had to find out the hard way about Johnny being married, she got a call from his wife. Molly was devastated and totally lost it when Johnny came home. They hadn't been together long but hadn't spent a night a part since the night they met. Molly was still so broken from losing her parents and all the hell Joey had put her through since their separation; finding out Johnny was married, was enough to drive her over the edge. The short time she had spent with Johnny being happy for the first time in her life seemed like a fairy tale after she got the phone call from his wife. The thought of being a home wrecker haunted her mind daily but being without Johnny when she pushed him away made her sick inside.

Molly said, *"Looking back I realize now God wasn't punishing me, I was punishing myself. If I had known then what I know now, I think things would have been a lot different. All those feelings of shame and condemnation didn't come from my Lord, they came from the enemy. God doesn't shame us or condemn us, he chastises those whom He loves and draws them to repentance. The enemy knew my chastisement so he tormented me daily with shame so I would run even further away from my Lord than I already was. He knew my Love for the Lord, as well as he knew my Love for Johnny and he was out to destroy them both at the same time. After all those years I spent trying to figure out if Johnny was sent to me from heaven or hell I think I finally figured it out. I think God is all knowing but He doesn't stop us from doing anything that we really want to do; and He doesn't change things just so it will work out for us unless we are living inside His realm of safety. I believe, if we are living our life for the Lord and not for our flesh; He will detour us from trouble and lead us down the road to happiness. However, if we are living each day to satisfy our flesh, He won't hold us back; He will let us have the free will rope to hang ourselves. The bible say's to be absent from the body is to be in the presence of the Lord. I think sometimes He has to let us hang ourselves so the spirit inside us will start fighting to live. Do I think God knew when I walked into that bar that night I would meet Johnny, He would leave his wife and we would spend the next 10 years of our life hurting each other? Sure, I know He knew it! Do I think God wanted that to happen? "No! Do I think He could have stopped it? Yes, and He would have if Johnny and I had not been living in Sin! Do I think the enemy lured us to the same place and knew what would happen if we got together? Yes, and I'll tell you why he did it. I think the enemy knew we would fall in love because he knew us both pretty well; he makes it a habit of knowing* the children of God. I think he knew Johnny and I were soul mates and he could tear our souls apart because we weren't living the life our Father wanted us to live. Do I think it all went according to his plan? No! He thought he would throw every dark spirit he had on us until we were so consumed we either killed each other or killed ourselves, but it didn't work! That is when our Father stepped in and said, NO, not this time you don't, not this child you won't! Our Father still had plans for our lives! Whether his plans included Johnny and I being together again someday, only Jesus knows. Never the less, He has called us to do His will so He spared us from the strong holds of the enemy for that season. It's like the footprints in the sand, just when we think He isn't there, He is carrying us.

I feel like God must have been saying,......"**Molly! You weren't supposed to let the enemy talk you into hanging yourself with the free will rope I gave you! You were supposed to use it to pull someone out of the pit!**"

However, the bible also say's what Satan meant for our harm, God will use for our good; and it was the years I spent battling the demons of my life with Johnny, that gave me the courage to fight the ones to come."

Johnny had been called to be a Preacher when he was young. Although Molly wasn't sure what God wanted her to do with her calling, she knew God gave her a warrior Spirit. Molly wondered if God was calling her to fight the spirits of darkness that tormented Johnny so he could preach.

Molly said, *"Johnny was always afraid of the spirit realm and didn't like it when I talked about it; if only I had known then how to cast out his fears in the name of Jesus; both of our lives could have been so different. It's hard to fight a battle when you can't see the enemy and I can't see the enemy that Johnny battles now that we're apart."*

Molly wondered if Johnny had matured enough in his walk with the Lord to fight his own battles or if he still needed someone to fight them for him. She prayed for the day she would hear he was back in church, preaching the Gospel, so she would know he was safe.

Molly said, *"I know the Lord has kept this Love for Johnny in my heart for a reason, because I have asked him many times to take it away. If Johnny still holds a piece of my heart because the Lord knows he will need me some day to help him fight his battle, I will gladly take on that fight! Those demons already know my name and where I live. They have lost the battle at my house because now I can do all things through Christ who strengthens me! I blacked their eyes and sent them packing so they don't even want to get close to Johnny again if I'm around. They know I have reloaded and I've got a lot more ammo than I had before. Only time will tell if Johnny and I will ever cross each other's path again, but this I do know; from now on, my spirit will be my guide and if his spirit is in trouble, the Holy Spirit will lead me to prayer."*

Just as the Holy Spirit led Molly to prayer when Nick was in trouble, Molly had learned to hear the voice of the Lord when others needed her to pray as well. She had finally figured out who she really is on the inside and what her purpose in life truly was. She finally knew why God had put a desire in her heart to write since she was a little girl. It was because He knew someday she would have a story to tell and He wanted her to write it down so all the world could see how she managed to find a way where there seemed to be no way out!

CHAPTER 5

Not only in life, but also in death

Johnny wasn't the first addict Molly had fallen in love with. There seem to be something inside her that drew her to them and them to her. Molly's first love was an alcoholic/drug addict named Gene, she fell in love with at fourteen. Gene was only nineteen, but had several miles on his body by then. Most everyone in the family but Gene's mother was alcoholics who didn't think twice about having a little whiskey for breakfast. His parents worked nights when he was a baby and left Gene at home with his older brothers while they worked. The older boys didn't want to deal with a baby at night, so they would put beer in his baby bottle to make him go to sleep so they could have fun. By the time Gene was 19 he was told by the Doctors if he didn't stop drinking he wouldn't see 21. Molly had known Gene since she was a little girl but hadn't seen him for many years after her family moved to Stilesville.

Molly said, *"The last time I had seen Gene before we ran into each other again was when I was about 7 and he was about 12. Gene had just been in a car accident that almost killed him and had to have his head shaved. I found out when we got together years later that he was drunk and so was the driver when he was in that accident. At the time, I had a crush on his best friend and did since I was three years old; but*

I still remember how he smiled when I saw him that night and he said, **you don't know who I am, do you?"**

Gene and Molly only lived about a mile apart when her parents bought the first house she can remember living in. Gene was one of her Sister Robin's boyfriends and played at her house all the time with his best friend Jamie, who was also one of Robin's boyfriends. Robin and Jamie were 7 years older than Molly; but Gene was only 5 years older than Molly.

They used to have coloring contest and let Molly be the judge since she was too young to color in the lines. Molly would always pick Jamie as the winner even though Gene was the best at coloring. Molly and her family moved from that house when she was five and the house burnt. It had been a couple of years since she had seen Gene that night at the skating rink and she didn't recognize him, but he recognized her. Gene told Molly when they got together that he always knew she would grow up to be beautiful. Gene said, **"I always loved you Molly, even when you were running around in just your underwear."**

It had been 7 years since the last time Molly saw Gene when her parents moved her away from Stilesville. Now Molly looked like a woman and Gene was already a man.

Molly went to the fair one night with her cousin Maria who had a really bad crush on Gene that she had carried since she was 3. Molly and Maria were only 6 months apart and had always been like sisters. Even though Molly was sad they moved away from Stilesville, Maria was glad she had moved back to Bloomingdale so they could be close again. They had always planned when they grew up they would steal Gene and Jamie away from their rival Robin. Maria had a feeling this night would be the night all their dreams would come true at the fair. She had kept up on the Jamie and Gene dirt all through childhood because her parents bought the land where Molly's house had burnt. Now that Maria was in the neighborhood she could keep Molly posted on any Gene or Jamie sightings over the phone. The night had come and they were making plans to run into their true loves at the county fair. They walked the circle time and time again and finally there they were. Maria went into fits shaking her hands whispering *"there they are, there they are!"* Molly didn't have a clue where they were because she was looking for the faces she remembered, not the faces of two grown men. Maria kept shaking as they walked closer and without missing a beat she reached out, grabbed Jamie by his arm, grabbed Molly by her arm, pulled them into each other and said, *"Jamie, this is Molly, Molly, this is Jamie!"*

Just as their eyes started to meet there was a voice that drew Molly's attention away. She looked up to see who had spoken and locked eyes with Gene. From that moment on, Gene had her heart.

She didn't want to look at Gene because she knew how crazy Maria had been about him for so many years, but she couldn't help it. She tried her best to focus on Jamie but Gene had her spell bound. Over and over in her mind she kept telling herself not to look, he belonged to Maria. The guys didn't stick around for long but as they walked away, Molly looked back and so did Gene. Their eyes met again, he smiled and said those words again. Molly quickly turned her head and listened to Maria go on about how gorgeous they were, asking Molly if she still felt the same way for Jamie because she sure did for Gene. Molly was so disappointed but didn't know how to tell Maria she had chosen the wrong boy when they were little. It wasn't Jamie that took her breath away anymore, it was Gene; but how could she tell Maria? Molly decided a plan was a plan and she had to stick to it. After all, Jamie was quite gorgeous himself and it wasn't that she didn't like him anymore; but that she had just got taken away by Gene.

Maria's Dad just happened to be friends with Gene's brother so they got invited to Gene's parent's anniversary party the next day. Molly and Maria were up all night making plans of what they would wear and what they would say when they saw the guys. Molly kept telling Maria she couldn't believe how gorgeous they both grew up to be and Maria kept telling Molly she better stay away from Gene! Molly was supposed to be with Jamie because that was their life long plan and Molly better not forget it. Scared to death to tell Maria what she was feeling because she didn't want to make her mad, Molly just kept it all inside. Molly had a really low self- esteem and couldn't imagine either one of them would want her anyway. Molly thought they were just living in a fantasy world while they were making plans; so it didn't matter if she was secretly crushing on Gene.

However, the next day gave Molly a little more to think about. By the time they got to the party they were both a nervous wreck. Since most of both Gene and Jamie's families like to drink a lot, there was a lot of drinking going on at the party. They of course could have drunk all they wanted but they were only 14 and too afraid at the time.

Molly said, *"I'm not really sure why Maria and I didn't get drunk that day. Maybe it was because her Dad wouldn't let us, I really don't remember, but I know Gene asked me if I wanted a drink. I remember the way he kept looking at me and the little things he would say when I walked in a room. When we played Volley Ball, Gene picked me to be on his team and I could hardly breathe. I think I told Maria I was glad I was on Gene's team so I could look across the net at Jamie, but that wasn't the truth. Gene kept flirting with me, saying sweet little things when he walked behind me on the court. I never told Maria about any of it, maybe I should have but I couldn't stand the thoughts of hurting her."*

The days went by and Maria had one plan right after another for them to run into the guys, but most of them failed. Maria finally managed to get Gene to meet her and Molly at the drive Inn one night, but there was no Jamie to keep Gene away from Molly. Gene had managed to get really messed up that night and tell Molly how he felt. He knew Maria had always liked him so he waited until Maria wasn't paying attention to tell Molly he didn't want her to go out with Jamie, he wanted her for himself. Molly told him to be quiet because Maria would kill her if she found this out, but Gene insisted he wanted to be with her and said he would tell her himself.

Molly said, *"I'll never forget how he leaned over to me and said all he wanted was to be with me, I thought my heart would beat out of my chest. I told him there was no way that could happen and then Maria came back."*

Sometime that week Gene went to the neighborhood where Molly lived and parked his car in a parking lot by the neighborhood pool. It was a beautiful day and he thought Molly might be hanging out at the pool. She wasn't there so he parked his car and waited until she walked down the sidewalk on her way to a friend's house. Molly didn't see him but she heard his voice saying that cute little thing he would always say every time he saw her.

Molly said, "When I heard his voice my heart skipped a beat and I dropped whatever was in my hand. When I bent over to pick it up, I ripped the rear right out of my skin tight jeans and thought I would surely die. I turned around in humiliation, to see if it was really him and if he noticed. He was standing there smiling that smile, staring at me with those big Green eyes that lured me closer to him. I walked over to his car thanking God my rear was behind me. He made a joke about my pants; we laughed then talked for a while. That was the day I knew, there was no denying it, I was in Love with that man. I didn't even think about Maria or anybody else until we parted ways that day; but as soon as we did, reality hit and I didn't know what to do. It wasn't long until he was back in my neighborhood again sitting in a parking lot waiting for me to walk by. There was a girl I knew at school that was living with one of his friends, she was an 18 year old senior and had her own place. Gene told me to say I was spending the night with her so we could all go out. Of course I did and that was when my drinking career started. Gene was a perfect Gentleman outside of getting me drunk. I remember asking him that night how old he was the first time he got drunk because I was feeling guilty for being so drunk. I'll never forget the look on his face when I asked him that question or the answer he gave.

Looking very sad, He said, **"The first time I remember being drunk I was 5."**

I couldn't believe my ears! Five? I said

He sort of grinned and said, **"Yeah, my brothers thought it would be funny to take me to the top of a hill at the bluff and tell me to ride down it on my trike when I was drunk so they could see me crash, that's why I remember it."**

I remembered feeling so bad for him but he didn't seem to think there was anything wrong with it. We snuck out a few more times to our friend's house and during that time we were planning a Birthday party for Maria at my friend Rachel's house. Maria wanted Gene to come so bad in hopes he would finally see how much she loved him and they would be together. Although I knew Gene would be there to see me, I told him he had to pretend he was there to see Maria or it would break her heart. Looking back, I realize the way she found out broke her heart much worse than if I would have had the guts to tell her the truth. I didn't know what to do, I was in love with him too and he sure seemed to be falling for me. He kept telling me he would tell her himself but I knew how bad that would crush her and kept telling him no. It was the day of her 15th Birthday party and he and I snuck off for a while during the day. He bought me some booze for the party, a fifth of Mr. Boston screwdriver to get me started. Gene being there was supposed to be a surprise for Maria and what a surprise it was! Well, it was many years ago and I was really drunk that night so I don't remember exactly how it all went down; but I do remember by the time he got there I had it in my head I didn't like the fact that she liked him anymore. My Mom always said, the truth comes out when you're drunk and boy does it. I remember I kept telling myself I had to keep my feelings under control because it was Maria's birthday and I didn't want to hurt her; but the more I drank the less I could control my feelings. Needless to say, Gene hadn't been at the party long before Maria figured out she wasn't the only one in love with him and her birthday was ruined! If only I had listened to Gene and let him tell her he wanted to be with me, maybe things could have turned out different. Maria wasn't just my cousin, she was my best friend and almost like a sister. I loved her so much if there would have been any way I could have got out of hurting her, I would have. Looking back on the situation I realize, it would have helped if I had just stayed sober that night and kept my feelings for Gene under control. I thought I had it all planned out so she could just see Gene for her birthday and that would make her happy. The problem was I couldn't figure out how I was eventually going to tell her he wanted to be with me and I wanted to be with him too. So instead of thinking things all the way through and finding a way to tell her the truth, I tried to find a way to make both of us happy. When Gene and I were together that day he told me he didn't want to go to the party if he wasn't going to be able to be with me but I insisted he had to go so she could just see him for her birthday. As the old saying goes, the road to hell is paved with good intentions. Although I know in my heart I had good intentions of making her happy for her birthday, I know now I also paved that road to hell I was on for the next several years!

Needless to say, Molly's deception had opened the door for Maria to make Molly's life a living hell. She had half the family against her when she told everyone about Molly being drunk and ruining her birthday party. She had almost everyone at school hating Molly for breaking her heart. She even managed to make Genes mom hate Molly and she didn't even know her. Molly continued to sneak and see Gene but it was pretty hard since Maria had managed to have everyone in the family watching every move she made near Gene. Molly was on a downward spiral from the moment she fell for Gene. She was scared she would get caught every time she snuck out to see Gene, so she just drank some liquid courage and did it anyway. By the fall Gene's pancreas was getting worse by the day. By the time December rolled around he was taking more and more drugs to take away the pain of drinking so he could drink some more. The doctors had told Gene he had an abnormal pancreas but no one knew why, not even his mother.

Molly said, *"Gene's mother once told me Gene was born with an abnormal pancreas and it just couldn't handle all of his excessive drinking; but she had no idea he wasn't really born that way! I didn't find out until many years later after his mother was already gone what the real truth behind Gene's illness was. After his mother passed away I was taking care of Gene's dad and his older brothers would often come to spend the night and get really drunk. It is amazing how much truth comes out of the mouth of a drunk. One night as we all sat around the table drinking and talking they began to tell stories of how they would put beer in Gene's baby bottle when their mom and dad would go to work and leave them to baby sit. It all became perfectly* clear to me then of why the doctors assumed Gene was born with an abnormal pancreas. My guess is, he wasn't born that way at all! His pancreas just wasn't able to develop properly as he grew because he was unknowingly being fed poison by his older brothers. The really sad part is, they still never realized they were the reason he wasn't able to be the man they all expected him to be.

I will never forget the last night I saw him as the gorgeous man I fell in love with. I was supposed to be spending the night with my friend in the neighborhood but had her older Sister's boyfriend drive me to see Gene at one of his friend's house. It was December30ᵗʰ of 1983 and it was bitter cold with a lot of snow that night. They dropped me off so I didn't have a way home if I would have wanted; but I had no intentions of ever leaving that night. It didn't take long before Gene was more messed up than I had ever seen him. He had just turned 20 but had the miles on his insides of a 41 year old alcoholic that got started at 21. He always said something cute when I walked in a room with that crooked little smile like he did when he lay there on that bed I later left him on that night. Since I only got to see him on the weekends I was so happy to be with him; but his friend really creeped me out as soon as I walked in that night. I had to start drinking pretty heavy if I wanted to catch up with Gene so I went for the straight vodka and chased it with Little Kings malt beer. It didn't take long into my buzz before the phone rang and I had been found. Still to this day I'm not really sure how it happened but for some reason my Dad decided to check up on me that night. When my friends got home their Mom asked where I was and gave them no choice but to tell. When they told their Mom where they left me, she told my Dad and he called my cousin Maria to get Gene's parents phone number to find out how to reach me at his friend's house where I was dropped off. Looking back, I was never really sure if my Dad checked up on me on his own or if he was put up to it. Never the less, I was had and things went downhill quick. My heart breaks when I think of the horrible things I said to my Dad that *night. The more he threatened to kill Gene if I didn't come home, the madder I got. There was no one going to get me away from him that night, I had to much liquid courage and I would have fought a bear to stay with him. However, I think God saved me from myself that night as well."*

Just as the phone started ringing nonstop, Gene began to pass out. As Gene faded in and out of consciousness his friend got creepier. Then about the time her Dad had given up calling Molly came to her senses and remembered the rumor about Gene's crazy friend raping some girl. She couldn't get Gene to respond when she told him to tell the creep she wouldn't be sleeping with both of them and then reality set in. She called her Dad back and told him she would be willing to take a cab home if he would pay for it. When Molly got home that night she was ready to fight. She knew she had it coming but she was too stubborn and too drunk to back down. She was in love and thought she was an adult since she had been taking care of things at home for so long. She felt the only reason her dad was acting this way about her and Gene being together was because of the things Maria had told them about Gene. She was tired of Maria turning everyone against them being together and was tired of hiding how she felt. She was about to make a stand and fight for the man she loved even if it meant fighting her own Dad that she loved more than anything. She stormed in the door with her fists clinched tight, but wasn't ready for what she walked into.

There her Dad sat in a chair, with tears in his eyes flowing down his face like rain. He looked up at her and said, **"My little birdie is ready to leave the nest and I can't stop her."**

Molly's heart was broken when she saw her Daddy cry. Molly said, *"It couldn't have hurt any worse if he had punched me in the face, I wanted to crawl off in a hole and die."*

The next day Molly was too ashamed to show her face in the house. She didn't want to come out of her room and have to face her Dad again. Needless to say, eventually she had to come out but to her surprise not much was said. The only person who had anything to say was her Sister's boyfriend who threatened to kill Gene if he didn't stay away from her. Molly didn't care much for her Sister Robin's pip squeak boyfriend anyway because he had beaten her Dad's face beyond recognition not to long before. She told him it was none of his business and walked out. Molly's Dad never held a grudge on anyone and had forgiven the lunatic for what he had done to him; but Molly never forgot the brutal beating he gave her Dad and wished she could give it back to him that day. His threats toward Gene only made her despise him more. Molly waited patiently to hear from Gene but he never called or showed up in her neighborhood looking for her like he usually did. Although it didn't take long it seemed like forever before Molly found out why Gene hadn't contacted her. He had been put in the hospital and had an emergency surgery to keep him alive the next day after she last saw him. His excessive drinking had finally taken him down.

The day the Doctors predicted had come and the Gene she knew would soon be gone. They had to cut him in so many places to fix all the problems it looked like he had been slashed in a knife fight. They had to take out part of his pancreas which eventually made him become a diabetic. They had to take out his gallbladder, his spleen and appendix. God only knows what all they had to repair to keep him alive and He was never the same again. While Gene was in the hospital fighting for his life, Robin's lunatic boyfriend decided to call and threaten to take what was left of his life if he ever saw Molly again. Molly had no idea any of this had happened for a very long while. She just kept thinking Gene forgot about her and that he didn't really love her at all. Molly was convinced she wasn't good enough for Gene because he was the most gorgeous man she had ever laid her eyes on. All she could think about was his big green eyes and sun kissed hair against his golden brown skin. The sweet little things he would say when she walked into a room and how good she felt to be in his arms. Her heart ached for days until she found out why she hadn't heard from Gene and then it ached for months when she found out he was gone from her without even saying good bye.

Maria was the one who broke the bad news to Molly that Gene had been in the hospital. She probably couldn't wait to tell Molly how Gene had got so sick from the last night they were together that he almost died. It probably gave Maria even more pleasure to let Molly know about Gene's new girlfriend.

Molly said, "Not that I didn't deserve Maria enjoying my pain for the pain I had put her through but at the time I didn't understand how she could take so much pleasure in seeing me hurt when I knew how bad it hurt me to hurt her. Now I understand, my falling in love with Gene didn't hurt her near as much as me hiding it from her and the way she finally found out. We can't help who we fall in love with but if I could turn back time; I certainly would have done things different. Maybe it wouldn't have mattered but I would give anything if I would have had the guts to tell her in the beginning. I've always heard the truth can set you free and I would love to know if my telling the truth could have saved us both from all that pain."

Gene had somehow met a girl Molly and Maria went to school with and wound up hooking up with her while he was in the hospital. They sent him home with instructions to never drink again unless he wanted to die. They made sure he had enough pain meds to over dose a horse and he took over his dose every day. Gene decided if he couldn't drink alcohol he would get drunk on his medication and when that ran out he was on the hunt for more. Molly had to see

Marissa every day at school and get it rubbed in her face that she was Gene's new girlfriend. Of course the story was going around how much in love they were, which hurt Molly even more. Since Molly hadn't heard from Gene she had no reason to believe it wasn't true and tried her best to move on.

Molly and Maria finally made amends but their relationship was tarnished to say the least. Molly met a new boy who stole a piece of her heart from Gene, but he was way too wild to tame. He had more girlfriends than the law should allow and never made Molly feel as special as she felt with Gene. Time went on and Molly wondered if she would ever see Gene again; if she would still love him when she did or if they would someday get back together. It took over a year but when Molly was 16 she found her way back to Gene. By this time Gene was so far gone on the drugs he was near death again. Molly thought she could help him but all she managed to do was enable him to get worse. Gene barely weighed 100 pounds, he was like a skeleton with skin stretched over it and all of Molly's friends asked why she even wanted to be with him anymore.

Molly always said, *"When we get old neither one of us are going to look very good and I'll still love him then, so what does it matter now?"*

Gene was far from being the gorgeous man she fell in love with but Molly loved him still the same. As time went on things kept getting worse and Gene kept using stronger drugs to ease his pain. He started drinking again even though the Doctors warned him not to or he would die. Everyday Gene was on the hunt for some more drugs and every night Molly feared he wouldn't wake up this time. It got to the point he was sneaking behind her back putting needles in his arms until finally one night he died right in front of her.

The evening started with them riding his motorcycle into town to see her Sister Robin. Gene was acting weird on the ride through town. Telling Molly to stop trying to jump off the back of the bike and that if they hit a pebble on the road or a manhole cover they would get killed. Molly thought he was goofing around at first; but then she realized he was serious when he started dodging pebbles and manholes.

Molly said, *"I remember praying all the way to my Sisters that God would keep his hand on us so we didn't wreck again."*

It wasn't but a week or two before that Gene had gotten messed up and drained all the oil out of the bike. When they took off on the bike it locked up on the highway and they crashed.

Molly said, *"I remember when we crashed I looked up and saw Gene laying in the road and a big truck was coming, I reached over and pulled him out of the way. When we got the bike off the side of the road I begged Gene to let me call my brother to come and get us but he wouldn't let me."*

Gene begged Molly to get back on the bike because he was afraid her brother would kill him if he found out he had wrecked Molly. They got back on the bike but didn't make it very far before it locked up again on another highway. This time Gene managed to throw the bike to the side of the highway and Molly jumped off without getting hurt. Molly refused to get back on this time, they were only a few miles from Gene's house and Molly insisted she would walk there to get his Mom because Gene was hurt. Gene made Molly promise she wouldn't tell anyone about the wrecks and told her to take his drugs and hide them in case the cops showed up. On the way to Genes house Molly had a little time to think about how stupid she was for riding around on a motorcycle with someone who was screwed up on drugs with an 8 ball of cocaine in her pocket. How would her parents feel if she got killed and they found drugs in her pocket? How would they feel if they knew she had been doing the drugs too? Molly began to pray and ask God to help her find a way out of this. It didn't take long before Molly's prayers were answered and God made a way for Molly to get out of that situation.

The night they were on their way to see Molly's sister, Molly began to think as she prayed for them to make it there alive. She thought about how many Demerol pills Gene had taken in the past week. She thought about all the cocaine and the marijuana he had done. She thought about the day her nose began to bleed while they were visiting the drug dealers and how embarrassed she was most of the time. When they made it to her Sisters house Molly had decided to take it easy that night and not get too high or drunk. They hadn't been there very long when Molly found out Gene was in the bathroom shooting up some dope with Robin's friend. When Gene came in the kitchen and sat down at the table with Molly she began to question him about what he was doing in the bathroom. Molly knew Gene had just got a prescription for 100 Demerol pills two days before and Gene usually took about 30 pills a day. She started nagging at him about all the pills he had taken and what he was doing in the bathroom. Gene had a few pills left in his pocket and tried to give them to Molly to get her to not be mad at him.

Molly said, *"I'll never forget him sliding what was left of the pills across the table to me and saying, "Here, you can have them". I was so angry, I shoved the pills back at him and said, I don't want your damn pills! He slowly slid them back to me again and then he went stiff as a board and fell straight back in the floor. I started screaming for someone to help me. My Sister's friend was a nurse and she came running to the kitchen, she checked his pulse but couldn't find one. I immediately began to cry out to the Lord and beg him to forgive us.*

I was running around the house, pouring out the booze, throwing the pills in the trash, shooting the syringes filled with dope into the air and begging God to let him live! Gene still lay there stiff as a board, no breath, no pulse, no nothing, for several minutes. I repented, I begged, I pleaded, I promised God I would never do anything wrong again if he would just bring Gene back.

Then suddenly Gene began to go into a seizure, he was reaching for a fan, foaming at the mouth and convulsing. Then suddenly Robin's friend began to seize; then another teenage girl that was there started to seize. I thought I had slipped off into the twilight zone and didn't know anything else to do but pray!"

By this time someone had gone to the neighbors to call the paramedics and they were on their way. Gene finally snapped out of it but was pretty lifeless when it was all over. Molly got him to a bed and continued to cry and pray until the paramedics arrived. Gene couldn't understand why they were there. He thought they were telling him he had to go to the hospital to have another surgery and kept refusing to go. Molly begged him to go but he wouldn't and as long as he refused and was able to tell them who he was, they couldn't take him. Molly sat up all night and worried he would go to sleep and not wake up. The next day they went home to Gene's house and were watching a TV show that showed someone having a seizure.

Molly said, *"I told Gene, that is what you did last night and he couldn't believe it."*

Gene explained to Molly he didn't understand what they were saying the night before. He told her if he had known that was what had happened he would have gone to the hospital. Molly was so scared she didn't know what to do anymore. Gene had gotten so bad he was shooting sleeping pills in the muscles of his legs in the middle of the night.

Molly said, *"I was horrified when I was lying in bed one night, I felt Gene move, looked over and saw a needle in Gene's hand coming down on his leg in the moonlight shining through the window. I rolled over, cried and begged God not to let him die next to me. That was a lot for a 17 year old girl to go through and I know I couldn't have made it through it without the Lord. Shortly after the night at Robins and the wrecks on the motor cycle, Gene and I went out with one of my best friends and her boyfriend. We stayed the night at Rachel's house because her parents were out of town. Gene and I slept in her parents room and of course we were all pretty messed up. A few days later, Rachel's step Dad said He had a very expensive gun missing from their room and questioned Rachel who was in the house while they were gone. When Rachel told them that Gene and I spent the night and slept in their room, Gene got the blame for stealing the gun. Looking back, I know now that Gene didn't really steal that gun. Rachel even told me years later they suspected her step dad lied about the gun being stolen to collect insurance money. Never the less, at the time Rachel said her mom wouldn't let us be friends anymore because I was with Gene. I was looking for an excuse to get out of the relationship anyway because I couldn't take that life anymore. I thought if I broke up with Gene Rachel and I could still be friends and there could be a chance I could get on a road to a better life; but that didn't happen either. The truth is, I wasn't strong enough in the Lord to help Gene fight the unclean spirits that ruled his life and they were taking control of mine too. Somehow I knew I wasn't strong enough to battle the road to addiction I was on and help Gene with his battle too; so this seemed like a way to get out and try to save myself. Gene swore He didn't do it and I know I broke his heart when I refused to believe him. The truth Is, I really did believe him but I thought if I didn't have a good excuse to leave him, I would have to admit the truth and that would hurt him worse! My heart still aches when I think of how I failed that man. Now that I know all the things I didn't know then, I realize if I had told him the truth, he might have had a reason to try to quit. If only I had known how to fight the spirits of fear and addiction, maybe it could have turned out a lot different. If only I had believed I was good enough for someone to love in their right mind, maybe Gene could have found strength in our love."*

When Molly told Robin Gene had been accused of stealing the gun from Rachel's house; Robin decided to fill her in on a few more things she didn't know. Robin told Molly Gene had been coming over to her house asking for dirty needles late at night when Molly wasn't with him.

Robin said, ***"He begged me not to tell you Molly, but He is really strung out and you just need to stay away from Him before you get AIDS!"***

Molly's heart was broken because she wanted to believe Gene didn't steal the gun, but she knew even if he didn't steal the gun she was taking a chance on putting her life in even more danger if she went back to him now. Molly knew she would always love Gene but it would be better if she loved him from a distance.

Shortly after Molly left Gene, he went to the Mayo Clinic to get off the drugs. Gene never called Molly while he was there and then he moved to Ohio with his brother when he got out. Molly kept thinking he would call and ask her to come to Ohio but time went on and he never called. Maria always had the scoop on Gene because she hung out with Gene's sister in-law. She always hated Molly and told Maria Gene had found a good girl friend in Ohio and he wouldn't be coming back. She bragged about how good he looked since he had gotten off the drugs and how pretty his new girlfriend was. She told Maria the Doctors told him to never come back if he wanted to stay straight and he was very happy there. Maria was sure to let Molly in on all the details and sometimes Molly wondered if she took pleasure in seeing her hurt. Molly loved Gene so much all she really wanted was for him to be happy and well; but she didn't understand why it couldn't be with her. She secretly prayed he would come back to her someday like a knight in shining armor to take her away on his motorcycle to Ohio.

It had been almost a year since Molly saw Gene and she was severely depressed. She went looking for love in all the wrong places and had decided it wasn't Gods will for anyone to love her. She was now 18 and more depressed than she had ever been. The only other guy she cared anything about was the wild one who stole a piece of her heart when she lost Gene the first time at 14. She had bounced back and forth between the two of them for the past 4 years, but Con was still as wild as ever and on his way to be a rock star. Molly didn't understand why Con would make her feel so bad but hold on to her so tight when they were alone. They were both stubborn and couldn't admit their feelings to save their own souls. They would say things to hurt each other in front of people; then love each other to death when they were alone. After Gene was gone Molly went to see Con but he was feeling like being mean that day and told her he had slept with Rachel while she was off with Gene. Molly had already broken up with Gene because of Rachel, but she hadn't hung out with Rachel since the gun episode. When Con told Molly he slept with Rachel, she was devastated and believed it to be true since Rachel had dumped their friendship like she did. Molly didn't find out until many years later that Con only told her that to hurt her because she had been back with Gene. Molly and Con had a young and crazy kind of love that often drove them to hurt each other. They were only 2 days apart in age and were so much alike they couldn't see the forest for the trees. By this time Maria and Molly were on pretty good terms and Maria suggested Molly pay Rachel back by going out with Joey. Rachel had a big crush on Joey and he was one of Rachel's "Hands off" boys. Molly thought Maria had a pretty good idea since Rachel knew Con was her "Hands off" boy and thought she had slept with him; so Molly set out for revenge.

Molly said, *"Looking back, I now see why my life got so bad; could it be because "vengeance is mine", says the Lord? That pay back date lasted 8 years but at least I got two beautiful children from it. It just goes to show that what the bible says is true; what Satan meant to harm us, God will use for our good. I know now, that spirit of depression Satan put on me was what kept me with Joey all that time, but God used it for my good when he gave me those children."*

It didn't take long for Gene to find out Molly was with Joey. Within a few months of her being with him Gene called to tell her he thought she would come to Ohio. Molly didn't know what to think or what to say. She told Gene she thought he would have asked her to come and he told her he thought she would have just come to find him. She told him it was a little late for that now that she was living with someone else.

Molly said, *"I'll never forget what Gene told me that day that made my heart melt.'*

Gene said, **"I'll be coming back there soon and when I do I'm coming back for you."**

It didn't take long until Gene was back in town and called Molly again. He asked her to come and see him and of course she did even though she knew it wasn't right to do that to Joey. However, she had already caught Joey cheating with his ex-girlfriend by this time so she thought he had it coming. Besides that, she knew she still loved Gene with all her heart and if he had actually changed she would leave Joey in a heartbeat. She went to see Gene and prayed all the way there that things would finally be good; but the enemy must have heard her prayers and screwed things up before she got there. It hadn't been more than a couple of hours since she talked to Gene on the phone and he sounded great; but by the time she got there he was wasted. She asked him why he was messed up when he sounded fine on the phone. He told her he got nervous about seeing her and just thought he would have a drink to get the nerve to see her again. She was so angry, she told him she wouldn't leave Joey for him and she left. Gene never stopped drinking and doing drugs again. He tried several times to get Molly back over the years but every time he came close, he got messed up and ruined it. When Molly had Nick, Gene found a girlfriend and got her pregnant shortly after. He called Molly and told her he was going to be having a Son like she did. Then Molly had Sarah and Gene found another girlfriend and got her pregnant. He called Molly again and told her he was going to be having a little girl like her and he begged Molly to come and see him. Molly went because he sounded straight on the phone but when she got there he was really messed up lying in bed sick.

Molly was so upset with him, but she tried to keep her cool and find out why he wanted her to come to his house so bad. He had a quilt on his bed that his Grandma had made him before she died that was called the wedding ring quilt. He told Molly his Mom had just given it to him because he was finally out on his own, living with a girl. He told Molly he wasn't supposed to get the quilt until he got married but it didn't look like he was ever getting married so his Mom gave it to him anyway. Then he said, **"If we would have gotten married, Mom would have given us this quilt as a wedding present from Grandma."**

Then he began to get sick and throw up in a basket beside the bed. Molly was so upset she started saying, *"Why are you doing this to yourself? When are you going to stop doing this Gene?"*

Gene looked up at her with those big green eyes and said, **"When you marry me!"**

It tore Molly apart to see him that way again. She thought her heart would break in two; but at the same time she didn't know why he would say such a thing to her. She thought it must be the booze talking because he never asked her to marry him when they were together. She wondered why he would say he wanted to marry her now that they were both with someone else. She was in a state of confusion and didn't know what to say or what to do. She told him she had to go, he begged her not to but she left anyway for fear his girlfriend would show up to find her in their house with him dead.

Molly said, *"I remember driving home that day begging God to help him and wondering if he meant what he said. I wondered if I could be strong enough to go back and help him get straight. I wondered what our life would be like if he got straight, we got married and raised the four kids we would have with other people together. I prayed all the way home, asking God to help me to know what to do. Telling God if Gene meant what he said to please make him get clean so we could be together; because I wanted out of the relationship with Joey so bad. What a state of confusion I was in that day. All I could think about was all those years I wasted praying Gene would get straight only to wind up in a relationship with a more functioning alcoholic! Now here I am, 25 years old with two children in a relationship with a cheating, alcoholic that doesn't even believe in God and I can't stand to be with anymore. How could I even be thinking about going back to a drug addicted alcoholic that can't even tell me how he feels when he's in his right mind; but wants to lay this on me when he is messed up? What about my children? What about me? Why can't anything go the way I want it to? The more I thought about it, the angrier I got! I just didn't understand why I had to feel this way. Why did I have to feel guilty for wanting to be happy? Why wouldn't God just supernaturally change my life the way He knows I want it to be? Why didn't I deserve to be happy? Why didn't anyone ever love me unless they were messed up?"*

Seeing Gene that day only put Molly into a deeper depression than she was already in. As soon as he found out she left Joey he started calling and begging her to come see him again. Molly then found out how bad she had hurt Gene that day when she walked out on him.

Molly said, *"Still to this day I feel so bad for hurting Gene like that. I know how hard it must have been for him to finally get up the nerve to tell me he wanted to marry me after all those years of us being apart. I will always wonder if I could have made a difference in his life, if only I had known then what I know now."*

When Gene found out Molly had finally left Joey he tried his best to get her back again but he couldn't stay straight long enough to get the job done. Molly was determined she would never be in a relationship with another alcoholic, drug addict or atheist again. No matter how mad she got at God or how far she ran from Him, she knew that couldn't be what He wanted for her life. Now that she was free it was going to take someone who was willing to prove his love to her before she would ever give another piece of her heart away again. Gene kept trying on up until Molly met Johnny, but she shot him down every time he called or came around. She was a woman scorned and out to seek only whom she could devour.

Molly said, *"Looking back, if I had known then what I know now, I think I could have used the Love Gene had for me to help Gene get well. I think there was a real good chance he loved me enough that he might have been alive still today if I had only been where I needed to be with the Lord."*

Molly had been with Johnny about 9 months when Gene passed away. Although she was already in love with Johnny in a way she had never known before, she thought she would die with Gene for a while.

Molly said, *"Looking back, I think a part of me did die with Gene, the innocent part that holds on to love in hopes of a brighter day."*

Years later, Molly found out that Gene had stopped taking his insulin because the Doctors had only given his Dad a year to live. When Gene heard the fate of his Dad he said, **"I'll die before you do, because I can't make it without you."** Gene stopped taking his insulin and then drank himself into a diabetic coma.

When Molly got the call from Jamie that Gene was in the hospital in a coma she fell apart. Johnny didn't understand why Molly was so upset and got angry with her because she wanted to go to the hospital alone. Molly didn't want Johnny to see her falling apart and knew she needed to do this alone; but he was very upset about her going. She went to the hospital without him anyway and was glad she did when she got there. She went into Gene's room and all the family was there. Gene had been in a coma for two days by the time Jamie called Molly. She went to his bed side, holding back her tears she put her hand on his and said with a trembling voice, *"Gene, its Molly."*

It must be true that a coma patient still has their hearing because as soon as Molly spoke, Gene opened one eye and stared straight at her.

Molly said, *"I don't even know if I spoke again, it was like I was frozen in time falling apart inside myself. I just remember the way he looked at me with that one eye and hearing the family say, "**Oh my God, he opened his eye for Molly**". His Mother walked over to the* bed, grabbed me and said, **"He has been in a coma for two days and you're the only person he opened his eye for."** *I think I told him I loved him and ran out of the room. Johnny was paging me every minute so I ran to a phone in the hall to call him. I did my best to pull it together long enough to make the call and I remember seeing one of our good friends step off the elevator. I hung up with Johnny and walked back in the room with him. As soon as we walked in the room the family started talking about Gene opening his eye when I came in the first time. We walked over to the bed and again I put my hand on his, Mark put his hand on Gene's chest and said, **"Gene it's me Mark and Molly here."** Again, Gene opened one eye and looked straight at me and again I was frozen and falling apart inside myself. I didn't stay long because I didn't want to make things harder on everyone else by me falling apart. I don't even remember the drive home, but I remember the fight I had with Johnny when I got back. He was so jealous that I was taking it so hard over Gene that he drilled me all night."*

Molly cried all night until she had a migraine and was throwing up. The next day Johnny told her they needed to get out of the house because the phone wouldn't stop ringing with people calling about Gene. She agreed to go with Johnny to his Dad's to watch a fight on pay per view in hopes she could stop crying and stop fighting with Johnny. She knew she had no control over what would happen to Gene because he was in the hands of the Lord now and she had to let the Lord take care of it. Still, she couldn't stop thinking about him all day and all night. Somehow Maria managed to get Johnny's Dad's phone number and call her late that night crying that she needed to get to the hospital quick because Gene was about to take his last breath. Of course Molly fell apart again and Johnny went over the edge again. He had no understanding of her pain and she had no understanding of his jealous behavior. She wondered how anyone could be jealous of a dying man that he knew she could have been with if she wanted to and he was beginning to make her wonder if she didn't make a really big mistake.

Molly said, *"Looking back I know the devil was dancing all around and jumping up and down at all my misery. He put the spirit of jealousy on Johnny so he could put the spirit of confusion on me. He had us both right where he wanted us and he was about to unload."*

When the day of the funeral came there was no way Johnny would allow Molly to go without him. Molly was so afraid to fall apart in front of Johnny for fear of another fight; that she felt she was choking on her own tears and emotions. They somehow made it through the day without a fight; but Gene's Mom could tell there was something wrong and called Molly out on it in front of Johnny.

Molly said, *"I'll never forget how she looked me straight in the eyes and pointed at Johnny and said,* **"Is he good to you? He better be!"**

Molly didn't tell her what was going on, but she really wanted to. Molly kept in touch with Gene's parents until they both passed away. She said she would always love them and knew they would be waiting for her to see them again someday.

Molly said, *"It took years before I understood why things didn't work out with me and Gene, why he couldn't get straight, why he had to die so young. It was like Gene had a target on his head at birth. His brothers putting the beer in his baby bottle when they had to baby sit was only the beginning. Could it be that Satan knew the spirit God had sent to Gene was one that had a calling to do great things? Could it be that Satan knew if Gene and I had spent time together with Gene being alcohol and drug free we may have been able to strengthen one another? Could it be, the very reason we loved each other that much without ever sharing the kind of love that Johnny and I shared was because our spirits somehow knew we belonged together?"*

It had been years since the thought of being married to Gene and living happily ever after had crossed Molly's mind. She remembered those thoughts from her youth and wondered why they had surfaced again. Why did it hurt so bad to remember his attempts at getting her back? Why did she ache inside when she remembered the way he looked at her? These were things she took for granted at the time. The way he looked at her seemed to be so trivial compared to the way he looked for drugs. Sure, it made her feel good for a moment; but then she felt so unimportant when he picked up a bottle, a pipe, or a bag of drugs.

Molly said, "*I always felt Gene loved the alcohol and drugs more than he loved anyone or anything in the world. When Gene was in his right mind he was in so much torment he couldn't even think of love or affection. He was in so much pain, he couldn't think of anything but how to silence the thought of where to get his next fix. Now I know, he didn't know how to express his love without it; because he didn't really know how love was supposed to feel in his right mind. There is no doubt in my mind the enemy used his family to destroy him because he knew the sweet and tender spirit that had been sent from God to dwell in Gene's body. It wasn't their fault, they knew no better and I know how much they loved him. They were all afflicted with unclean spirits of alcoholism except his Mother. She was a wonderful woman but she didn't know how to fight the battle; so she just tried her best to clean up all the messes. Oh how my heart aches when I think of all the things I could have done different. Tears fill my eyes, when I think of how different it all could have been; if only I had not run away from the voice of the Lord. My heart kept leading me back to him every time he would call; but my head would tell me to go, because he would never change. If only I would have been the spiritual warrior God created me to be back then. I could have fought that battle for Gene, called on the name of Jesus and commanded those unclean spirits that tormented his soul and destroyed his body to leave! If only I had fell in love with*

*Jesus first before I fell in love with Gene at fourteen; maybe I would have understood the love I had for Gene in my heart. Despite the fact most would argue with me that Gene couldn't have been saved because he never went to an alter in prayer and turned from his sin; I know he was. I know he was because I know how he cried for his Aunt Rose in the middle of the night because he knew she was a Christian. I believe that was the very reason he wanted me in his life; because he knew when I was beside him, I was silently praying for God to help him. I didn't know how to fight the good fight back then, but I knew how to call on Jesus to help us get through it. I believe now, Gene must have known when I put my hand on his back at night I was praying for him to be saved and I think he felt safe with me. Matthew 7:7 says, **"Ask, and it will be given you; Seek and ye shall find; knock, and it will be opened to you."** Yes, I know our Father in heaven had mercy upon Gene and took him out of his torment. Maybe God sent a warrior to fight the battle for Gene but the warrior God sent only knew how to call on Jesus, she didn't know how to listen to Him; so God had to take Gene out of the fight before he was devoured. As the old saying goes, "only the good die young", have you ever wondered why?"*

Maybe the good that die young are part of the lesson we need to learn. If we all have a purpose and I believe we do, then maybe that is their purpose. Maybe there are those who are sent to love and those who are sent to be loved. Maybe those who are sent to fight the good fight need those who are sent to be loved to fight for. It is usually those who love the most who are the most fearless. If it weren't for the love of something there would be nothing to fight for. Those who are led by the wrong spirits find it fit to fight for the love of money or power. Those who are led by the spirit of God fight only for what is right in the eyes of God. After years of wondering, Molly finally knew her love for Gene was not only right with God but it was also the will of God. For it was the will of God for her warrior spirit to fight for the spirit of the meek like Gene, to claim the power in the Blood of the Lamb and victory in the name of Jesus! Even though Molly had not yet understood her calling while Gene was alive, she never stopped praying for him. Maybe that was her only purpose where Gene was concerned. God is all knowing! Therefore, He must have known Molly wouldn't make it to be the person He wanted her to be while Gene was alive. Could it be that Gene was part of God's plan? Could Gene have been one of many teachers sent from God to prepare Molly for the ultimate battle? Just as Almighty God hid the secrets of the crucifixion from our enemy and allowed him his time to gloat. Could He also have allowed the enemy to think he had won the battle with Gene and Molly? Could our all knowing, Sovereign God of all creation, have tricked the enemy once again into thinking he had one up on him? Yes, He could have and I think He did! He hid the secrets of the crucifixion so well the enemy actually thought he had won when God's chosen people sent His only Son to the cross. Can you imagine the look on his face when Jesus showed up in hell to set the captives free and fill him in that he had just saved the world?

It brings joy to my soul and laughter to my lips when I think of the fear on Satan's face when he saw my Lord and Savior had the keys to death and hell in his hands. I bet he had his moment of laughs when he saw all the pain he put Gene and Molly through for so many years. I bet he was laughing all the way to the grave when he saw Gene take his last breath, right up to the moment he saw Jesus. I can hear him now being the accuser he has always been, cursing every breath of Gene's life, condemning him to an eternity of torment. Just as I can see my Lord Jesus saying, "***NO! Not this one you don't! I paid the price for his sins and he called upon MY NAME to have mercy upon him, so get behind Me Satan!***"

Molly said, *"Our Lord Jesus made a promise that the meek shall inherit the earth, the pure at heart shall see God and the poor in spirit shall obtain treasures of the kingdom of heaven. I know Jesus doesn't lie; so Gene will surely see God, obtain treasures and be one of the inheritors of this earth on judgment day. Glory be to God for hearing my prayers and setting him free."*

CHAPTER 6

I was asleep while the enemy invaded my camp and stole my Son!

It was the first week of July 2008, Molly couldn't remember the exact day. She was driving in her car when the spirit of God hit her in the gut like a piercing sword that went all the way to her heart. She had a very strong feeling to pray for her Son. As she began to pray she knew in her heart something was very bad wrong. Without knowing why, she began to rebuke the enemy and demand him to get away from her Son.

"He is my Son, she declared! He is mine and he belongs to my Lord and Savior Jesus Christ! You can't have him, do you hear me? You can't have him and I will fight you tooth and nail if you think you can!"

She drove for miles declaring her Son unto God. She couldn't remember how long this went on, only it seemed to have been a long while. When the spirit of God left her that day she went on with life as usual. Finishing her work, going home and doing whatever came next, it was just an average day of the week. The weekend to come was the 4th of July holiday and she had plans to go to a party on Friday the 4th and fireworks Saturday the 5th. She went on with her plans and didn't really think too much more about what happened in her car. Her Son was 19 and she usually only saw him in passing.

She saw him briefly after her experience in the car and casually asked him if there was anything going on that she should know about.

Of course his reply was, **"No, is there supposed to be something going on?"**

Molly replied with her usual *"You tell me, is there something going on? Have you been doing things you're not supposed to be doing?"*

Nick replied, **"No, have you been doing things you're not supposed to be doing?"**

Molly just dropped it as usual, for fear he might nail her about the things she was doing wrong. Besides, Nick never really thought she needed to know about anything that was going on in his life and she knew it was too late to change things now. Nicholas was always very quiet and secretive. He rarely told his Mom or anyone else what was going on in his life or in his head. If he told his friends they weren't telling her and even if they would she only knew one of them. Nick had battled with drug addiction since he was 15 but Molly didn't find out until he was 17 and he got in trouble at school. Not long before that Molly got one of those gut feelings that Nick was slipping away and prayed for God to help her get closer to her Son. Nick was a loner and Molly didn't know how to get him to come out of his shell. She was convinced he was just a quiet person like his Dad and there was nothing she could do about it. Molly regrets she didn't do a lot of things different while the children were young.

Molly said, *"Looking back, I was sleeping while the enemy invaded my camp and stole my child"*.

It all started when Nick was about 2 and Molly's Dad died of cancer. Molly didn't even realize it at the time but her grief had taken quite the toll on her life. She remembered being angry all the time and often taking her anger out on Nick when he would act up as 2 year olds do.

Molly said, *"I was angry about my Dad not being there to see Nick grow up and I was angry that Joey didn't show Nick the kind of love my Dad did when he was alive. I was lucky if I got a few hours of sleep a night and then I was rushing in the morning to get Nick to day care so I could get to work on time. The only thing I can remember during the first few years after my Father passed away is feeling like I was all alone in the world and Nick was the only thing I had to live for. Being mentally tired from grief and physically tired when I got off work, dealing with an energetic 2 year old that was no doubt starving for attention was more than I could handle. I remember trying my best to be a good Mom but nothing ever seemed to be good enough. Looking back, I realize now, Nick couldn't feel my Love because my Love was lost for a while in the grief. I was going through the motions of being a Mother but wasn't capable of showing him the Love every child needs to be able to grow up and be a loving person. Joey wasn't any help because he never knew how to love and that made matters worse for me. Nick was just trying to get someone's attention by acting out and I was too lost to see the signs.*

It was Sunday July the 6th 2008 when life as Molly knew it changed forever. Molly had gone to a gambling boat after the fireworks on Saturday night and didn't get home until about 5:00 a.m. When Sarah woke Molly up to go to church Molly was too tired to go and told Sarah to ask Nick if he would drop her off and then Molly would pick her up after service. Molly went back to sleep and had no idea that Nick had actually decided to go with Sarah to church. When it came time for Molly to pick Sarah up, Sarah told Molly Nick had gone to church with her and she would be going to her boyfriend's house after church so she didn't need to pick her up. Nick came home after church and told Molly he had been saved at church. Molly felt numb and didn't understand why she wasn't jumping for joy but there was something weird about Nick's countenance that she didn't understand. Molly was about to go with her boyfriend to his house so he could feed his animals and asked Nick if he would like to go; to Molly's surprise Nick said yes.

All the way there Nick had a heavy spirit upon him that Molly could feel but couldn't quite figure out. She wondered if he had taken some kind of drugs before he went to church that he was struggling to get out of his system. When they got to Clay's house, Nick wondered off in the woods alone while Molly was in the house. He asked Clay if there was a pond or creek in the woods and Clay said yes. Clay told Nick that he and Molly would meet him down by the creek when he got done feeding the animals. Molly came out to help Clay feed the animals and asked him where Nick was. When Clay told Molly Nick had gone on into the woods Molly had a very bad feeling. She didn't know why but she had a thought that the enemy would try to get inside Nicks head if he caught him alone in the woods. At that time, Molly didn't know how to tell the difference between her own thoughts and those that were spoke to her from the spiritual realm; all she knew was she had a bad feeling.

Molly and Clay took the four-wheeler down into the woods to look for Nick and it took a while before they found him. By the time they found Nick Molly could feel the evil all around her and was beginning to get a little scared. She cried out for Nick every time they stopped but he didn't answer for a long while. Finally Clay saw him down by the edge of the creek and again Molly cried out for Nick but he still didn't answer. Molly and Clay got off the four-wheeler and started walking towards Nick.

Molly said, "I just remember having this real weird feeling that there was something in the woods that was after Nick. I couldn't explain what I felt and I tried to ignore it but it didn't feel right and I felt very scared of whatever it was."

When Molly and Clay found Nick she asked him why he didn't answer her and he said he didn't hear her. Molly knew he had to have heard her because she was yelling so loud. She decided to drop the subject and they just started walking side by side along the creek.

Molly said, *"At one point Nick reached over and put his arm around me while we walked and I remember feeling uneasy that he was touching me."*

He said, **"You don't believe me that I got saved today do you Mom?"**

"Of course I believe you Son," she replied.

"Then why don't you seem to be happy about it?" replied Nick.

Molly replied, *"I am happy Son, I just don't know what to say, I never thought this day would happen and I think I'm in shock."*

Molly truly didn't know why She was feeling the way she felt. She had no understanding of how strong the spirit realm is at that time. Still wondering why she was speechless instead of jumping for joy, she couldn't help but to feel completely resistant to Nick that day. Molly began to wonder what in the world was wrong with her. The more Nick talked about getting saved the more Molly wanted to run from him. When they were in the car on their way back to their house Nick again reached out to hug Molly from the back seat.

Again Nick said, **"You really don't believe I got saved do you Mom?"** as He wrapped His arms around Molly from over the seat.

Molly said, *"I remember feeling like my skin was crawling when Nick touched me and I immediately wanted to pull away from him but felt wrong about doing so. I love that child so much and on any other day I would have given anything to have a hug from him or even just a conversation. This should have been the happiest day of my life because it was a day I had waited for since before he was even born so the feel the way I was feeling, was more than I could understand! Please don't get me wrong, it wasn't that I thought my son was evil or that I thought he was lying about getting saved. I truly believed he had decided to give his heart to the Lord which was the greatest news he could have ever given to me; but this presence I felt was so strong, it was robbing me of my joy! At the time, I didn't understand it and thought there was something wrong with me. My son was truly innocent in all that was going on. When Nick sets his mind to something, he puts his whole heart into it! He had finally made a decision he had struggled with all of his life to dedicate his life to Jesus Christ and there is no doubt in my mind he took that decision very serious!*

However, Satan had no intentions of letting him go that easy! He knew what a valuable asset Nick would someday be in the Kingdom of God and he couldn't take any chances on letting that happen. So Satan sent every dark force he could send to surround us that day and play tricks on both of our minds. He knew darn good and well I wasn't where I needed to be in my relationship with God to figure out what was going on or what to do about it; but he also knew I had a sensitive enough spirit inside me to feel the presence of his darkness; and that is all he needed to get me to do what he was planning for me to do!"

When they got back home Sarah was there and Nick went in Molly's room to talk to Sarah. It didn't take long before Sarah was calling for Molly to come in the room. When Molly went into the room, Nick was laying on her bed crying. He had been pouring his heart out to Sarah and asking her to help him. When Molly went into the room she knew something was very wrong. Molly had seen allot of people get saved in her life but had never seen any of them so broken the day they got saved. Nick was crying and confessing He had done horrible things that Molly just couldn't believe. As Nick told her of these things, Molly felt she was being told a lie but couldn't imagine why Nick would tell such horrible lies on himself. Nick had a lot of problems with drugs but he was never a liar.

Molly said, *"Yes, Nick was a very secretive young man so I wondered if the things he was saying could be true but it just didn't feel like it was. I can't explain it but a Mother just knows when her child is lying even if they don't want to believe they are, they still just know. I knew*

Nick really thought he had done these things but my gut was telling me he had not! Later, I went to the people Nick said he had done bad things to and they confirmed to me that none of those things ever happened. By this time, I was starting to understand what was going on with my Son. The enemy was lying to him about everything! He was out to get my Son because I had waged war on him a few days before. The enemy underestimated the power of the Holy Spirit in me because I had danced on his play ground for so long, but I was not that easy to deceive!"

Not knowing what else to do, Molly began to talk to Nick and tell him this was the enemy trying to bring him down.

Molly said, *"Nick, we need to pray and rebuke the enemy in the name of Jesus to leave you alone!"*

They knelt down by Molly's bed and began to pray but the words of their prayers kept getting twisted.

Molly said, *"I remember, instead of saying Satan I rebuke you in the name of Jesus we were both saying Jesus, I rebuke you in the name of Satan. No matter how hard I tried for the words to come out the other way, they kept coming out wrong! Nick and I both knew it was going on and tried our best to fight it but there was a stronger force controlling our tongue and we kept saying the words wrong. The more Nick cried the more I felt numb, I felt like I was caught up in a whirl wind that I couldn't get out of. I would give anything if I knew then what I know now because I would have blacked the enemy's eye and sent him straight to the pits of hell where he belongs. However, I didn't know then what I know now about spiritual warfare, all I knew was something wasn't right but I didn't know what it was or what to do about it."*

Molly knew Clay must have been freaking out at what was going on in her house that night. Although she worried about what he might be thinking, she was more worried about what was going on with her Son. Then Molly made another big mistake and told Nick he just needed to go to his room and go to sleep, and everything would be alright the next day. When Nick went to his room Molly tried to figure out what was going on but what was going on in Nick's room was worse than what had just happened.

Molly said, *"I can't imagine the mental torture my Son must have went through that night in his room. While I stayed awake in my room wondering what was going on, the enemy was attacking my Son in his room all night long."*

By the next morning Nick was so oppressed by demonic forces he didn't know if he was coming or going. He had been awake all night and was convinced he had been called by God to go out and save souls.

Molly said, *"It breaks my heart to think of what my sweet and loving son went through that night. He had the Holy Spirit speaking to him in one ear and the spirits of darkness speaking to him in the other. He had just given himself over to Christ which was a major decision for him to make but instead of having the chance to feel good for a while like most people do when they make that decision, my son fell under an immediate no holds bar attack from the enemy. I know now how important my son is to God because Satan wouldn't have fought so hard to destroy him if he weren't! I may have not known what to do then and I know I went about things all wrong when my son was under attack; but the enemy surely must have under estimated my love for Nick when he picked that fight!"*

The next morning Nick took off on his bike on a mission to save the lost. By early afternoon Molly was getting phone calls that Nick had stopped by to see some of her family members. Everyone was surprised at how Nick was so passionate about God and made mention of how much he had changed. Still Molly felt numb and didn't know why. With each phone call she felt more and more unrest about Nick finding the Lord. When Nick came home, he was a mess. He hadn't showered in at least 2 days and it was over 90 degrees outside. As the day went on Molly began to realize not only had Nick not took a shower or brushed his teeth, which was very unusual for him because he was a very clean person with good oral hygiene; but he had also not eaten or drank anything since before he went to church. Now this was Monday and Nick had been running around on his bike in the blistering heat and sun all day. Molly knew he had not slept all night on Sunday night and he was beginning to look and smell really bad. Monday night Molly went to her room to pray and think about what to do. She was exhausted from the craziness of the past two days and thought Nick would go to sleep if the house got quiet. Just as Molly was about to fall asleep Nick opened her door, and stepped inside her room.

Nick said, **"Mom, you think your parents went to heaven but they didn't."**

Once again, Molly felt numb to what Nick was saying; she looked at him in confusion and said, *"What did you say?"*

Nick then smirked at her and said, **"Well, from what you have told me, your Dad may have went to heaven but I doubt it and I know for sure your Mom is in Hell."**

Molly couldn't believe her ears, she just looked at Nick and said, *"Get out of here I won't listen to that non-sense."*

Nick left Molly's room but didn't go to sleep again that night. Molly barely slept either all night and was running on nervous energy all the next day. When she came out of her room the next day Nick was gone on his bike again. It didn't take long until the phone started ringing with family members calling to tell her how Nick had been by their house again. By this time Molly knew there was an evil force leading Nick all around town on his bike. Molly began to pray and call on the power of the Holy Spirit to lead and guide her in the right direction.

Molly's phone continued to ring throughout the day and with each phone call Molly knew there was more and more darkness leading Nick's path. People were telling her of how Nick came to their house and told them they needed to pray to be saved. He would insist that they get down on their knees to pray with him and most confessed that when they prayed they felt something they had never felt before. When Molly heard them say they felt something they had never felt before and it was weird she knew there was an evil force behind those prayers. Molly had been around the Holy Spirit her entire life and she knew what it felt like was not described as anything but wonderful. The more phone calls she got, the more she prayed and then she got the call that would lead her to the power of the Holy Spirit. Nick called Molly and told her he had found a church downtown that had a service that night at 7:00. Nick saw the sign at the church on his way to Leon's house so Molly told Nick to wait there for her to come and go with him. Before Molly could get to her brother's house Nick started getting so weird her brother had to make him leave. Molly was on the road when her brother called to tell her what had happened. She asked him where Nick had gone but all he knew was Nick was trying to force him to go to some church nearby. Molly knew Nick must be on his way to the church he told her about earlier so she was headed in that direction when she got another disturbing phone call from one of Nick's friends. Nick's friend was so freaked out at what had just happened he was about to cry. He told Molly he had met Nick at some church and Nick began to pray for him to be saved. The boy said he felt something he had never felt before and started to cry. He said when he began to cry and repent for his sins, Nick began to growl at him and was saying very hurtful things; He got very scared of Nick and ran away. Molly told the boy to stay away from Nick because there was something bad going on that he didn't need to be exposed to and she asked him to tell her exactly where the church was that they went to.

Molly said, *"There is no doubt in my mind Satan would back off from Nick long enough for the Holy Spirit to shine through him and get these people to pray with him; but as soon as they did, those dark forces would take control of Nick's mind and make him think he was being led by God when he was scaring people or freaking them out.*

Nick had no understanding that people were even afraid of him. Still to this day, Nick's memory of that week is far different than mine or anyone else's that came in contact with him."

When Molly arrived at the church she found Nick standing in front of the church surrounded by 5 ladies and the Pastor of the church. She walked over to them and heard Nick talking in a voice she had never heard before. It was like he was in a trance and was talking like a disciple to those people. When Molly walked up to them Nick turned and looked at her but just kept on talking as if he didn't know who she was. His eyes were hazed over and he had a look on his face like he was in a trance. One of the ladies interrupted Nick and asked who Molly was. It was then that Molly knew it wasn't her Son talking to those people.

Nick looked at Molly and said, **"Let us pray for her because she is a sinner."**

He then dropped to his knees and started crying out to the Lord to save this sinner woman. He cried out for the Lord to save his father and his mother from their sins.

Molly said, *"I didn't know what to do or say, all I could do was stand there frozen and cry. Then one of the ladies touched Nick and asked him why he was calling his mom a sinner and he sprang back to his feet. I could tell by the look on her face that she knew something was wrong with him. While the* woman was talking to Nick I looked at the Pastor of the church and quietly asked him if we could talk in private. The Pastor then led me into the church where we could talk alone and asked me what was going on with my Son. I began to tell him all that was going on and what I thought was the reason for him acting so strange. Thinking this man was the Pastor of a church that didn't really believe in the power of the Holy Spirit, or the forces of darkness; I tried my best to choose my words carefully. It didn't take long before Nick was in the church talking in that strange disciple tone again like he was still in a trance.

Nick said, **"I know what I must do, come, we must go now."**

When Molly asked Nick what he must do, He said, **"Come, I must find Him, we must go now."**

Then she asked who he must find and Nick said, **"I must find him, I must find Joey, I must leave now."**

Then He walked out of the church and Molly could feel her heart beating in the top of her head. She tried not to be rude and just run out on the Pastor of the church but she knew she had to stop Nick before he found Joey, or it wasn't going to be good. As Molly and the Pastor of the church were walking toward the door she saw the ladies that were outside with Nick waiting by the doors for them to get done talking.

Molly said, *"I wanted to just run past them and get to Nick before he got too far away and I couldn't find him; but God had another plan. When I got close to them one of the ladies reached out to me and said,* **"I have to tell you something, It was no mistake that you wound up here today. Your Son came to this church today because he saw the sign and thought it was Monday and we were having a meeting for drug addicts; but it is Tuesday and we don't have meetings on Tuesdays. Earlier today, the Lord told me to call some ladies to come and meet me at this church. I didn't know why I was being led to call the ladies to meet me but now I do. God led you and your Son here today so we could pray for you and I would like to pray for you before you go."**

Molly was so desperate for help, she welcomed the prayers but wondered what would happen if she began to pray with these people from a Methodist church. Molly had been raised in a Pentecostal church and received the gift of tongues when she was a child. She often prayed in tongues when something bad was going on and feared she would freak those people out if the spirit fell upon her. They began to pray and Molly was holding back the spirit until the spirit fell on one of the women who was praying with her; then Molly just let the spirit flow from her as well. When they got done praying a woman in the group took off her necklace and told Molly she wanted her to have it. It was a beautiful gold necklace of the Star of David with Jesus written in Hebrew across the star.

Molly said, *"I can't take this from you, it is such a nice necklace."*

The woman insisted she take it and said, **"Please, I want you to take this because you're going to need it."**

The women explained to Molly that they didn't all usually attend that church. There were 5 women there that day, all from different denominations. All of those women just happened to obey the voice of the Lord and go to that church that day without knowing why. Molly left that church with a prayer cloth they had anointed with oil and prayed over together, feeling like she was filled to the top with the Holy Spirit and Praising God for what He had just done.

Molly prayed the Lord would lead her down the right road to find Nick and it didn't take long before she found him. Nick was still in a trance when Molly drove up on him riding his bike to find Joey. She pulled up next to Him several times and begged him to get in the car but Nick just looked at her as if he didn't know her and couldn't hear what she was saying and kept on peddling. The sky was filling up with storm clouds and starting to turn green. It looked like a scene from The Wizard of Oz! Molly knew there was a huge storm on its way and kept begging Nick to get in the car before it hit with him on that bike. He just kept ignoring her and riding along as if he were still in a trance. Molly continued to drive alongside him until the traffic would force her to pass him and then she would turn around and get beside him again all the way to his Dad's house. Molly had already called Joey and told him what was going on but Joey wasn't at home and said he wouldn't be for a while.

When Molly and Nick arrived at Joey's house, Molly said, *"See, I told you He isn't home, now put your bike in the car and let's go before this storm hits."*

Nick still appeared to be in a trance and just ignored what Molly was saying. He kept walking toward the door and said, **"I must rest now."**

Molly said, *"You can rest at home, you can't rest here because your Dad isn't home! I already talked to him, he won't be back for a while!"*

Nick continued to walk to the door as Molly followed him saying, *"You can't get in Nick, the door is locked!"*

When Nick realized he couldn't get in the house he looked at Molly and said, **"We must pray now."**

That was a big mistake on the devils part because Molly had just got filled up with the Holy Ghost at that church and she had on her full armor of God!

Nick knelt down to pray and Molly walked over to Him, put her hands on his head and started calling on the name of Jesus!

Molly said, *"It was like I touched him with a hot poker when I laid my hands on his head. He sprang to His feet and swung his arm around like he was going to knock me out of his way; and about that time his Dad pulled up. Joey got out of his truck not realizing what was going on and began to tell Nick he was acting crazy."*

Joey said, **"What the Hell do you think you're doing boy? Running all over town on a bike scaring people to death! You're acting crazy and you have got to stop this stupid crap! It's one thing for you to go to church but you can't be going around trying to force religion on other people!"**

Nick stood there silent with his head down and then Molly spoke up and said, *"I have to agree with your Dad Nick, your acting crazy and you can't be doing this!"*

Then Molly started to walk toward Nick's bike to put it in her car. Nick took off running toward the bike, jumped on it and took off down the hill in the opposite direction of how Molly was parked. By the time Molly got in her car and got turned around Nick was long gone. By this time the sky looked like something in a horror movie. Molly started to panic because she had never seen the sky so green or storm clouds that big moving so fast. She called Joey and told him if Nick came back to his house to call her because she lost him and had no idea where he was. Joey still didn't understand what was going on and told Molly not to worry about Nick because he was a grown man now and she just needed to go home and let him take care of himself. Grown man or not, there was no way Molly was going to let go of her son that easy!

Molly cried and prayed for God to keep him safe all the way home in the storm. When she got to her house Nick called and was talking in his normal voice.

Nick said, ***"Mom, I wanted to let you know, I'm here with Dad and I'm all right. I'm going to stay here tonight so don't worry."***

Molly got off the phone and was praising God for bringing her Son back safe and for making him normal again.

Molly said, *"Although I was so happy to hear my Son talk in his normal voice; I still couldn't stop thinking about what had been going on"*

Molly's sister was at her house and kept insisting Nick had gotten a hold of some really bad drugs because he wasn't acting normal. Molly kept telling her she didn't think Nick was on drugs and something else was going on with him. Lynn wouldn't hear anything Molly had to say because Nick had stopped by her house earlier and had her husband down on the ground praying. Jose was one of the people that had called Molly and told her about Nick stopping by. Jose was a very soft spoken sweet hearted guy that didn't talk too much about God. He wasn't the kind to go to church so he had no idea what was going on when Nick showed up and wanted him to pray but he was nice enough to do what Nick asked. When Jose called Molly and told her he felt something he had never felt before when he prayed with Nick and it was intense, she hoped it was the spirit of God but something told her it wasn't! Molly still hadn't completely figured out exactly what was going on but she knew it was something to do with dark forces. She could tell by the way Nick looked, by the way he talked and by the way he jerked away from her when she called on the name of Jesus, the Holy Spirit had nothing to do with his behavior or the things people expressed they felt. Molly had known the Holy Spirit long enough to know the presence of it is easily described as wonderful not weird or scary!

It was storming terribly bad outside as Molly and Lynn sat and talked about Nick. At the peak of the storm Joey called scared to death as he told Molly what had just happened at his house.

Joey said, **"Nick asked me to pray with him so we were praying and I started feeling really bad about all the things I had done wrong as a father. I told Nick I was sorry for all the things I had done wrong and I really felt bad for it. Just as I began to pour my heart out to him and cry he got really angry and started calling me a liar. He really scared me Molly! He was growling and screaming at me, liar, liar, liar as he squeezed my arms. I was really afraid things were going to get physical and then he ran out the door and took off on his bike.**

Molly said, *"You mean he is out there in this storm on his bike?"*

"Yes, and I left my house because I was afraid he would come back and kill me" Joey said.

"Oh my God, where is he at?" Molly said.

"I don't know and I don't plan on going back there tonight because I'm afraid he'll come back and kill me," said Joey.

About that time Joey said, **"Oh no, there he is, he has found me! What the Hell am I going to do?"**

Molly said, *"Joey, ask Him to get in the truck and just keep telling him how much you love him; Perfect Love cast out all fears!"*

"I'm afraid to let him in the truck!" Joey replied.

Molly replied, *"Just let him in the truck and keep telling him how much you love him Joey! You'll be fine until you get him home to me".*

Molly got off the phone with Joey and started praying for God to protect them and bring Nick home to her. She knew she had a better chance to deal with Nick than Joey did because she had the Holy Spirit on her side. Her sister just kept telling her to give it up because Nick had taken something that sent him on a bad trip that he wasn't ever coming off of. Molly tried to talk to her and listen to what she was saying but just kept praying in her mind for God to lead her and guide her on what to do when Nick got home. Although Molly didn't know exactly what was going on, she was sure it wasn't drugs that had Nick behaving this way. She knew the answer was in prayer and the Love she had for Nick. As she waited for Nick and Joey to arrive she continued to pray and the storm stopped right before they pulled in.

Molly ran out to the truck to talk to Joey and could tell that Nick was back in that trance as he walked past her to go in the house. Joey told Molly he didn't understand what had just happened. No matter what Joey said to Nick on the way to her house Nick just replied with **"You Liar!"** in a mean voice.

When Molly got back in the house Lynn looked at her and said, **"Molly, don't go in that bedroom! Nick is gone, the lights are on, but nobody is home in his head."**

Molly just walked past Lynn and headed for the bedroom. Lynn was behind her the whole way saying, **"I'm telling you Molly, he has gone on a bad trip and he's not coming back. You need to just call the authorities, it is too dangerous for you to go in there!"**

Molly went in Nick's room and began to tell him what had happened at the church when he left earlier. She told him how the women anointed this prayer cloth with Hebraic oil and they prayed over it. She told him how the Holy Spirit came down when they were praying over the cloth and how the woman gave her the necklace that she wanted him to wear.

Nick just looked at Molly while she talked and only said, **"I must rest now".**

Molly told him she would let Him rest but she wanted him to put on the necklace and put the prayer cloth on his head board. She reached over and put the necklace around his neck, put the prayer cloth over his head board, kissed him, said *"I love you Nick and everything is going to be all right".*

She shut his light out, walked out of his room and shut the door.

Still Lynn was behind her saying, **"I'm telling you Molly that boy is gone! You need to call the authorities and have him checked out before someone gets hurt!"**

Molly walked in her room and sat down. Lynn was still talking but Molly was lost in silent prayer and couldn't pay attention to what Lynn was saying anymore. Suddenly Molly knew God was talking to her. He said, **"Go brush the cigarette smoke off your mouth."**

So Molly got up and went to the bathroom to brush her teeth. Lynn was still talking this whole time but Molly wasn't hearing what she was saying.

Then Molly got done brushing her teeth and the Lord said, "**Go in the living room and start singing Power in the blood.**"

Molly started to walk out of the bedroom and Lynn said, **"What are you doing?"**

Molly looked back at Lynn and said, *"I'm going to fight the devil!"*

Molly went to the living room and began to pace the floor singing Power in the Blood. She paced back and forth several times singing that song and noticed Lynn looking at her like she was crazy; but Molly just kept singing.

Molly said, *"At one point I remember looking over at Lynn kneeling down by the chair praying and I knew she was clueless to what was about to happen. Then the Lord told me to go to Nick's room and ask him if he wanted to pray. I was singing very loud and I knew the enemy was getting agitated at my singing. I marched down the hall, singing all the way, slung the door opened and said, are you ready to pray now Nick? Nick came up out of that bed and made a dash for the door like he had just seen a ghost. I grabbed him because I knew if the enemy got him outside of my house he would probably take his life. It was like the Holy Spirit had taken over my body and I suddenly had super human strength. On a normal day there would be no way I could have over powered Nick, he is a very strong young man! However, with the Power of the Holy Spirit inside me, he didn't have a chance of getting* loose! I was speaking in the **"Language of God"** during this whole battle except for the time when the word **"Freedom"** came out of my mouth. I could tell my voice sounded like that of a man and I was speaking with great authority! Suddenly the window flew open and Nick was half way out it. He was trying to get my bible out of my hand as he went through the window. The spirit inside me said, **"Don't let Him take your bible."** I couldn't hold on to Nick and my bible at the same time so I had to make a choice, my Son or my Bible; I chose my Bible and let go of Nick. When I let go of Nick the Holy Spirit left me and I became very afraid. I ran through the house locking the doors and windows and telling my Sister he was down the road gaining strength but he would be back. I didn't know what to do, I didn't want to let him back in but I didn't want to let the enemy have my Son."

While Molly was running through the house praying, locking the doors and windows; Lynn was on the phone calling her husband and then she called the cops. Just before the cops arrived Nick came back and walked in the house when Lynn opened the door for Jose. He told Molly he wanted his bible she had given him and his cell phone. Nick no longer looked like He was in a trance He looked very angry! Molly told him he couldn't have his things and that made him angrier. Nick demanded Molly give him his things because they belonged to him but Molly stood firm that she paid for them and he couldn't have them. Then Molly called him Nick and His countenance changed as he spoke in an evil sounding voice and said, **"Why do you call me Nick? My name is Nicholas!"**

Molly said, "Because if you were Nick, you would know that Nick doesn't like being called Nicholas, Now who are you?"

Then the spirit inside of Nick told Molly, **"I am Jesus Christ!"**

"You're not Jesus Christ!" Molly said in a firm voice.

Then Nick lunged at her and grabbed his cell phone out of Molly's hand. Nick ran out the back door and was surrounded by cops with guns. Molly stood in the door watching as Nick ran into a swarm of cops. She could hear the clicking sound of the guns being cocked to fire if he moved another muscle. Lynn was screaming in fear as Molly stood frozen in the door way and watched Nick kneel to the ground with his hands in the air saying, **"all I wanted was my phone".**

Molly said, *"I can't explain the way I felt at that time. It was like I knew he was my Son and I should have been afraid for him but I was so freaked out over what had just happened I was glad they were there. At that point in time, I was convinced my Son was possessed by demons and I felt relieved to see him put in hand cuffs. After they took my Son away and I had time to calm down is when the emotions hit me. I can't tell you how much I cried or how guilty I felt that I didn't run out that door when the cops were getting ready to shoot my Son down. There is no doubt in my mind that I really made the enemy mad when I waged war on him and then used the Power of the Holy Spirit to fight him off my Son that night. He tried every dirty trick he had to destroy my mind after that night. He tried to make me think I was the one who had evil spirits on me. He told me I didn't love my Son or I would have run out that door when the cops pulled guns on him. He tried his best to convince me my Son would be better off if I weren't in his life.*

However, the bible say's **"Thou shall not curse what I have blessed."** *And since I have been covered in the blood of the lamb, God has always shown a light on the enemy when he tried to bring me down. The Lord revealed to me that I wasn't prepared for the battle I started with the enemy that day in my car but it was the Holy Spirit inside me that knew I had to fight for his life. He told me when the spirit prompted me to wage war on the enemy He planned on using my Love for Nick to show me I couldn't make it without Him. He told me I was frozen in the door way when the cops pulled their guns on my Son because He didn't want me to step out the door. God told me the reason He instructed me to not let Nick have the bible is because*

Satan planned on twisting the word of God around in Nick's mind to get him to do bad things."

God said, **"I had control of their guns and there was no way I was going to let them shoot our Son down. Don't let the enemy fool you, I had control over you and them!"**

When Molly and Nick were fighting the spiritual battle in Nick's room Lynn stood frozen in the door way.

Lynn said, **"It was like there was a glass wall between me and them that I couldn't get through."**

Lynn and Molly were very close and they would never stand back and watch one another get hurt without trying to help.

Lynn said, **"It looked like Nick was going to break Molly's neck while they were wrestling on the bed and I wanted to help her but I couldn't."**

Lynn told the police that night that she thought Nick was going to kill Molly. She said Nick was slamming the window down on Molly's head when he was trying to get away from her but Molly didn't feel a thing and didn't want to let go of him. Lynn told Molly she would be black and blue the next day from the way Nick was slamming the window down on her and choking her when they were on the bed; but Molly didn't have a mark on her.

Molly said, *"I'm not certain Nick was the one opening and shutting that window. I'm not sure how he could have been because we were wresting when it came open. I believe it was the forces of darkness in that room that opened that window because it was closed and the next thing I knew it was open and Nick was half way out it. I know there is no way my son would ever try to hurt me or anyone else! I'm sure Lyn saw the window opening and closing like she said and it most likely appeared to her it was Nick because she couldn't see the forces in the room; but I don't know how it could have been possible for him to do that. Isn't that just like the Lord to protect me from being hurt in battle? He also protected Lynn because she wasn't filled with the Holy Spirit that night; so God put a hedge of safety around her so she wouldn't get hurt. God allowed Lynn to witness the battle to confirm it actually happened but He kept her out of it because she wasn't spiritually equipped for battle."*

When the cops took Nick away that night he began to pray in the car and they felt there might be something wrong with his mind. They took him to the Hospital and told them what was going on. The doctor then called Molly and asked her to tell him what had happened. Molly was an emotional wreck by then about what had just happened and told the doctor her Son told her he was Jesus Christ. She pleaded for them to help him but they didn't know anything about spiritual warfare and diagnosed Nick as Psychotic. Molly had been attacked with a spirit of fear when Nick was taken away that night and she was too afraid to stay home alone. She went to Lynn's house and they talked about what had happened. Then suddenly Lynn turned on Molly and told her she thought she was the one who caused all this to happen because she went in that room.

Molly said, *"I think Lynn and I both were under attack from the enemy for several days. Lynn began to doubt what she saw was really real and began to think I was the one who was really crazy. There is no doubt in my mind that the enemy sent spirits of fear, confusion and doubt to torment both me and my sister."*

Molly battled the spirit realm to get any sleep at all for the next 4 nights after Nick had been taken away. Every time Molly would start to nod off she would be awakened by God telling her to read her bible or pray. She knew she was under attack and God was trying to warn her of the enemy's presence while she slept; but she was exhausted. It had been more than a week since Molly had a decent night sleep by the time she was set free. Every day she went to the hospital to see Nick and every night she stayed at Lynn's or Clay's to keep from going home alone. For the first few days Nick was very angry when she went to see him until the hospital drugged him up so he would be to out of his mind to be angry. By Friday, the doctor had filed a court order to have Nick committed as Psychotic.

The doctor was leaving for vacation on Friday and didn't want Nick to be released when his 72 hour hold was up on Saturday. Molly and Joey went in for a meeting with the doctor on Thursday, Nicks second day in the psychiatric ward. Nick was still combative and very bitter at Molly for being in that place; which didn't help Molly out at convincing Joey he wasn't really psychotic. Molly tried her best to convince Joey and the doctors that Nick wasn't psychotic and explain this was an attack from Satan; but Joey didn't want to hear about that stuff and warned Molly if she didn't shut up she would wind up being put in there with Nick. Molly knew she didn't have a chance in hell against those doctors and without divine intervention her Son would be walking around the mental hospital like a zombie the rest of his life. She kept praying and reading her bible all weekend seeking the divine wisdom of God. She called preachers and prayer warriors to intercede on behalf of her Son and vowed she would get her Son out of that place. Molly had stepped into a realm she knew very little about and had to take a crash course in spiritual warfare before she lost her son forever.

Molly had called her best friend Beth to help her pray for Nick. Beth had been going to church and getting closer to the Lord for the past 10 years and Molly knew God had anointed Beth for intercessory prayer. Beth had contacted a prophetic man of God that Molly had met when she was visiting Beth the year before. Beth told Molly she sent him a message to call her but she didn't tell him what was going on; only that Molly needed him to pray for her and call her A.S.A.P. On Sunday July 13th 2008 Molly was at Clay's sitting in the yard reading her bible. Nick had been in the psychiatric unit of the hospital since early Wednesday morning and it wasn't looking like He was going to be released anytime soon. Molly hadn't slept more than 12 hours since the Sunday before when all this started. Mentally and physically exhausted she kept searching for answers in the bible. She would pray every time she opened the book for God to lead her to the answers to help Nick. God had led her to read Matthew chapter 10 and she had just got done reading it when her phone rang. The prophetic man of God Beth had contacted in Florida was calling to tell Molly what God had told him.

When Molly answered He said, ***"Molly, I don't know what is going on with you but I always pray about things before I call people and God told me to tell you to read Matthew chapter 10."***

Molly knew this man was spiritually gifted and was expecting him to tell her exactly what to do to help Nick; not tell her to read a chapter in the bible she had already read. Molly told Him God had already led her to that chapter but she needed to tell him what was going on. She began to rattle on about the events of the past week when he very calmly said, ***"Molly, I don't mean to be rude but you need to listen to me; God told me to tell you to read Matthew chapter 10"***

"I already read Matthew chapter 10 but listen to what is going on here" Molly exclaimed as she began to rattle on again.

"Molly, again, I don't mean to be rude but SHUT UP! God told me to tell you to read Matthew chapter 10!" he exclaimed.

"But I already did and I didn't get any answers out of it!" exclaimed Molly.

"Well I suggest you go back and read it again." He said.

Molly was so upset and disappointed when she hung up the phone. If this prophetic man of God couldn't give her the answers then who would? Then she felt a very strong feeling to take his advice and re-read Matthew chapter 10.

She went back to the lawn chair, looked up at the sky and said, *"God, please help me to understand your word and show me a way to help my Son."*

That was the day Molly knew what it meant to be born again. She re-read Matthew chapter 10 and realized God was telling her she had the power to cast out the demons that oppressed her Son. She was jumping for joy when she got this revelation.

Molly said, *"That day was the most beautiful day of my life. I remember exactly what the sky looked like that day; it was a bright baby blue with big white puffy clouds. The sun was shining like the glory of God and the Holy Spirit was sweeping over me in the gently blowing breeze. I couldn't stop praising the Lord for what He had done. I knew at that moment that He had everything under control and all my fears were ripped from my soul by the calming of the wind."*

Shortly after Molly was born again of the spirit Nick called from the hospital. He sounded so good on the phone and asked Molly if she would be up to see him at visiting time.

Molly said, *"It was like the Holy Spirit had visited Nick at the hospital at the same time He was visiting me at Clay's house. I felt like we had both been set free at the same time and couldn't wait until it was time to see him."*

Molly got off the phone with Nick and went to tell Clay what was going on. She knew Clay was a little freaked out about everything that had happened in the past week and what she was telling him now probably didn't help matters any. Molly just had to tell someone because she couldn't hold back the joy in her heart and Clay was the only one there. Molly told Clay she was going to take her things and go home after she visited Nick because she wasn't afraid anymore. Clay told her she didn't have to go home and be alone but Molly could tell he needed a break from what was going on and wanted to take her house back from the enemy anyway. She left that day knowing that it wouldn't be long before Clay wanted out of the relationship but she had more important things to do than worry about that.

Molly headed home to bless her house and run out any dark spirits that thought they had claim to it. All the way home, Molly commanded the enemy to flee from her home and leave her Son alone in the name of Jesus. She went in and went through the house anointing every door and window with oil. She told the enemy that house belonged to her and he wasn't welcome in it. Then she commanded him to leave in the name of Jesus and claimed a hedge of safety around her home. Then Molly went to the shower singing Power in the blood and got ready to see Nick. This was the first visit Molly had alone with Nick since he had been there. They had a wonderful visit and for the first time in a week, Molly knew for sure that Nick was saved. She knew he had been washed in the blood of the lamb and he had been set free of the demons that tormented his mind. Molly told Nick she knew everything was going to be o.k. now and God would make a way for him to get out the next day. Before Molly left that day she asked Nick what he did with the necklace she had put around his neck that night.

Nick said, **"I took it off when I was down at the corner and then put it on the deck when I came back to the house to get my bible and phone."**

"Why did you take it off?" Molly asked.

Nick said, **"I don't know why I took it off; all I know is I went down to the corner and thought I was going to get my phone and my bible and go to the cave to get some sleep. Then I laid it on the deck when I walked back in the house."**

Molly couldn't wait to get home and see if the necklace was still on the deck. She knew that necklace had been blessed by God and it was very special to her. Molly went home and found the necklace right where Nick had left it, shining bright in the evening sun. She walked in her house without a care in the world, read her bible and went to bed to get a good night sleep.

The next day Molly got up and called the only doctor in the hospital who believed her when she talked about spiritual oppression. She knew that woman just had to be a Christian because she told her the day Molly argued with the head doctor that she believed her. Molly knew God had put her in charge while the head doctor was on vacation because He knew Molly would be born again on Sunday and take authority over the demons that oppressed her Son. It was really no surprise to Molly that she agreed to release Nick in her custody. Molly ran as fast as she could go to get Nick out of that place and bring him home. Although Molly had won this battle, the war was far from being over. There were conditions on Nick's release that he continued to take the psychotic medication he had been given in the hospital and report to mental health the next day. Molly agreed to take him there because she didn't think it would hurt for Nick to get some counseling somewhere; but only agreed to give him the medication to get him out. Molly didn't really want Nick to take those meds because she knew he didn't need them but felt she would talk to him about that later when they got home.

Molly and Nick talked about Him taking the meds and Nick said he didn't want to take them because he felt like a zombie when he did. Nick told Molly that he knew if he could just go to the counseling at the church he found that day and start going to church on a regular basis he would be just fine and Molly agreed. Molly knew Nick didn't need those meds and she wasn't going to force him to take them. She also knew going to mental health wasn't going to help Nick near as much as talking to Christian counselors at the church. Molly told Nick they would still have to go to the meeting at mental health and he would have to do what he had to do to get out of the system.

When they got to mental health Nick said, ***"Am I court ordered to be here?"***

The receptionist said, ***"I don't think so but I'll check."***

She made a phone call to the hospital and found out Nick was not court ordered to be there. She informed him that the doctor advised him to go but there was no court order to do so.

Then Nick said, ***"If I'm not court ordered to be here, I'm not going to waste my time doing this because I know all I need is to depend on the Lord to help me, and go to church."***

Molly could tell by the look on the receptionist face she didn't like that answer, but thought there was nothing she could do about it, so they left. Within a few days the doctors had sent a non-compliance report to the authorities and there was a warrant issued for Nick's arrest. Because of the statements from Molly and Lynn on the night Nick was taken to the psychiatric ward the Prosecutor filed criminal charges of battery against Nick so they could put him in custody for not complying with the doctor's orders. Molly was at work when Nick called to let her know the cops were at their house placing him under arrest for battery against her.

Molly said, *"I couldn't believe this was happening; how could they file charges of battery against my Son, on my behalf without me pressing charges against him? How could God let this happen to him after the brutal attack from the enemy he had just endured all because he had given his life to the Lord? Was my son going through this because of me? I knew this was another one of Satan's little tricks to turn my son against me but what I didn't know was why God was allowing him to do it! On up until now, I questioned God quite often as to why He allowed this to happen to my son, but I finally figured it out. God had spoken to me when Nick was in the Psych ward of the hospital one day about a patient I saw walking down the hall heavily medicated on the drugs they were trying to make my son take.*

*God said, **"This man is not psychotic, he is a victim of demon possession and all he needs is someone to deliver him of those demons."***

At the time, I was too concerned with my own son to take time to ask God if there was anything I could do for that man. Later Nick told me that is why he didn't want to take the drugs they sent him home from the hospital with; because they turn people into zombies that have no feelings, memories or emotions. Still to this day, I have never forgotten that man in the hospital who walked around the halls like a zombie with no expression or emotions about anything. I know now, God had to allow this to happen to Nick so he would go back and help those afflicted with what he went through that horrible week."

Molly went straight to the prosecutor's office and demanded to talk to the prosecutor who issued the warrant for Nick's arrest. While

Molly was waiting to see the prosecutor a woman leaned over to her and said, **"I couldn't help but over hear what you were saying to the receptionist; and I wanted to warn you to not say a word about anything spiritual to the prosecutor or they will try to put your son away for life."**

She and Molly shared their stories and Molly took her advice when she went in to see the prosecutor. The prosecutor wouldn't listen to Molly and insisted it was in her best interest that Nick be locked up. Molly tried to tell her if anyone should be in jail it wasn't Nick it was her. Molly explained that she was the one who tackled Nick that night because he was trying to leave but Molly didn't say a word about why she didn't want him to go. Molly got nowhere with the prosecutor; she wouldn't let Nick out or even lower his bail.

When Molly was leaving she saw the woman she was talking to sitting in the waiting room with her Son. The young man looked like an angel who had fallen from heaven and had the sweetest spirit Molly had come in contact with in years. The woman had told her son Molly's story and they were waiting for Molly to come out so her son could talk to Molly. He first asked Molly if she had the money to get Nick out of jail and Molly said sarcastically, *"Does anyone ever really have that kind of money to throw away?"*

The young man then turned to his mother and said, **"Do you have the money to give this woman to get her Son out of jail until we get home and I will give it back to you?"**

Molly immediately said, *"No, No it is o.k., I have the money to get him out!"*

The young man said, **"But you just said you didn't have the money and I want to give it to you so your Son doesn't have to stay in there."**

Molly replied, *"Thank you very much and God Bless you for caring but I just meant I'm really angry that I have to waste my money to get him out when he shouldn't be in there to begin with."*

The young man could relate to what Nick was going through because He had been arrested for trying to help a child that was tormented by evil spirits. Molly knew as soon as she met the young man that he was an anointed man of God and Satan was trying to destroy his life so he would be out of the way. She expressed her gratitude to the young man and his mother for wanting to help her and they all agreed to keep each other in their prayers.

Molly said, *"You see God told me Nick would be a psychiatrist one day and he would help many with the same trials he has faced. As hard as it is to see my child struggle and suffer through all of these trials, I know God doesn't lie! Experience is our best teacher and my son has experienced enough mental torture in his life to write a book on psychology called* ***"What every psychologist needs to know to cure mental illness."*** *Nick has not only overcome, but he has also endured the pain and consequences for things he did not even do. I know every mother thinks she has the best kids in the world and love is blind when it comes to our children; but this child is truly special in ways I cannot even explain. It absolutely amazes me how he silently deals with his pain without ever complaining.*

Nick once told me a wise man said, ***"I have often regretted when I spoke, but never that I kept silent."***

We sarcastically call him silent Nick because we long to hear him engage in conversation. When Nick is at peace, there is no sweeter human being on this earth to have a conversation with. He listens, he cares and he responds with words of wisdom and compassion when you need him most. When his soul is not at peace, he remains silent because he cares too much for others to allow them to share in his pain.

Molly had the money to get Nick out of jail but it would have taken every dime she had so she decided to pray and ask God what to do. God told Molly to not throw her money away getting Nick out of jail because He would get him out when He went to court. Molly decided to trust the Lord and waited until Nick went to court.

When Nick went to court Molly went in and there was a different prosecutor in court than the one she had talked to. Molly knew this was a blessing from God because that other prosecutor would not have let Nick out without bail. Molly requested to talk to the prosecutor and told her Nick wasn't guilty of this crime. She told the prosecutor she wanted Nick released immediately because he never battered her or anyone else. The prosecutor had Molly stand before the judge and swear under oath this didn't happen and Nick was released in Molly's custody once again. Molly left the court room praising God for Nick's release and feeling another battle had been won. However, Nick was very agitated at Molly when he was released from jail. They had shown him the statements Molly and Lynn signed the night he was taken to the psychiatric ward and he blamed Molly for everything that had happened. Although Nick was released from jail, he still had charges pending against him for battery against Molly. Molly knew Nick had every right in the world to blame her for what had happened to him and she didn't blame him one bit. Now the next battle begins, getting Nick to stop resenting her for what had happened.

Molly said, *"Still to this day I know the enemy torments my son's mind with spirits of resentment that speak into his thoughts against me. I'm certain they speak thoughts into his mind like* **"What kind of Mother would do something like that to her own son?"** *Or* **"She is crazy if she thinks she hears from God, there is no way God would speak to a sinner like her."** *Nick hasn't yet come to an understanding of God's grace and mercy. He still thinks God's gifts and His love has to be earned. Nick suffers from what I have learned to be called* performance depression. *Meaning, these tormenting spirits of depression speak thoughts into his mind if he does this or that, he will feel better and suddenly all of the things he thinks are the reasons of why his life isn't the way he wants it to be, will all be taken care of. So he works really hard to accomplish whatever it is that this tormenting spirit convinces him he needs to do to make it all better; and then when* *he accomplishes his task and he still doesn't feel any better, he resorts back to what he knows works...... drugs and or alcohol! It is a repetitive cycle for people who suffer with this type of depression. The incredibly strong spirit that lives inside of them is constantly fighting to find a way out of the misery they feel each and every day. Suddenly they have a very persistent thought that seems to be the answer they have been looking for. So they work really hard to accomplish whatever it is that they truly believe will solve all of their problems. But their problems are never going to be that easy to fix because their problems are caused by forces of darkness they don't even believe exist."*

Within a few days of Nicks release from jail he started going to the addiction classes at the Methodist church and attending church there on Wednesday and Sunday. Molly knew Nick was trying his very best to get on the right track but she also knew he was having a hard time dealing with the pain of what had happened to him when he turned his life over to the Lord. It was clear that Nick blamed Molly for all that had happened. He didn't really believe he was under spiritual attack from the enemy when he got saved and deep down he thought it was Molly who caused this all to happen. Molly tried to talk to Nick about it several times but he didn't want to hear anything she had to say about what had happened. When Nick started attending the Methodist church Molly wanted to go with him but he didn't seem real enthused when she asked if he wanted her to go. For a while they were driving separate to the church on Sunday morning because Molly had to take Sarah to the Pentecostal church she attended and drop her off. Nick didn't want to ride with Molly so she would go to the Methodist church and look for him after she dropped Sarah off. Molly felt it was important that she be there for Nick and support him in his new walk with the Lord; but Nick seemed to feel different about it.

Molly said, *"I remember feeling like Nick didn't want me to sit by him at church every Sunday. I would sit there praying God would anoint him with so much love that I could feel he wanted me to be* there, but I never did. Then one Sunday morning Nick went over to the Pastor after church and asked him something. I sat there wondering what they were talking about and waited for him to finish so I could ask him what was going on. When Nick walked away from the Pastor I followed him and asked what he was talking to him about.

Nick never even stopped to answer me, he just kept walking and said, **"I wanted to get baptized but He can't baptize me today."**

I was in shock! I couldn't believe that he could act so self-centered over something as important as this! I had been waiting for this day to come since the day he was born and he hadn't even told me he was ready for it! I continued to follow him out of the church trying to talk to him about his decision to be baptized but he just kept walking and said very little about the matter. He was acting as if I had no concern in the matter and it was none of my business to know when he was getting baptized. Nick didn't come home after church that day and didn't bother to tell me where he was going. Later on that evening Nick called and told me he was about to be baptized at a Pentecostal church that he had never attended and they made him call and tell me before they baptized him. I begged him to wait until I could get there but he laughed at me and said, **"There is no time to wait, they're waiting for me and this doesn't have anything to do with you."** My heart was shattered in a million pieces like a glass that had been thrown against a wall. I had been robbed! I was robbed of the most important day of my Sons life and it wasn't funny to me!"

When Nick got home from church that night Molly was very upset and crying. Nick told her she was being ridiculous about the whole thing because it didn't have anything to do with her; it was between him and God. The more upset Molly got, the more Nick laughed about it and told her she was crazy. Molly went to bed that night feeling angry, feeling hurt, and feeling like a fool for even caring after the way Nick had acted. Once again she prayed and asked God to tell her why Nick would cheat her out of this celebration.

Molly said, *"It was like I had not been invited to his wedding but much worse because I had waited for this day his whole life. What would make a kid do something like that to his mother? How could he possibly love me at all and not wait for me to get there or make plans for another time when I begged him to not do it without me? Even the Pastor of that church knew how important this celebration should be to his mother when he made him call me. I'm sure they would have been happy to wait on me to get there or make plans to do it another day! To be honest, I really felt this was another attack from the enemy to bring me down. He knew how long I had waited for Nick to come to the Lord and get baptized; and he knew it was inevitable that Nick would get baptized now that he had accepted Christ. I really believe he took that opportunity to throw a dart at my heart! The enemy knew how special that day would be if we had time to plan and he didn't want that to happen. In a way, it was like we both had won the battle that day. I was victorious because my prayers had been answered, but he was victorious in keeping me from the celebration."*

Although Molly had not been included in the victory celebration of Nick's baptism, she knew there would be more to come, many more to come!

Molly said, *"Since that time in our life God has revealed to me many things about His purpose for Nick. God told me, **"Nick is my son and I have him in the palm of my hands!"** Many times since then God has told me He has got Nick in His hands and He has big plans for him. He told me Nick has a spirit like that of King Solomon and He has anointed Nick with the gifts of knowledge and wisdom that he will use some day to help others who have gone through the same spiritual battles he has gone through. God said, **"Nick has to go down this road to get on the road I need him to be on".** I can't tell you how many times since then God has had to remind me that He has our son in the palm of His hands and will keep him safe while he is on this journey; because the mother in me wants so much to see him happy, healthy and prosperous. Every parent wants nothing but* the best for their children but we often fail to remember they belonged to God before He gave them to us to love. He knows what is best for them just as He knows what is best for us. There is no doubt in my mind, God has a great purpose for allowing our son to go through all of this spiritual oppression that I see as mental torment and yet I still struggle with wanting to end this fight. God told me Nick loves others as He loves them and that Satan uses Nick's love to grieve him. One day when I was praying for Nick, God gave me a scripture to speak over him every day. The scripture is, **1ˢᵗ John 5:3... For this is the Love of God, that we keep His commandments and His commandments shall not become grievous.** Jesus said in John 15:12 "**This is my commandment, that ye love one another as I have loved you**" Because Nick loves so deeply God wants him to remember His commandment and know it is not meant to grieve him."

I was given the John 15:12 scripture in Bible school when I was a little girl to memorize for a ribbon. I spoke that scripture almost every day of my life since I memorized it as a little girl. It became part of the prayers I said over my children when they were little. It wasn't until I began to seek the Lord about Nick that God revealed to me why I had learned that scripture as a little girl. God told me without even knowing what I was doing, I was speaking His love into the heart and soul of my children when they were small that would bless them with a heart full of love that would eventually lead them to be who He had planned for them to be. God also told me Sarah was anointed with a warrior spirit like that of King David that would defeat the enemy through song and Praise."

God said, "Just as David cleared a path for Solomon to live in peace and use his gifts of knowledge and wisdom to help my people, so shall Sarah clear the path for Nick through the power of song and praise! Sarah will use her gift of song and praise to go into battle for my people just as King David went to battle against the enemy for my people. Sarah will use her warrior spirit to defeat the giant that is out to destroy Nick's

gifts of knowledge and wisdom. Then shall Nick break down strongholds on my people by shining a light on the truth through his knowledge and wisdom of the spiritual realm he has been through. Greater things than you have done, I have saved for the two of them!"

Praise God I now know my son loves me so much he keeps silent instead of hurting me with the thoughts the enemy constantly puts in his mind against me. Satan would love nothing more than to destroy the relationship I have with my only son. He has set out many times to destroy my relationship with Sarah as well. Sarah and Nick are complete opposites when it comes to how they deal with me. Sarah has my warrior spirit so she will come after me and fight it out. Nick has the other side of me; the side that would rather love from a distance than to fight with someone he loves. There is no doubt, I have learned as much from my children as they have learned from me! One day the three of us will join our forces of spiritual strength and use the knowledge we have learned from each other; and what a glorious day that will be!

CHAPTER 7

Spiritual Boot Camp

It didn't take long for Molly to realize Nick was still under attack and she needed to find some answers on how to help him. Although Nick seemed to be doing well and was going to church every time the doors were open; there was still a wedge between them that she just couldn't move! It didn't take but a couple of months and Nick had been faced with more and more temptation he wasn't ready to handle. What seemed to be a blessing at the time, turned out to be the door of temptation the enemy put in Nick's path to get him on a downhill spiral that could take years to get off of. Nick had gotten a job working with his dad on a big construction site making more money than he had ever made. He felt so good about himself to be able to get up every morning and go to work doing a "man's job"!

Molly said, *"I know Nick was not only proud to be working a job that he felt good about but it also made him happy to be able to see his dad every day".*

Molly hoped and prayed this job would be the missing link in their relationship. She was so happy that Nick was going to church and seemed to be moving in the right direction but she feared him being around all those men who were drinking and doing drugs would be more temptation than Nick could handle.

Molly said, *"All I knew to do was pray and trust in the Lord that He wouldn't allow Nick to stumble and fall."*

Molly prayed Nick would get through to his dad and he would be saved as well. She hoped her fears of them rubbing off on Nick would be wrong and he would rub off on all of them instead.

Molly said, *"Looking back, I think I knew in my heart I was wishful thinking and this job was not going to be good for Nick. If I had known then what I know now, I would have been praying those strong holds down every day! It got to the point Nick was working so many hours a week, he wasn't able to attend all of his meetings and church services and I knew that couldn't be good for him. He was trying so hard and I wanted so desperately to believe everything was going to be o.k. that I refused to listen to my gut."*

It didn't take long until Nick was faced with the ultimate temptation that he just couldn't refuse. He went to his grandma's house one day after work with his dad. He was getting ready for church and needed to iron his shirt. When he got in the closet to look for grandma's iron the enemy was staring him in the face! His grandpa had been given a prescription of pain pills for one of his surgeries and put them in the closet where the iron was. Nick had taken this kind before when he was doing drugs and knew they would get him high. Later Nick told Molly he tried his best to walk away from them; but the temptation to take them was so strong he decided he would take them with him to church and pray about it.

Nick said, **"I left the pills in my car when I went in the church; and begged God to take them out of my car while I was in the church if He didn't want me to take them!"**

Nick told Molly he felt like God had let him down when he got out of church and found the pills were still there. That was when it started all over again and the next few months would change Molly's life forever!

Nick ran off to Florida on a bus with very little money in his pocket. He was on the streets of the ghetto the first night until God led Beth down the right road to find him. Nick then stayed with Beth and her girls that were just like family to him for the next few months.

He seemed to be doing pretty well while he was there but he still had battery charges hanging over his head from that night in July that he would eventually have to come back and face. Molly began to isolate herself from friends and family so she could quit drinking and smoking. She spent every moment of her free time seeking the Lord and reading His word. She knew the enemy was out to get her son and she had to figure out how to stop him once and for all! She fasted and prayed for answers and was growing stronger every day but still didn't know how to end this war and was getting tired of these constant battles.

Then one day Molly decided she needed more information than what she was getting from the word of God. So she prayed and asked God to lead her to the right source of information that would help her figure out what to do about Nick. She felt compelled to go to this certain book store and get a book.

She walked in and said, *"O.k. God, I'm here and you have to lead me to the book you want me to read"*.

Molly never liked to read and had never read a book that she didn't have to in her whole life; so this was way out of her comfort zone! She immediately went to this book that she later bought but argued with God about the title. Molly was terrified of snakes and this particular book just happened to be called **No Small Snakes**! Molly just knew there was no way God could be telling her to buy a book about snakes so she immediately put it back on the shelf and continued to pray for God to lead her to the right book.

Molly said, *"No matter what book I picked up, God just kept telling me **No Small Snakes** over and over in my head! Until finally I said, God, are you really trying to tell me to buy a book about snakes? So I went back and read the introduction and realized the book was actually about spiritual warfare and a man's quest to find his purpose in God's plan. I was so excited because I knew God had led me to that book; that I couldn't wait to get home and start reading it! I could* hardly put that book down from the time I opened it to the time I finished it!"

It took Molly a few days to finish the book and it took her a few more to completely understand why God lead her to that book.

Molly said, *"I remember being in the bath tub one night and asking God questions about things the writer had gone through in the book and how it pertained to my life. It was like the windows of heaven opened up and God just started telling me all kinds of things. Of course at that time in my life, I was never really sure if it was really God or if I was just crazy, so I had to check out everything I thought He was saying. Much to my surprise, I really was hearing from God, and that gave me hope!"*

Molly didn't stop there; she continued to seek out as much information as she could. She bought c.d.'s & d.v.d.'s more and more books and continued to talk to God in her bathroom; because that seemed to be the place where He most often answered.

After a few months Molly found herself taking on a responsibility she did not want! Her uncle had passed away and her 80 year old aunt needed someone to care for her. Molly told God over and over, *"I don't want to do this!"*

She felt she needed to be alone and feared if she took on such a big responsibility she wouldn't have time to spend with the Lord and get where she needed to be.

Molly said, *"My house was too small, I didn't have room for another person, not to mention all of her things! I just kept telling God, if you want me to do this I will, but I don't want to! I told Him over and over, if He wanted me to do this, He was going to have to change my mind and give me peace about it! And that is exactly what he did!"*

Molly's aunt Lorene had gotten upset with her sister Lynn and left. Lynn and Robin had moved their Aunt & Uncle in with them a few months before when it got too hard for them to care for themselves Molly's uncle had already gone to the nursing home because he was sick with cancer and Aunt Lorene was still staying with Lynn, Robin and the kids.

Molly said, *"It didn't seem like there was a day that went by after they moved in with Lynn that she wasn't calling and complaining about something they had said or done! I felt like Moses must have felt when he was trying to lead the children of Israel out of bondage! Every day Lynn would call and complain about how they were driving her crazy and I would most often have to go over and help with something. It wasn't the helping part that was driving me crazy, it was the constant turmoil the whole house seemed to be in every day!"*

Molly's uncle was dying of cancer, so he had enough drugs to fill up a pharmacy and Robin was a drug addict. Lorene was old and set in her ways, and she didn't like the way Lynn lived her life so she wasn't very nice to Lynn. Robin had always been the black sheep in Lorene's eyes, but for some reason she suddenly felt safer with Robin than she did Lynn.

Molly said, *"It didn't really surprise me that Lorene felt safe when Robin was there because Robin just had that way about her of making everyone feel safe when she was around; but it was still really weird considering the way Lorene had always treated Robin when she was growing up. Robin had never really liked Lorene either, but something happened that brought them close in the last few years of Lorene's life and I believe her death had a greater toll on Robin than it did even me. I believe that something was the will of God that brought Lorene and Robin together. I think it may have even been part of his plan to get Lorene here with me."*

After the 80 year old Lorene got mad and left Lynn's house with her step son, Lynn wouldn't let her come back. Lynn called Molly and asked her what she should do and Molly said, *"Don't give in to her, it would be best if she went to the nursing home to spend what little time she has left with Ron. Besides, it will be much easier for her to stay there after he is gone, if she has him there while she gets used to it."*

Molly couldn't understand why she would tell Lynn to not let Lorene come back when she had no intentions of taking her in herself and knew darn good and well she couldn't make it long at her step son's tiny little apartment.

Molly said, *"I had no idea why I kept encouraging my sister to get rid of them. Every time she would call me and complain about what they were doing to make her life miserable, I would give her what I thought was bad advice and then question why I did it after I hung up the phone. I was convinced there was no way I could take them in because I didn't have the room or the time to take care of them; even though I had always promised I would never let my aunt go to a nursing home! I was so angry at Lynn and Robin for moving them out of their apartment into Lynn's house. I kept telling them it was a bad idea and then one day, they just went over and started moving them into Lynn's house and called to say they needed help."*

Molly knew from day one this wouldn't be a good idea because Lynn didn't have the endurance to take on two old people that needed a lot of attention and had a lot of drugs in a house with 4 kids and a drug addict! After all, any one of the 3 is like having another full time job; so how is someone who liked to have her free time going to pull this off? Needless to say, she didn't, but she did put Molly in a position that she had to pick up the slack that she didn't want to pick up; and that seemed to be exactly what God wanted Molly to do. However, before all hell broke loose in the house and Lorene left; she had managed to send Robin to the store after she had eaten a bunch of Ron's pills and Robin got arrested. That was the beginning of the end for Robin and was the straw that almost broke the camel's back for Lynn.

Robin was back in the legal system after several years of staying with Lynn and keeping out of trouble. Lynn and Molly were both beside themselves with anger at the old people feeding Robin the drugs but Molly was trying her best to understand and seek God.

Within a couple of weeks of Ron being taken to the nursing home, Lorene had Robin take her on another adventure *"this time in Lynn's car"* after she had given her more of what Lorene called *"nerve pills"*. They got pulled over by the cops because there was a wreck; but this time, Robin got lucky and they let Lorene drive them home.

Molly said, *"Robin was scared straight that day after riding a block with an 80 year old Lorene, and told her to pull the car over as soon as they got away from the cops."*

Lynn came home a little later and found both Lorene and Robin looking like a couple of little kids in separate rooms ashamed to lift their heads. Of course Lynn called Molly having a fit and the turmoil in the house started all over again! Within a couple more weeks all hell broke loose and the 80 year old Lorene packed her bags!

Within 2 weeks Lorene called Molly and asked if she could come over and spend the night. Without even thinking about it Molly immediately said yes! But as soon as she hung up the phone with Lorene she started to panic and immediately started to pray!

Molly said, *"I couldn't believe I had just fallen into this trap! I knew Lorene was only asking me to spend the night because she had called Lynn and asked to come back but Lynn turned her down and she was miserable in that little efficiency apartment with her step son. I knew she was going to ask me if she could stay and I was praying she wouldn't! I prayed on up until the moment she got to my door that God would make her want to go to the nursing home with Ron so I wouldn't have to break her heart by telling her she couldn't stay with me."*

Robin had been calling Molly almost every day worrying about Lorene and saying she couldn't believe Lynn wouldn't let her come back. Molly felt like a yoyo stuck in the middle of it all. Although she felt the same compassion for Lorene that Robin did, she knew Lorene going back to Lynn's house would just be more turmoil; and wondered if Robin's motives were sincere.

Molly said, *"From the moment I began to pray, my anxiety went away. It didn't take long before Aunt Lorene had arrived, and within a few moments of her being in my house, I knew she would be here to stay; and I felt totally at peace that she was right where God intended her to be."*

Molly was still going through what she called her spiritual boot camp when Lorene came to stay. She had no idea Lorene would become a very important part of her journey and wondered if her journey may be over. Within two weeks of Lorene being at Molly's her husband passed away in the nursing home. His battle with cancer was long and hard but it was finally over! Molly had been there with him through it all from the very beginning but felt absolutely nothing when he passed.

Molly said, *"I expected I would fall apart when he passed, but by the time he finally gave up, my heart no longer knew him. It made no sense to me at the time but I think I may understand it now. How could I spend that much time with someone I loved, taking him to every doctor's appointment, staying by his side through radiation and chemo, talking to him about the Lord and praying so hard for his healing and salvation, only to feel nothing when he passed? But I wasn't the only one who felt that way, so did Robin and Lynn. We all tried to understand it but couldn't. It was almost like he never existed once he finally passed.'*

So now Lorene was faced with finding herself in a brand new life. She was only able to bring her clothes and a few small things to Molly's, so she not only lost her husband but also all of her possessions. Molly really didn't think Lorene would make it as long as she did, but prayed God would help her to feel at home and not be scared for the time she had left. Lorene had lived most of her life in fear of something. Her childhood was a nightmare in itself, and then she spent several years with an abusive husband that only added more pain to her already deep seeded wounds. Molly always looked up to Lorene as a child and wanted to be just like her when she grew up. Lorene was the one who took Molly to church when she was a small child and introduced her to the Holy Spirit. Lorene was twelve years older than Molly's mother Sue and loved Sue like her own child. Lorene had adopted Sue's two oldest children when Sue was too young to be a mother and always said she would have loved to take Molly too but Sue and Ray wouldn't let her. Molly spent allot of time with Lorene when she was a child and always promised she would take care of her when she was old.

Molly said, *"I've always tried my best to keep my word and I was so glad, I got to keep that one after she was gone."*

Although Molly didn't understand how it was going to work out with her having to sleep with an 81 year old woman in her 40's and sharing her space, she just knew it somehow would, and it did! However, Molly was faced with challenges far greater than sharing her space, she didn't know would exist. Over the next two years Molly remained in spiritual boot camp through helping Lorene deal with her demons.

Lorene had been afflicted with a spirit of infirmity at a very young age and Molly didn't even realize what this spirit was until the Lord revealed it through Lorene. She had also been in bondage with spirits of fear and religion for most of her life. As time went on the Lord revealed these spirits to Molly and Molly revealed them to Lorene. Molly spent countless hours teaching Lorene the power of the spirit realm; and how she had the power to fight the spirits of darkness that had controlled much of her life through the Holy Spirit. Lorene was terrified of death because the spirit of religion made her feel unworthy to make it to heaven. She was so afflicted with the spirit of fear she couldn't stand the thought of being alone at night or being in the dark. She feared everything from storms and starvation, to hell and damnation!

Molly said, *"It was like looking into the eyes of a little child when I would teach her about the word of God. She would hang onto my every word and want so badly to believe what I was saying. I would think she has finally got it now and then as soon as I would leave her alone she would start calling people to have someone to talk to or calling me to see when I would be home. I should have known her time was near when she started staying at home alone without being afraid. But I foolishly thought she was just becoming a big girl now and things were going to get easier for me."*

Little did Molly know her home was the beginning of the end for Aunt Lorene or that Aunt Lorene's stay would be the beginning of her finding herself.

Molly said, *"It seemed like every time I would find an answer to help Lorene I would be another step closer to finding myself. Now, that I know now, what I didn't know then, I'm really not surprised at how God used her to help me. After all, His word says, He will use all things for the good of those who love Him; and Lorene and I both, love Him very much!"*

Sometime during the first few months of Lorene being with Molly, her finances were looking very grim. Molly began to pray for the Lord to open a door for her if she needed to get a second job or make a way for her to stay home with Lorene. As usual God began to talk to Molly when she was in the bathroom.

Molly said, *"He just kept saying, **write the book and the money will come!** Of course as always, I thought I was crazy because I didn't know how to write a book so it would make no sense for God to tell me that. It never failed, every time I would get in the shower and start praying, I got the same thought..."**write the book and the money will come."*** For several months of me questioning my sanity and arguing with God that He can't possibly be telling me to do this because I don't know how to write a book, I finally surrendered. However I first went on like this for months questioning and doubting and finally came to the conclusion He must be telling me to go to school and learn how to write a book. *So I started asking Him if he wants me to go to school and He finally said to me, "**I am the great teacher, let me be YOUR teacher."***

Molly began to tell Lorene what she thought God was telling her. Although Molly believes Lorene even thought she was crazy, she said Lorene told her, ***"If God told you to do it; you had better start writing the book before we wind up starving to death!"***

So Molly finally surrendered for fear they wouldn't make it much longer and asked God to use her hands if he wanted her to write a book because she had no idea what she was doing.

Molly said, *"I couldn't believe it when I sat down in front of the computer and prayed it was like all of these memories I had locked up inside, just started flowing out of me. The more I typed, the more I understood things I had put in the back of my mind because I didn't understand why they had happened. I would stay up until day light typing away on this book because I really thought I would have a best seller when I was done since God was helping me write it."*

Molly had a goal to have the book finished by her 41st birthday, but failed miserably when she stopped writing to go see her favorite preacher Perry Stone in Florida.

Molly said, *"I couldn't understand how the words were flowing so freely before I left, but then I get writers block after going to the most spiritual church service I had ever attended in my life!"*

Then Molly decided God didn't mean the book would be a best seller when he told her the money would come; He simply meant he would bring her buyers to her business that had seemingly gone under before she started writing. She had received a few good paychecks from selling houses and thought that was because she was obedient and started writing the book that was obviously just meant for her to learn from. After all, God had revealed many things to Molly through her writings and she finally felt her spiritual boot camp had come to an end! It wasn't until Molly started writing the book that she finally understood what role I had in her life, nor did I understand what role she had in mine.

During the time when Molly was reading the book "**No small snakes!**" God had revealed to me, through Molly what my name meant to Him. God told Molly that my first name "Marcella" meant Warrior of God and my middle name "Jean" meant Grace. You see I always hated my name because it had no meaning; and I was named after people my mother barely knew; who seemed to be the center of laughter among my family members. One night when Molly was taking a bath she was asking God about names because she had read in the book "**No small snakes!**" how important names were to God. The man in the book had been given a family name but later found out on his spiritual journey that God called him something else. So Molly began to look up names and their meanings on the internet and questioned God this particular night how I wound up with a name that meant "Warrior of God" and "Grace" when my mother didn't even ask Him what to name me or even pick the name out herself.

After all, that sounded like a name that God would have picked out; but how could He have picked the name if my parents didn't ask Him? She asked Him what my name was supposed to be because she knew how important it was to me to find out who I am to Him and what my purpose in life really is. That very night Molly found out who I am to God but didn't know who she was until sometime later!

God told Molly it was really Him who had given me my name because I was sent to be a spiritual warrior of God so He called me Marcella. However, my mother was taking drugs at the time of my birth, *which was a plan from the enemy to take my life because he knew God had sent me to be one of his worst nightmares of our family;* so I was actually on the verge of being still born!

That is when God stepped in and said, ***"Not this child Satan! I have a plan for her!"*** And then God breathed the breath of life into my little body and gave me the middle name of Jean which means God's Grace because it was by His grace that I was born!

Molly said, *"I will never forget what God told me that night"*.

God said, ***"You had to fight your way into this world like the warrior that you are but it was by my grace that you made it!"***

He then told Molly that He gave that name to my grandmother while my mom was still out of her mind on the drugs because I was so very special to Him that He wanted me to be called by my ***"given name"*** and that was the name He gave me. He knew if my mother came to her senses she would have never named me Marcella Jean. I can't tell you how good it made me feel that God gave Molly this information. It was almost like I had been reborn or had taken on a whole new identity! God also told Molly all about how Satan tormented my mother with addiction to try and destroy all God's plans for her children. He told Molly of how my mother prayed when I was in her womb that God would take care of me and let me be born healthy. He told Molly of how she had prayed for Leon while he was in her womb and He heard her prayers so she could stop worrying about him. He told Molly that Sue had prayed over all of her children and He heard all of her prayers.

The Lord said, ***"Do you think your mother never prayed for you? Do you think she never prayed for them? Why do you think I have always been with you? Why do you think I sent her a warrior child that would help her fight the battles she was too weak to fight on her own?"***

Molly was so excited to find out about my purpose she could hardly sleep that night. She remembered all the times God had spoken to her in the past and gave her little clues that she didn't pick up on because she thought it was her own thoughts. It was like the flood gates were opened and her mind was flooded with memories of things God had told her in the past that she never understood before. I'm not for certain how long it took after Molly found out about me before Molly asked God who she was to Him, but I know for certain what He told her.

One night when Molly was writing the book, the thought came to her mind to look up her name and see what Molly meant. Now that she knew who I am, it made no sense that she was Molly. The meaning she found for the name Molly meant *"Sea of great sorrow".* After she looked up the meaning of her name she went to the bathroom and asked God why her name meant sea of great sorrow. I will never forget what God told her that night.

God said, *"Because in the beginning of your life, you lived in a sea of great sorrow but it is time for your sorrow to end so you will be the warrior of God you were created to be Marcella!"*

You see, Molly is I and I was she. When God told me to write this book I had no idea I had lived in a sea of great sorrow. Although God had revealed to me why I had been given the name Marcella while I was reading the book He led me to, I never understood about Molly until that night. When I first began to write this book I gave the Lord complete control and my name became Molly in this book. At first I just thought He was giving everyone a different name so no one would know this book was about our life. Then as time went on certain people had the name I felt led to give them and certain people had the name they were known by and I began to question why I was called Molly in this book. That night when God revealed to me why I was called Molly in the beginning of this book it all made perfect sense. You see I didn't really become Marcella *"the warrior of God"* until I was born again during Nick's battles in 2008. On up until then I was still drowning in the sea of great sorrow.

How ironic that a girl who has done everything backwards in her life would go into her first big battle as a warrior of God before she even went through boot camp! Sometimes I wonder if God is looking down on me laughing and saying, *"There she goes again, my backwards little child who has to do everything the hard way".*

I know God is an all knowing sovereign God who knows our next move before we make it but sometimes I wonder if He gets tired of me making all the wrong moves. When I think about how different my life could have been if only I had been born again as a child, I have to wonder if I would have anything at all to write about right now. All throughout this book I have said, *"If only I knew then what I know now"* but I have to wonder, if I knew then what I know now if I would have ever gotten myself in the situations I was in to be able to do anything different. If you think about it, would anyone who knows how hard they will have to fight for the person they love willingly put themselves in a position to even fall in love if they knew it would be a long hard battle?

If someone had said to me, **"You can have this man that will make you feel more love than you have ever known but you will have to go through hell to keep that love, are you willing to fight for it?"**

I think I might have said, *"How good could it really be to be worth all that?"*

The point I'm trying to make is most humans have to already love something before they are willing to fight for it. The reason my desire to fight for Nick was so strong was because I loved him with all of my heart and I knew I had a right to fight for him because he belonged to me!

My mother in all of her wisdom used to always tell me, **"You will never lose a fight if you're in the right"**.

I have found that to be true so many times in my life. However, my biggest regret is all the times I gave up without a fight because I felt unworthy to have the right. My greatest hope for this book is that the readers will know there is nothing in this world more valuable than understanding God's love for you and learning to hear His voice.

The Lord said, **"My sheep hear my voice"**.

Although God doesn't tell us every move to make He does eventually speak when we seek Him. The hardest part is learning to wait on Him to speak and not letting our own thoughts or the thoughts that the spirits of darkness will put in our mind get in the way when we are waiting on Him. The bible tells us to test the spirits. Sometimes we want something so bad we convince ourselves God has spoken when He really didn't. Sometimes we dismiss His words for our own thoughts when He tells us something we don't want to hear.

However, the bible says, **"Seek and ye shall find, knock and the door will be open unto you"**. If we keep seeking Him, He will find a way to get our attention when He speaks.

CHAPTER 8

Demons with strong holds don't like to let go

I think it was the fall of 2009 when my aunt Lorene came out of the bedroom crying one day. I had never seen her as distraught as she approached me in the living room and practically fell in my arms. Her frail little body was trembling and she was crying so hard all she could say was, *"pray Marci, something is going to happen to one of our son's, we have got to pray"*!

I just felt numb and didn't know what to say to her. I hadn't been feeling like anything was going to happen and God hadn't alerted me to pray for anyone. However, I knew God had surely spoken to Aunt Lorene because she wasn't the type to fall apart like that for no reason. We prayed for a while and then she began to calm down and tell me what the Lord had told her.

She said, *"I was sitting in bed asking the Lord how much longer do I have to stay on this earth and be a burden to you."* *"I told Him I don't want to live like this anymore and I just want to know how much longer do I have to be here before I can go home."*

The Lord spoke to her and said, *"You must face one more death and it won't be much longer until he is gone."*

Aunt Lorene was certain the Lord had to be speaking of either Leon or Nick because they were the only males in the family she could think of that could possibly be doing anything that would warrant an early death. Leon and Nick were very close and they were often drinking too much together and keeping Aunt Lorene and I upset. She cried on my shoulder for a very long time before I was able to convince her I didn't feel like anything bad was about to happen to either one of them. I told her all we could do is pray for them like we always do and trust in the Lord to take care of them. She agreed I was right so we prayed some more and put this situation in the hands of the Lord.

It was the spring of 2010 when my brother came to fix my closet that had been damaged from a hot water heater leak. I knew he didn't look like himself and could tell there was something not right. What I didn't know is that he was very ill and it would be the last time he would come to my house. My brother Raymond was always grumpy when he was working but he was grumpier than usual that day. However, I could tell it wasn't his normal grumpy; it was much more than that. My sister in-law had told me a few years before he had been having some health issues that he didn't want her to speak of. My brother and I rarely saw one another unless it was a holiday. We had our ups and downs over the years and I was reluctant to pry in his life unless he volunteered information. Even then, I was careful not to ask too many questions. When he came to help me that day my heart felt burdened for him but I wasn't sure why. He got me through the bad part and said he would come back to finish the doors and trim that had been damaged once I got the new dry wall painted. When I got done painting I called to let him know I was ready for him to come back but he didn't show up when he said he would. Then I knew something was wrong and decided to go to his house one day after a few weeks had gone by and I hadn't heard back from him.

When I got to his house in the middle of the day I found him lying on his sofa looking pretty bad. I knew he must be really sick to be on the sofa in the middle of the day so I immediately began to pry; but of course he tried to blow it off as nothing serious. Before I knew what had hit me I began to cry and beg my brother to please go to the doctor because I was afraid something was seriously wrong. He said he couldn't go because he didn't have insurance and he had already been to the emergency room but they couldn't help him. I told him I would help him get health insurance through the state if he would let me. For the first time my brother actually admitted he could use my help for something and that made me feel pretty good.

My brother had always worked in construction and never had a retirement fund. He liked to drink and gamble allot so he didn't have anything saved back to help him through a time like this. Thank God he had my sister in-law May! She was his rock and she had always been a hard working woman anyway. Although I know how much it killed her to leave him at home sick every day; she knew what she had to do and she did it! It seemed like the months flew by from the time I realized what was going on until the time it got so bad; but I know it felt like eternity for my brother and May. Raymond was a strong man who never let anything get him down but this illness took the life right out of him. By the time we managed to jump through all the hoops to get him the medical insurance he needed to be seen by a doctor, he had gotten so sick he had to be taken to the E.R. a few more times.

He didn't want to talk about it much but May knew it was bad and she told me, ***"This time I have to tell you the truth, I don't think he will make it to get the insurance or the help he needs"***.

The poor woman was a wreck and it had to be the strength of God that got her through that alone. She was the only one working and paying the bills. She was the only one cooking or cleaning and she was the only one my brother wanted taking care of him. I offered to come while she worked but he said he was fine and I felt he may need the time alone with God.

By the time he got the insurance in July, it was too late. He had already been in and out of the Hospital several times. They couldn't deny him treatment when he went into E.R. but could only make him comfortable and keep him stable without the insurance that would pay for them to find out for sure what he needed. When the insurance finally came through, my sister in-law May and I took him an hour away to one of the best hospitals in the state to see a specialist. They said they thought he could be too far gone to help him and they didn't really know what to do for him without doing exploratory surgery to find out if he really had cancer. From the reports they had received from Bloomingdale it looked like he could have cancer of the liver but without knowing for sure, they couldn't treat him. When we left there that day, we all knew his time was short and it was a very long drive back to Bloomingdale. Before it was time for his next appointment with the specialist May had to take him back to the Bloomingdale E.R. After about a week in the hospital the doctor told May he would only have about 2 more weeks to live. They sent him home with hospice and that was when I knew what I had to do!

You see my brother and I had different mothers and he wasn't raised to know the power of the Holy Spirit or to have a love for Christ like I was. He wasn't raised to call on Jesus for everything or to plan his days on this earth to reach the goal of getting to heaven. Raymond rarely ever even spoke of God and when he did it usually wasn't very nice. However, God heard our prayers for my brother and did not leave him alone or let him go before he was ready. The only other time I had witnessed to my brother since he had been sick was the day I found him on the couch. That day I told him Jesus loved him and He would never leave him or forsake him if he would just call upon His name and believe. Throughout those spring and summer months of my brother being too sick to do anything but

145

think, I think he was thinking about what I said that day. There were a few times I heard him ask God to forgive him when he would get angry and say bad words in the hospital and that melted my heart. But the day I decided to go to his chair and ask him if I could pray for him was the day I knew I would see my brother in heaven again one day. He actually welcomed my prayer with open arms and the power of God fell in that room in a mighty way. No, he didn't get healed that day but I know he felt the presence of the Lord and he felt safe in that presence. I know he knew when it came his time that presence would be what he wanted to feel and with Jesus, was where he wanted to be!

The next couple of weeks felt like a whirl wind as time flew by so quickly. May knew she had to call his kids to let them know their Dad was sick so they could have a chance to come and say goodbye. I knew I had to call our brother and sister to let them know he was sick so we both decided we would do it whether Raymond liked it or not. On up to that point we had hope he would get well and there would be no need to upset him by telling the family he was sick. We both expected to hear his wrath when he found out we had told; but he was so sick he barely grumbled at all. His 3 children and our sister flew in town within a few days but our brother didn't want to believe it was as bad as I said since Raymond had told him I was making a big deal out of nothing. I believe Raymond was glad we made those calls so he could see his kids and our sister one last time. It broke my heart that we had to wait until he was that sick to call them; but I'm so glad they all got to say their goodbyes.

They had only been there for a couple of days when I went out to visit. Everyone was trying to laugh and enjoy their time together but my brother was too sick to even speak at that point. May looked like she was going to fall over with exhaustion and all I could think of was I wish things would get quiet so they both could rest. I didn't stay long that night because I wanted the kids and my sister to have a chance for some alone time with Raymond. When I left one of his friends who had been staying with them to help May take care of him and one of his boys were drinking and playing cards in the family room. I remember thinking to myself, that I wished everyone could refrain from drinking when my brother was so close to passing from this life to the next. It is so hard to believe in things that others don't believe in and not know how to share your views on life without coming off like a fanatic. I understood that they were just trying to get through it the best way they knew how; but I also know when people indulge in alcohol or drugs they become willing vessels for dark spirits to hide in without even knowing it. My brother had enough of his own demons to deal with on his way out of this world without having to deal with those brought into his home by others. Never the less, my speaking my mind would have accomplished nothing but making people resent me and most likely upsetting my brother. Therefore, I did the only thing I know to do and went home and prayed God would send the spirits of peace, love and mercy to camp around my brother; so when he left this world he could follow those spirits of light!

The next day was August 11th 2010 and I went back to see my brother again after work. Our 2 sisters met me there so I had my boyfriend drop me off and planned to ride back with them. When we pulled up to the house there were squad cars in the drive and my heart sunk with fear I had waited too long and missed my chance to say one more goodbye! To my surprise they weren't there to carry my brother out; they were there to take a statement from his granddaughter who had claimed his friend tried to molest her. The house was filled with family members that were there to spend those final hours with Raymond and be of help to May.

So here my brother is suffering like no man should ever have to suffer and the woman he dearly loves is going through complete hell at the hands of tormenting and unclean spirits! As soon as I stepped foot on the porch the Holy Ghost inside me rose up with anger! Have you ever heard of righteous anger? Well I had it! The Holy Spirit in me was angry, so the human side of me was livid! I felt like I needed to start kicking butt and taking names on anyone and everyone that dared to be a willing vessel for the wiles of Satan! As if it wasn't enough my brother had to suffer and die for the willing vessel of darkness he had been for so many years; now those same dark spirits that he entertained are going to have a party in his final hours! I don't think so!!!! Not on my watch they're not!

As soon as I walked in the door and took one look at him, I knew what I had to do. So I began to go through his house singing songs of Praise unto the Lord because I know darkness can't stand it when we Praise the Lord. I walked through the house from room to room, singing softly so that only the Lord and those tormenting spirits could hear. All the while I was praying silently in my head asking the Lord to give me wisdom and knowledge on what I needed to say or do to cast those dark spirits out of my brother's house. As time went on throughout the night I could feel the power of darkness gaining ground. It was like the more I prayed and sang the songs of praise the more demons I felt entering his home. The more demons I felt entering his home, the more miserable I could see my brother getting. Our older sister, who doesn't believe the same way I do, kept telling our brother he had done a good job here on this earth and it was time for him to let go and be at rest. Every time I heard those words come out of her mouth I wanted to scream *"NOOOOO!!!!!"* as loud as I could. I kept trying to tell her he wasn't ready to go yet but I knew she didn't understand why I was saying it. She has a nursing back ground and knew his body was ready to give up. But she just didn't understand why he was fighting so hard to live was because his soul and spirit was scared to death of the demons he could see when he tried to leave his body. The house was filled with unclean, tormenting and downright EVIL spirits that were on an assignment from Satan to drag my brother's spirit of life off to the pits of hell as soon as he left his body!

My other 2 sisters that were raised with the same mother as me knew there was something going on that wasn't right in the house but they felt helpless and just wanted to scream. After hours of going through the house praying and singing I told my 2 sisters there is power in numbers and I needed them to go outside and pray with me. We needed the power of God to come down on that house in a mighty way and remove those demons so our brother could die in peace; and see the spirits of light he needed to take him home. So the 3 of us went out back and prayed in the prayer language of God; but when we went back in the house our brother was still fighting those demons. Our other sister was still trying to get him to give up and let go; and May was so tired of seeing him suffer I think she was just ready for it to be over. My sister Robin who had not been blessed with the power of the Holy Spirit like Lynn and I had, was looking to me in fear asking what are we going to do? Lynn was feeling that same righteous anger as I was but didn't have a clue how to fight this battle. Everyone else in the house believed the explanation of the nurses that it was just part of the dying process; but the 3 of us knew there was more to it than that!

They had given him enough morphine to kill a horse but every little bit he would come up out of his bed swinging with this horrific fear in his eyes like something was trying to kill him. I knew it was demons in the house trying to drag him into darkness; but I also knew my brother had made his peace with God and that wasn't where he was supposed to go. If it had been, he would have not feared them so! However, all those years of his life he had spent as a willing vessel for those spirits to dwell in him and in his home; had now given them a strong hold that they weren't going to let go of willingly without a fight. At this point I knew Satan had sent a legion of dark spirits to try and lay claim to the soul and spirit he thought he had a right to. However, I knew I wasn't going to let them take my brother to a place of torment for one second without fighting with all the power God had given me; even though I knew Jesus had already paid the price for his sins and they couldn't keep him for long. In complete desperation I went outside alone and cried out to the Lord to tell me how to fight this battle for my brother. In an instant I heard the voice of the Lord telling me to cry out in a loud voice for Michael and Gabriel to come and help me fight off those spirits of darkness.

Without even thinking twice I began to yell out to heaven, *"Michael, Gabriel come forth, I need you!!"*

It didn't take long until I felt a rushing mighty wind go past me and I felt the spirit of peace. So I stood outside praising the Lord for a while because I knew the Calvary had shown up to win the war! Then I opened the back door and walked toward my brother's room.

My nephew looked up at me and said, ***"I think the morphine is starting to work, he seems to be calming down."***

I turned and looked at my sisters and said, *"We can leave now"*.

They had no idea what had just happened outside and assumed we were leaving because the morphine had calmed him down; until I told them later in the car. I knew from that moment on, I was no longer needed to try and keep those demons at bay when his spirit left his body; because Michael the Arc Angel had showed up and kicked some demon butt! I'm not 100% certain why God told me to call on both Michael and Gabriel because I'm sure there isn't a demon in hell that is any match for Michael. My guess is that Gabriel was there to give my brother the good news to ***"Fear Not"*** that he was going home very soon to be with our Lord Jesus. They said after we left he slept very peacefully without another single drop of morphine until he passed. Of course they all thought he had just finally gotten enough in his system to rest in peace but I knew the truth! I couldn't help but smile when I heard he was gone. As tears of joy ran down my face I felt like doing a victory dance as I smugly told Satan, *"Ha, ha, ha, ha, ha, you didn't get my brother!"*

Don't get me wrong, I didn't want my brother to die! However, I know where he is now is so much better than where he was on this earth; that I do not weep! I rejoice in knowing Satan lost another soul to the power in the blood of Jesus!

CHAPTER 9

Learning to turn it over to God

The past few years had been pretty rough but with each trial came more understanding. Just when I thought I could handle just about anything I found another mountain to climb. After battling cancer for a year, my uncle had passed in 2009 and left me to care for my aunt; which I regretfully admit was not a job I wanted to do. But isn't it so God to put you in a place you think you don't want to be to show you the beauty in the breaking? Although I begged God not to give me that job it turned out to be the most rewarding job I ever had. My aunt Lorene was 80 years old when she came to stay and she was scared to panic of dying. She had asked me many times to not let her die alone and of course I promised to be right by her side when the time came. She was very much in her right mind for a woman who had been on one of the strongest anti-anxiety medications known to man for over 30 years. She knew the bible and had been faithful to believe for as long as I could remember. She took me to church and taught me a lot about Jesus when I was a small child. How ironic that I would be the one to teach her about being in relationship with Jesus in her final days. Looking back, I realize it was God's way of blessing her for what she had done for me; by taking me to church and helping to plant seeds of faith in my tender heart. In a way I guess you could say she had paid it forward. Just as the bible promises to bless us tenfold for our good works; her blessing has become mine.

We spent almost 2 years together watching the Price is Right and Jeopardy while we drank our coffee every morning. Holding hands and praying before bed every night; and countless conversations about the Love of God and His precious mercy. My aunt knew a lot about religion; but as it turned out she didn't know as much as I did about having a relationship with God. Looking back, I realize my spirit of rebellion had given me no other choice but to find a relationship with Him because being rebellious is a conflict with religion. Whereas those tormenting spirits of fear and religion had her bound to this earth with no hope of being good enough to enter into heaven. This is not to say that it is better to be rebellious than to be religious by any means. I believe it can be good for people to live a religious life as long as they have the relationship with Christ to discern what He wants them to be religious about. Religiously reading God's word is the best way to understand His ways. Religiously talking to Him daily is the best way to build a relationship with Him; just like it is with anyone else. It is impossible to have a best friend that you don't talk to. It is impossible for a parent to know and understand their child if they don't spend any time together. Just as it is impossible for a child to know what they can and cannot do unless their parents communicate with them what their rules are. It is impossible to have a good marriage unless you spend time making love to your mate. This isn't meant to be thought of in a sexual way but rather in an intimate way. We are supposed to be the bride of Christ and yet most of us have never spent a moment of intimacy with our husband Jesus Christ.

In my opinion that is what religion is supposed to be about. If we don't religiously spend time alone in intimacy with our mate, we will most likely find ourselves in a rocky relationship. Marriage isn't supposed to be about one person being in control of the other. It is supposed to be about 2 people joining together as one unit and becoming more powerful together than they were apart. How can you possibly become one unless you spend time alone touching one another and creating that bond that only the two of you can have? There is only one you; there is only one Him or Her and there is only one God! There are many forms of religion my friend, but there is only one God and there is only one you; so find what works for the relationship you have with Him. Just as Jane and John Smith don't have the same relationship as Mike and Mary Moore; your relationship with God doesn't have to be the same as mine. However, He loves us all the same and wants the same thing from each and every one of us, ***"Our Love and Our Time"***. Therefore, if you feel it is necessary to find a religion that works for you, so you can dedicate a certain amount of time each week building your relationship with Jesus, please do so!

Personally I spent lots of time in church as a child and that is where the foundation of my relationship with Christ was built. I wouldn't take anything for the years I spent inside those little country churches. However, inside those churches wasn't where I truly fell in Love with the Lord in the way I Love Him now. The walls of our home where we share our most intimate moments were not built inside the safety of the church; they were built inside the storms. When I think of my Lord I think of several songs we used to sing in those little country churches like *"Power in the blood"* and *"He keeps me singing"*. However, some of the most intimate moments we've shared were when I sang country love songs to Him that I had changed the words around to fit my love for Him. Most of the time I sing Kenny Chesney's song *"That's all I need to know"* to Him in the shower. Sometimes I can see Him smile in my mind. Tonight as I sit here and write this story I'm thinking of the country song, *"Love say's they will"* by Tanya Tucker. The words of that song remind me of my life and how I often felt I was a sparrow in a hurricane. I had a head full of dreams and faith that could change anything; *"The world says they'll never make it, but love says they will"*. Then I think of the words that Noah and Allie said in the notebook and it often reminds me of Him, *"I think our Love can do anything we want it to"*. Anyone who has ever watched the Notebook would have to admit it is the greatest love story of all time. Their love was so powerful that they peacefully went to sleep and left this world at the same time *"you can't get any better than that"*! I used to watch that movie and hope someday that would be me & Johnny; but now I know that kind of love is spiritual and therefore it never really dies. Allie and Noah were an example of what love between a man and wife should be; which is also the way our Love should be for Jesus.

If there was one thing I learned over the last 2 years of my Aunt's life here on this earth, I learned how sad a human life can be without that kind of love. My aunt had lived a life of pain that was far worse than most of us could ever imagine. The spirits of darkness that had oppressed her entire family, "for God only knows how many years", had robbed her of the only true love she ever knew on this earth. Her first marriage was to a soldier that she barely knew because her parents wanted to make sure she would get his G.I. bill. That marriage was very short and then she met her true love that she was married to for over 29 years. I was a young child when they divorced but I can still remember the devastating impact that divorce had on her life.

Although she lived to bury 2 more husbands the majority of our conversations were still about Roy. There wasn't a day that went by she didn't mention his name. Over the years when she was married to the others and I went to visit, he somehow always managed to come up in conversation. Sometimes I felt really bad for my other uncles because it was quite obvious her heart and soul was still with him.

During our time together in her final 2 years of life I began to realize how Satan had used their love as a weapon against them. As time went on God would reveal things to me I had never understood before in all the countless conversations we had over the years since

155

they had divorced. As God revealed things to me, I revealed them to her, until one day I believe she finally found peace in what had happened to their marriage. She had carried that un-forgiveness and mental torment around for over 35 years. It was impossible for her to build the relationship she needed to build with Jesus until she was able to forgive Roy; but she couldn't forgive until she understood why he did what he did. Although I'll admit it got old hearing the same stories over and over; I realize now it was necessary for her to tell me that many times so I would cry out to God for answers. If I had just had the good sense to ask God to reveal this to me when I was a child, maybe I could have figured out a way to get them back together. If I had figured it out sooner, maybe I would have had the good sense to fix my own relationship with Johnny. Our stories were so similar that when God began to reveal to me what had destroyed them, I began to understand more and more about what had destroyed us.

You see those same tormenting spirits of depression, religion, confusion and control that opened the door for the unclean spirits of addiction and seduction played a major role in the destruction of both our relationships. Although their love was from a different era, the spirits of darkness know not time. Satan knows the most powerful weapon God has against him is love. Therefore, he will go after love with every dark spirit he has in hopes of destroying it before it destroys him. I'm absolutely amazed at how God managed to push me into writing this book several months after my Aunt Lorene came to stay and was able to reveal to me the root of her pain, *"as well as my own"* through sharing each other's stories. The amazing part of it all was that He was able to clean out and heal up a very infected 40 year old wound my aunt had in her heart; by ripping the band aid off mine. Once my wounds began to heal through writing this book, I was able to help Him shine His light on hers. Looking back, I now realize as I shared with her the things the good Lord had revealed to me in my writing, she began to see the light as well. It was almost like watching a caterpillar transform into a butterfly now that I think about how the forgiveness took her to a different level in her walk with the Lord.

I'm not sure why I was surprised that she waited until I walked out of the room to die. My job was finished and she was finally free to find her soul mate again in a place where darkness would never be able to tear them apart. My heart is filled with joy as I think of how happy they both must be in the radiant presence of our Lord. Now my aunt and uncle who played such a big part in molding me into the person I am today are back together in a world that is free of spiritual, physical and mental torment. They both have a brand new set of legs that they can dance on and a new set of pipes to sing with. She is able to soar with the birds she always loved to look at and smell all the beautiful flowers she always loved to get. I hope someday the good Lord will let her know how He inspired me to make her a part of this book. I know she couldn't wait for me to get it done and she always hoped she would be in it. Although I admit I had no idea this chapter would be about her "until He told me to write it"; and I wondered what on earth I would even say. I'm so very thankful that it is; because as He is always so wonderful to do, He has revealed to me something new Aunt Lorene as I write about you!

CHAPTER 10

The Devils Day

It was Monday October 31, 2011 and I was working from home. My best friend Beth stopped by and I was telling her how I couldn't sleep the night before. I felt burdened in my heart all day Sunday but couldn't figure out why. I kept asking God why I felt so empty and sad but never received an answer. After praying for hours and still feeling like someone I loved had died, I finally fell asleep somewhere between 5:00 and 6:00 a.m. When I woke up that day, the sadness was gone; so I discarded my feelings from the day before as hormones and went on about my day. Beth was sitting at the table working on her lap top and I was at the computer when Lynn called me on her lunch hour to see if I had heard from Robin. We talked about the weekend for a few minutes and how I had talked to Robin on Friday night and she had seen her on Saturday at a convenience store; but neither of us had talked to her on Sunday. As soon as I hung up with Lynn the thought crossed my mind that it was odd I didn't hear from Robin on Sunday; she typically called me every Sunday afternoon. Lynn said when she saw Robin on Saturday she wondered if she might be high and I wondered if that is why she didn't call. A few minutes later I got a call from her roommate's cell and thought it was Robin calling but it wasn't.

As soon as I answered and heard that shaky voice of her friend say my name, I said, *"Robin is dead isn't she?"* Suddenly it was perfectly clear to me why I had felt so vexed the entire day before and I just started screaming as soon as she said yes!

Beth didn't know what to do with me but she tried her best to help me get a hold of Lynn before she made it back to work. Every memory of every bad thing I had ever said to Robin came rushing through my mind. All I could think of was why didn't I let her stay with me when she asked or at least ask her to come after I got over being mad! Why didn't I think it was odd that she didn't call me on Sunday and why didn't I call her? But most of all, why didn't God answer me when I asked Him over and over that day why I felt that way? Why didn't He tell me I needed to go check on my sister when I asked Him over and over if there was someone I needed to be praying for or going to help!

Robin had issues with drug addiction most of her life but she had been doing really good for the past few years. She had been living with Lynn the whole time she had been straight but they had a falling out a few months prior because Robin had went *"on a mission"* as we called it, and relapsed. Lynn got really mad at her and told her she couldn't come back. Then Robin said some things to Lynn blaming me for Lynn not letting her come back and Lynn told me what she said. Then I got mad and wouldn't let her come to my house either. We foolishly thought we were going to punish her for relapsing so she wouldn't do it again; but all we did was throw her straight into the Lion's den!

So Robin went to stay with her friend that she had took off with the weekend she relapsed. Her friend seemed to need Robin there as much as Robin needed a place to stay; so it appeared to be a good thing for both of them. Robin seemed to be growing up and really trying her best to do the right things. She still called almost every day and didn't sound like she was high on the phone. She said she was going to work when there was work for her to do and she was still making it to drug court every day she was supposed to. She told stories of all the things she was doing with her roommates and appeared to be pretty happy. Looking back, I realize now she just didn't want us to think she needed our help. No matter how miserable she may have been or how much she really wanted to be with me & Lynn, she had too much pride to beg and neither one of us was offering to help her or asking her to come back and stay with one of us.

The first 24 hours after I got the news of her death I shut down and opted out of dealing with this one. I had been down this road before and knew there wasn't a funeral home in town that would take her unless she had insurance or we had thousands of dollars to bury her and we didn't have either! Lynn tried her best to find a place to take Robin but came back after hours of searching feeling defeated and hopeless. I couldn't stand seeing my baby sister like that so I pulled myself together and listened to where God had been telling me to call all day. Praise God for people in country towns that have a big heart!

Because she was only 49 and had no known health problems it was mandatory they take her away for an autopsy. The cops searched the trailer she lived in and took a few items that belonged to her roommate before we even got a call she was dead. I can't even begin to describe what all went through my mind over the next few weeks. I wondered if her roommates knew she had over dosed but were too afraid to call anyone because she was in drug court and they were afraid she would be in trouble. I wondered if they gave her the drugs and were afraid they would be in trouble themselves. But then when I went to prepare her body for the funeral and got to see her for the first time since she had passed my mind really began to wonder. As soon as I took one look at her I knew she had been dead for hours by the time anyone called the ambulance. Her face was badly distorted from where she had laid on one side until rigger set in. Her nose was bruised and she had a cut on her lip like her mouth had been busted. Her hand was all swollen like it may be broken and her hair was so matted I had to cut it! In my mind it appeared she had been in a fight and someone had pulled her hair, busted her nose and mouth and left her to die! I just couldn't believe her lifelong friend could be capable of doing something like this but the thought kept running through my mind, if she caught Robin stealing her drugs they could have got in a fight and she may have been too afraid to call me.

But that didn't make any sense to me either because I know Robin would have called me if they had been fighting that bad unless she was unconscious. My mind was racing and I couldn't even think straight enough to wrap my mind around what could have happened. I had too many unanswered questions and was mad at God for letting this happen! For the next few days I functioned on adrenalin and anger. Then about the third day Beth and I were heading across town to get flowers for the funeral and I was ranting to her how angry I was at God for not letting me know that night when I was crying out to Him for answers as to why I felt so empty like someone had died.

I will never forget the road I was on when He spoke so very softly to me and said, **"I was protecting you from yourself because I knew if you knew she was high, you would have said something mean to her and would have never forgiven yourself that your last words to her were mean"**.

I immediately looked up to heaven and said, *"Guilty Lord"*!

Then He began to tell me of how He had answered my prayers because He made sure she got so sick she would cry out in repentance before she took her last breath. He then told me her suffering was over and reminded me of when she had cried out to Him to help her to not be a drug addict anymore. He reminded me of how excited she was that she felt the Holy Spirit touch her when she cried out for deliverance. He said He had answered her prayers by not letting her go down that road again. He told me He knew she was never going to be strong enough to fight off that demon that had been chasing her for so many years. He told me He loved her too much to see her suffer over that spirit of addiction that had destroyed her relationships with the people she loved so dear for so many years any longer.

I felt so ashamed for doubting my Lord and being mad at Him for one second! I knew I had to make it up to Him for the way I had acted over the past few days; so I decided to use what Satan meant for our harm, for the glory of God! I pulled myself together and put together a sermon for her funeral that I hoped would put a knot on Satan's head for what he had done to my sister!

Robin started drinking when she was about 14 and managed to get into so much trouble the law was fed up with her by the time she turned 20. She spent her 21st birthday in prison and gave birth to her second child during that prison term. Robin was almost 7 years older than me and about 12 ½ years older than Lynn. She took care of us when we were little because our mother was so addicted to drugs and alcohol she couldn't half the time. I can still remember how Robin would cry when we were little kids and swear she would never do the things to her kids that mom had done to us. Looking back I realize now how depressed our mother must have been to just want to sleep all the time. She used to tell us she didn't like being in the "real world" and that was why she took a lot of sleeping pills so she didn't have to wake up. I can remember countless times we would pour pitchers of water on her head trying to get her to open her eyes so we would know she was alive.

Robin started driving when she was 11 years old so she could get to where mom was and try to save her. I will never forget the first time Robin showed up in our mom's car at a hotel room mom had taken me to on one of her drunken adventures. Robin was 11 so I must have been 4 or maybe 5. I just remember being in this hotel room with my mother and her being distraught without a car or any money to get us out of there. Then suddenly I saw Robin out the window pulling up in our mom's car, barely tall enough to see over the steering wheel. She got out of the car with a sack of groceries and a big smile on her face. Our parents had been drinking and got into a fight so our mom took me and left. I'm not sure why Robin wasn't with us when we left because she usually was, or even how we got to that hotel room. All I know is she was our saving grace that day when she stole the keys to the car and money from our dad while he was passed out. I remember she had a lot of junk food and we went and sat beside the pool. Mom was so happy to see her she didn't even get in trouble for stealing the car. Robin always had a way of making me feel safe in the worst of situations.

The first time I remember Robin making me feel safe was when our mom decided to take us on an adventure to Arkansas to see a woman she had met in prison. She snuck off from our dad and had her friend take us to the bus station one night. I remember at first she had us excited thinking we were going on a big adventure but the excitement soon left when mom took some sleeping pills and left us awake on that scary bus alone. We had layover after layover in big cities that were full of scary looking people. I can remember Robin holding on to me so tight when we walked through the bus stations trying to find a place to sit down. Mom would go back to sleep as soon as we found a seat to sit on; but Robin stayed awake the whole time and kept watch. It seemed like it took days to get to Arkansas and I remember being really excited when we finally arrived. However, it didn't take long for the excitement to turn into fear when the people from deliverance showed up at the bus station in a beat up old truck and took us to a place a million miles from civilization.

When we arrived at their trailer that sat on the side of a rocky cliff, we were told kids weren't allowed to stay in the house. They took Robin and me to a chicken house with dirt floors that had two twin beds and told us, ***"This is where the kids stay"***. Now you have to understand, our parents may have had alcohol and drug issues but we had a decent place to live and anything we wanted. Our parents never whooped us no matter how much we may have deserved it! These people were so mean their kids were scared to death to ask for a drink! I honestly don't think mom even realized how bad it was because she stayed comfortably numb the whole time we were there. I was very young and didn't realize how bad it was myself until Robin sat down beside me on our bed in the chicken house and began to cry as she sang a country song called *"Lord help me Jesus"* that was popular at the time. I will never forget her sitting on that bed with her arm around me crying and singing. Then I began to cry and tell her I was scared and she looked at me with those big green eyes and said, **"Don't worry, I'm going to get us out of here"!** Then she marched in the house and demanded that they better let her see our mom!

Mom was sleeping in one of their bedrooms and we marched down the hall demanding we were going to see our mother! Robin had sense enough to know mom would never stand for us not getting anything we wanted to eat, no matter how drunk or high she may have been. So Robin threw a fit and told mom she wasn't going to eat the garbage those people were feeding their kids.

She said, **"It's bad enough you are laying in here in a bed while we have to stay outside in a chicken coop but if you don't get me to a store I'm telling grandma what you have done when we get home"!**

So mom got out of bed and insisted someone take us to the store to get what we wanted to eat. Then one of those deliverance people took us to the store and Robin found a phone to call grandma. Our grandma was often referred to as Dick Tracey when she wanted to find mom and Robin knew if anyone could find us, Grandma could! I don't know for sure how she did it but it didn't take more than a day before my dad and uncle showed up on that rocky cliff with a bag of groceries like 2 White Knights!

My daddy was always my hero and I remember very well running out the door of the chicken house when Robin said he was there. I ran down the rocky walk way and grabbed a hold of his leg when he was walking in the house. I barely stood as high as his knee, but I can still remember the smile on his face as he looked down at me. There was no way those people were going to say we had to stay outside when our dad got there! By the time dad found us, mom must have sobered up and came to her senses so she was ready to go home. Dad got out the junk food and told us to share with the other kids but that mean woman said her kids weren't allowed to have pop and candy. That is when my sister got really bold and told that woman she may be mean and not let her kids have anything good to eat but our parents let us have anything we wanted! I'm sure those people were glad to see us leave because Robin wasn't about to obey their rules and when the white knights arrived, we knew we didn't have to! I don't remember the long ride home but Robin said it was miserable riding that far with three smokers. My guess is I was either sleeping or just so content that nothing could be miserable after what we had just been through.

It wasn't long after Robin started stealing the car that mom left dad and moved to an apartment in town. I remember my dad would come every day and bring us a sack of groceries in each arm and usually a coloring book for me. Robin made friends in the apartments and took me with her to their house most of the time. I remember going to one of her friend's house allot and listening to 45 records on her little turntable. We would dance in her bedroom and sing to Dianna Ross & the Supremes. Her mom worked hard at a diner so she would make sure the house was clean when her mom got home. I remember I loved helping her clean so she loved having me there. Then I remember our mom got pregnant with Lynn and we went back home for a short period of time until our house burnt. It was then that we moved into a trailer in town and things started to get really bad.

Lynn was born in December when we lived in the trailer court but we moved into another house shortly after she was born. Now I realize children often only remember the things that make an impact on them so I'm sure things weren't always as bad as I remember because I know what a wonderful person my mother was when she was in her right mind. However, I haven't got a lot of memories of my Mom coming out of her room during the day after we moved to that house. She didn't want me to go to kindergarten so I was at home with her every day while dad was at work and Robin was at school. I can remember hearing Lynn cry a lot in the bedroom and it would be so dark when I went in to check on her that I had to feel my way to the crib. I remember putting my little hands through the bars of the crib to feel for her bottle so I could see if she had milk in it. Sometimes I would find it empty and sometimes it would be like cottage cheese. So I would go into the kitchen and get a chair to get up to the sink and wash it out before I filled it up. Then I would go back to the dark room and put the bottle in her mouth while I tried to change her diaper in the dark. After a while I just started climbing over the bars and getting her out of the crib even though I knew I wasn't supposed to. I remember being so glad when Robin would come home from school and dad would get home because mom would usually wake up when one of them got there.

My aunt Lorene got a divorce while we lived in that house and came to stay with us for a while. Mom stayed awake more when Aunt Lorene was there because she would make her get up. However, Aunt Lorene couldn't take all the parties and taking care of kids so she didn't stay long.

By the time I started 1st grade we had moved into another trailer court where we lived until I was about 8. It was there that Robin started getting wild and my world really fell apart. By the time I was 8 and Robin was 15 our grandma died and both mom and Robin really went off the deep end. Robin was so devastated at Grandma's death she ran off for a few days during the funeral. When she came back she was never the same again. Mom had always struggled with depression and addiction but it got much worse after grandma passed. It seemed like the whole family fell apart in some way. I remember mom had started going to church when grandma was sick and that was my greatest memories of her. Looking back, I realize now she was trying to do everything she could do to get God to heal her mother and when that didn't work she gave up on trying at all.

Shortly after my grandma passed we moved again to a little country town that everyone in the family seemed to hate except me and my dad. We moved into a brand new house my dad built and dad bought mom all new furniture and a new car thinking it would make her happy. Robin said they had moved to Gilligan's Island and rarely ever came home. When she did come home it usually wasn't a good thing. She was full of anger and often only came home when she was drunk and wanted to fight with someone about something. I remember not long after we moved in she came in drunk and threw eggs all over our new white walls. From that day on it seemed our happy little home I was so excited to move into felt like a rat trap I didn't want to be in. There was always someone living at our house and some kind of chaos going on all the time. Either mom was wasted out of her mind on sleeping pills or there was a house full of drunks "or both"! My older sister Marie had 2 kids and they had moved in with us in the beginning. One was about 8 months older than Lynn and one was about 7 months younger. Since they ranged in age from 15 months to 3 ½ years old they really could have benefited from more suitable adult supervision. I can remember trying my best to keep them under control but they were like a barrel full of monkeys and I had already started getting depressed myself.

So over the next 5 years different family members moved in and out of our house in Stilesville. Grandpa came to stay for a while to keep from going to a nursing home but mom wasn't in any shape to properly care for him and I had to go to school sometimes. I remember trying to bathe and clean him up when he went to the bathroom was a real challenge since I was only about 9 years old. However, I did my best and he loved it when I made him cream of wheat and read him the bible. He always said my cream of wheat was the best because it was lumpy and he liked it that way. He would play his harmonica and I would sing church songs, we were quite a pair!

Then one day my aunt Lorene came and took him to the nursing home because mom wouldn't wake up to take care of him half the time, and it broke my heart. The first home he was at that was close to Stilesville wasn't doing a very good job so they moved him to another home close to Aunt Lorene and Aunt Mary. I begged mom to take me to see him every time we went to town and she would usually drop me off there for the day. I would take him up and down the halls in his wheel chair that he called a buggy and we had lots of fun! One day I took him out in the parking lot and was rolling him around when I lost control of his buggy and it started going down a hill. One of the nurses saw me trying to pull the chair back up the hill before he went out in the street and got really mad. After that, I wasn't allowed to take him outside anymore and it didn't seem like he lasted much longer. They said his heart gave out but I always thought his heart was too broken to live any more without grandma or anyone to bring him any joy.

Robin eventually came back home when she got pregnant with her first child at 18. For the most part it seemed like things were finally pretty good at home. Robin wasn't drinking so she seemed to be pretty happy most of the time and it seemed like mom wasn't as depressed when she was there. I can remember coming home from school and seeing the 2 of them out in the yard soaking up some sun. When mom was straight she was the most beautiful person in the world. She had the sweetest smile and loving eyes. She was filled with wisdom and had a heart of gold. Mom carried a light in her that people were drawn to and I think Robin inherited that light. I remember feeling so jealous when the two of them got together because I could see the love they had for each other and the bond they shared. Somehow it seemed like the more problems Robin got the closer they became. Maybe it was the mother instinct that made mom step up to the plate and protect her.

When the day finally came that we had all been waiting for I was at school. By the time someone took me to the hospital to see the baby they had already told Robin and my mom the baby may not live through the night. The baby had a bowel movement in Robin's uterus and was drowning in her own feces. By the time the doctors figured out what was going on; both Robin and the baby were about to die so they did an emergency surgery. The baby was born having seizures and that continued on through the night. My mom did what she did best and called everyone she knew that knew how to pray or might know someone who did. She trusted in the Lord to pull Robin and the baby through in that humble way that my mother only knew.

The next morning the doctor came in and said the seizures had stopped and the baby would live. I was at school the day they brought her home and was never so happy in all my life when I walked in my house and saw my whole family with our brand new blessing. They had named her Suzie after our mom and she was the prettiest thing I had ever seen. I was twelve when little Suzie was born and thought I was ready to be a mother myself. Lynn was a six year old pain in my rear by then and I couldn't wait to get my hands on that new bundle of joy. It didn't take long before Robin took off again because she was scared to death of Suzie and mom had taken over the role of mother to her. Needless to say, it didn't take long for mom to go back into depression and I got my wish of having a baby of my own. For the next few years I took care of Suzie when mom had her episodes and it was like Robin just had another little sister she would come home to see every now and then.

When I was 13 we moved away from Stilesville so I had to leave my church and my best friend Beth. Looking back I realize that is when depression really got its strong hold on me too. Robin was home a lot more when we moved back to town but that wasn't exactly a good thing. By now she and mom had become partners in crime when it came to drinking and taking pills. Robin had found herself a whole lot of friends that liked to do the same things so they seemed to always have an endless supply of something. Robin was always in trouble with the law and mom & dad were always spending money they really didn't have on getting her out of trouble. She had gotten involved with a man that had enough money to keep her drugged up most of the time. At first he appeared to be some white Knight that would take her financial burdens off of dad but the devil was surely in the details. Robin was in women's prison for her first sentence on her 21st birthday where she would continue to spend the majority of the next 10 years of her life.

As bad as it broke my heart to know my sister was spending her 21st birthday in prison it didn't hurt half as bad as seeing her shackled to a bed with chains when she had her second baby girl. After all, she wasn't a murderer she was just a drug addict that had just been caught too many times for driving under the influence without a license. So the man who paid for her drugs and alcohol most of the time so he could sleep with her when she got high was the father of the baby she had in prison. He took me with him to the prison hospital so he could get the baby out of the hospital by saying he was her husband. I remember feeling so sad for that baby as I held her on the way back home. Looking back I wonder if the Holy Spirit inside me was weeping at the life He knew that child would have.

Over the next couple of years Robin learned how to survive in prison by marrying the man she despised so he would provide her with the things she needed on the inside and bring her kids to see her. When she came out of prison she had a girlfriend and claimed to be a lesbian. Needless to say, it only got worse from there! The man she married was obsessed with her and was bound and determined if he couldn't have her no one would. He wasn't about to let her see the baby unless she was with him and expected everyone in the family to be on his side. The girl she was with had been a nurse and knew how to call in prescriptions to the pharmacy which is what she had wound up in prison for herself. It didn't take long before they became partners in crime on what they called "busting scripts". They would go to an expensive department store, grab a shopping bag and steal enough merchandise to get the money to buy the prescriptions they needed for the day. Then go right up to the service desk without even walking out of the store and return the merchandise they had in the shopping bag. They went from town to town and sometimes even traveled to nearby states doing their R & R's "Rip off and returns" and busting scripts.

Robin had never been on the needle before she met Linda and we all prayed they would get caught before they wound up dead. Within a couple of years they were on their way back to prison but this time they almost took our mom and Suzie's dad with them. Since mom was a drug addict herself she wasn't opposed to getting in the car with them when they took off on an adventure. Suzie's dad was a drug addict too and was at our house one day when the girls decided to go to another town and bust a script. Most likely already drunk or high themselves Mom and Mark decided to ride along. When the girls got caught mom and Mark were in the car with them so they went down too. I had to move back home at 18 to take care of Suzie and Lynn. I can't remember how long it took for mom and Mark to get out of jail but it seemed like forever since I was the only one to take care of the kids because dad was a mess. Robin made sure mom didn't get convicted of anything by making Linda testify that mom had nothing to do with it. However, Robin and her partner in crime didn't get out for a couple of years.

Shortly after Robin got out of prison that time, she got high and got ran over by a truck in 1989. When I went to see her in the hospital I didn't think there was any way she could make it through the night. I could see inside her skull and nearly every bone in her body was broken. She was bleeding from her kidney and was expected to be paralyzed for life if she lived. I remember standing there crying and praying as I said my goodbyes to her that night for what I thought would be the last time. My faith was very weak at the time and little did I know, God wasn't done with her yet. After she was sent home from the hospital with a wheel chair Mark showed up and told her he wasn't going to let her go down like that. She said mom was so high she was trying to give her a bath with a dirty sock so she was willing to do whatever Mark said to get out of that chair.

Mark had been in a bad motorcycle accident that was supposed to leave him paralyzed for life but he had his brother's put him in the bath tub and soak his body cast off; then crawled until he could walk again. He told Robin she had to be determined enough to try if she ever wanted to get out of that chair. He took her out to a parking lot and walked along beside her as she walked behind her chair. Within a few days she was walking on her own with broken bones and a dead kidney. In no time at all she was back to her same old stuff and I spent more time mad at her than being happy she was still alive like I should have been. I never failed to forget the pain I felt when I thought I was about to lose Robin, when she got drunk or high. I remember feeling the same anger towards Robin as I felt towards our mother; with very little compassion or understanding of the pain they both felt from being an addict. So many harsh words spoken that couldn't be taken back and days lost to anger that could never be replaced.

Although I can't really remember how many more times she went to prison after that I do remember her being home and being straight when our dad died. Shortly after Robin was hit by the truck, dad went to jail for drunk driving. He was taking the back roads home from the bar like he had done so many times before; but this time he forgot it was time for the county fair. When he started to turn on the road to home, he came up on a cop directing fair traffic. He sped off really fast and knocked the cops flash light out of her hand with the mirror of his car. She claimed he hurt her arm and was determined to see him put away for a very long time. Dad was never so ashamed in all of his life as he was when Mom and I went to pick him up in jail. I remember being so nasty to him and my mother scolding me for the way I was talking to my dad.

She said, **"Do you have no heart at all? Do you think he doesn't feel bad enough for what he has done that you have to talk to him like that?"**

My dad was so cold he was nearly blue and was shaking all over like he was about to go into shock. I loved him so much and had always feared he would either die in a bar room brawl or driving home drunk. My anger was derived from fear and hurt but those words I said to my dad later hurt me worse than anything he could have ever done.

Dad was the rock that our whole family depended upon. For the first time in our life, he needed someone and I was too selfish to see it at first. Thank God for my mother and her infinite wisdom that knew just how to chastise me when I was wrong. The next year was rough on dad as he went through detox and alcohol treatment. I was right there by his side as much as I could be and mom did her best to behave as much as she could. Almost a year to the day from the night he got arrested, my dad broke out in hives and his neck swelled up to the point he couldn't breathe. I was at the county fair with my son at the baby contest and just happened to call home right after they rushed him to E.R. At first I thought it was his nerves because he was about to be sentenced and would most likely go to prison very soon for a long time. Needless to say I went straight to the hospital and walked in right when the doctor was about to come out and give us his death sentence. My dad had a massive inoperable tumor on his left lung that was wrapped around the main artery to his heart. I felt like I had been given the death sentence because I thought there was no way I could live without my dad. How could this be happening after he had been sober for a whole year? My dad had never been sober more than a week in my entire life and now that he has been sober for a year he is told he is going to die in less than 3 months!

Somehow Dad's death sentence gave us the best year of our life; I guess God really does use all things for the good of those who love him. Mom got back in church and became the wife she was never able to be for very long periods of time. Robin managed to stay out of trouble and not give them much grief the whole time dad was sick. She even stayed home most of the time and helped mom take care of dad and Suzie. I quit smoking because I didn't want to smoke in front of dad anymore since he had to quit. Besides that, I thought if I did everything right God would heal my dad and we could all live happily ever after like I always dreamed we would. Looking back I realize I did the same thing my mother did when her mother was dying of cancer. I had prayed for as long as I could remember that God would do whatever he had to do to make sure all of my family went to heaven.

As the bible says in Matthew 18:8, ***"It is better for you to enter life maimed or lame, than to have two hands or two feet and be thrown into eternal fire"***. I figured dad suffering was just God's way of getting all of our family ready to go to heaven because He knew none of us could make it without the other. I was only 21 when we found out dad was sick so I had a lot to learn about life and about God. However, not a day went by that I didn't say a prayer that if God knew dad would go back to drinking if He healed him and then wind up in hell one day; He would just save his soul and take him home. Then when the day came that God decided to answer my prayer and take him home, I got mad as hell. I thank God Robin was there and managed to stay straight throughout the next few days of the funeral. I don't know if she ever knew how much I needed her then. Mom was a mess and couldn't handle making any of the arrangements; but Robin stayed by my side every step of the way and managed to be my strength like she had been all those many years before.

Although that wonderful year we had of pulling together would soon end as soon as dad was put in the ground, I will always treasure that time we had. It didn't take long after dad passed away for Robin to wind up in prison again. This time she came out with a girlfriend that had been in prison for murder. It didn't seem like that lasted very long before she was back home with mom and then shortly after married her second husband. I think Robin really loved him but she was so messed up at that time she couldn't be the woman he wanted her to be and he wasn't about to be the money source for her drugs. In less than a year of them being married Robin wound up being on house arrest but still couldn't manage to stay straight. She was on house arrest and lived in an apartment below me when our mother passed away, just 3 ½ years after we lost dad. Robin didn't find her inner strength when we lost mom and I feared I would lose her too. She tried to take on Suzie when mom passed away but she just didn't have it in her to take on a child who had the issues Suzie had. Suzie was 13 when mom passed away and had gone through more abuse than any of us ever knew.

Robin's first husband had been sexually molesting Suzie since she was a toddler but no one ever knew. She had been gang raped in a church parking lot that was near the place she lived with our mother when she was about 11 or 12 but was so used to being molested by her step father she never told anyone. When she started acting up after mom died, we all thought she was just grieving over losing both mom and dad within 3 years at the same time she started puberty. She bounced back and forth between Robin, Mark and me for about a year. Then the court took her away from Robin for not going to school and would only release her to me because Mark also had a record of being in prison. The really sad part was Robin was truly trying her best to take care of Suzie and get her to go to school. She would walk Suzie to the bus stop and then Suzie would get off down the road and take off. I had custody of her for over 2 years before I found out about the sexual abuse and still didn't find out about the gang rapes until years later. Looking back I have to wonder why God would have allowed me to get custody of a child who needed someone that could better see her problems and get her the help she needed. I was an emotional mess during that time in my life and barely had the strength to care for my own children. Suzie was doing things that I had no clue she was doing. Now I wonder how self-absorbed I must have been to not see how much more she needed than I was able to give.

The bible says a curse will continue on to the third or fourth generation until the curse is broken. Although I'm not sure how far back the curse of addiction went in our family prior to my own mother; I know Suzie has inherited the addiction curse to make at least 3 generations. Never the less, I vow to see Suzie set free and see this curse is broken before my time on this earth is through! I trust in my father in heaven to see our children through this just like He saw my mother and my sisters through it. He may have allowed them to their own free will that kept them from the blessings they could have had in this life time; but He was still only a whisper away. Although my heart is vexed at this time for the child I feel got left behind, I take comfort in knowing she has a hedge of safety around her. Suzie was baptized as a child and I know the Lord has His mark on her. Things may get much worse before they get better but I know some day we will all spend eternity together in heaven and that is all that really matters.

CHAPTER 11

Like-Minded Spirits

Sometime in 2010 I started having the same ongoing dreams about Johnny. This was after I went through spiritual boot camp and after God had started telling me to write this book. I don't remember exactly when the dreams started but I know I was still arguing with God that I didn't know how to write a book and that I must not be hearing Him correctly. The last time I had seen Johnny was in the spring of 2009 when he came to build my back deck. It was shortly after my Aunt Lorene had come to stay with me which was about 3 months after I had started spiritual boot camp. From the time I started my spiritual journey, the thoughts of being back in Johnny's arms again kept running through my mind. However, I dared not ask God to bring him back no matter how much I thought I was getting stronger in my walk with the Lord. I had made the promise I would never ask God to bring Johnny back again when He brought him back the last time if things didn't work. Even still, I wondered was God trying to tell me something with these dreams or was it just my sub-conscious where I kept Johnny hidden, coming to life in my sleep. But I wondered how could this be? The last time I had seen or heard from Johnny when he built my deck in 2009, I managed to royally screw up any chance I may have ever had with him when I disobeyed what God told me to do.

You see God had told me to hire Johnny to build the deck and I knew Johnny didn't have a whole lot of experience in deck building so I questioned whether or not I was hearing God correctly. However, Johnny and I had started building a friendship when we both lived in the same neighborhood in 2008. It seemed we had come to a place in our life that we were both willing to accept friendship over being completely without each other forever. He hired me to work with him remodeling a house when the market started falling and I desperately needed a side job. So when things started getting better for me, I hired him to do several jobs for me. The truth is I looked for any opportunity I could find just to call him or have him around. We were both single at the time and I hoped that one day when he came to do a job for me he would just take me in his arms and say he was sorry for all the things he had done so we could give it another try without me begging. After all, I had already gone to him and begged his forgiveness for everything I could ever think of that I had done wrong. Of course I had already forgiven him for all his wrong doings but in my mind if he didn't care enough to ask for forgiveness, he would most likely do it again.

I won't deny there were a couple of times our new found friendship wound up intimate; but I had not yet gone through spiritual boot camp and did not yet know how to rebuke the spirit of fear. Both times as I lay beside him feeling like I had died and gone to heaven; that tormenting spirit of fear would sneak into the room and tell me if I didn't sneak out of his bed and run back home while I had the chance we would be back together by morning and it would end up being bad again. I would get so scared at the thought of what had happened before, I couldn't breathe! I would lay there thinking, *"God I just wish I could die in his arms tonight so I could die a happy woman."* Yet all the while I would be scared to death he was going to get that control over me again. That hopeless feeling of wanting to die when it all went bad and he left me again. The thoughts of how much he and Nick disliked each other; and all that Nick was going through at that time, was more than I could consider dealing with. There was a time that Johnny would have come chasing me down when he woke up and found me not there, but not then. I lived less than a block away but instead of going back like I wanted to, I would lay in my bed the rest of the night wishing he would come after me. Wondering how being in his arms was still the only place that felt right to me and yet there still seemed to be more reasons why we wouldn't work out than why we would. The only reason I could think of that we should be together was Love; but Love just never seemed to be enough for us. How was it that we could tell each other anything until we decided we were going to give it another try? But as soon as we made that commitment we suddenly expected more out of each other than seemed to be possible. If only I had known then what I know now! If only I had the sense to rebuke that spirit of fear and claim the blessings of God on our life, but I didn't and I will live the rest of my life with that regret!

In August of 2008 I moved back to my old neighborhood and within a month Johnny had to move as well. He didn't have any work at the time so I sold his trailer to my niece so he could pay off some bills. He went to stay with some friends and that is when I kept calling him to work on my place. Most every time he came over to do a job for me I tried to find an opportunity to offer him a place to stay. He took me up on it one night, but both my sisters were staying with me at the time so he only stayed one night. I will never forget him sitting at my kitchen table when I walked into my bedroom and left the door open.

My sister said he saw my wedding dress hanging on the closet door and whispered to her, ***"What is she doing with that dress hanging on that door?"***

She replied, ***"I think she has it hanging there to torture you!"***

He replied back to her, ***"Its working!"***

Of course Robin broke her neck to tell me as soon as I walked back in the kitchen and we both got awkward. At that point I was ready to go to bed and Johnny was getting a little drunk. I told him & Robin goodnight and went to bed, but I could still hear their conversation. He was trying his best to convince her it would be better for him to sleep on the couch but she was already on the couch and refused to get up. I'm sure Robin did that for my benefit because she knew how bad I wanted to be in his arms. He finally came to bed and told me to scoot over because he wanted to sleep by the door in case he needed to make a fast get away. Then he told me to be sure and stay on my side of the bed and not touch him. He knew me well enough to know if he told me I couldn't I would have to show him I could; so I told him to shut up and let me hold him.

He laughed at me and said, ***"Oh is that how it's gonna be?"***

So I slid over close to him, wrapped my arms around him and said, *"Yep, it sure is, now shut up and go to sleep."*

He laughed and said, ***"Okay, but keep your hands to yourself!"***

I squeezed him a little tighter and fell right to sleep. I woke up the next morning and he was gone. When I woke up and found he wasn't there, I wondered if he was paying me back for the nights I snuck out of his bed. I wondered if I had screwed up by going to sleep so fast. Would he have said something I wanted to hear if I had stayed awake? I'm the girl who is a hopeless insomniac and yet I fall asleep before anyone that night! All I could say was "Why Lord?" I also wondered if I would ever get another chance to find out if he had anything he wanted to say about us being back together, but I never did.

That was a busy time for me because my uncle was going through cancer treatment and I was still pretty busy in Real Estate although I wasn't making any money. Not to mention all the side jobs I was doing to get by and all the things I had to do at home. Winter shortly came and I had run out of money so I couldn't call Johnny to do any work for me. So in complete desperation for love and financial stability I began to put my heart and soul into seeking the Lord for answers. That is when my spiritual boot camp began and God started preparing me to find my true identity. Right in the middle of my spiritual journey I had to go to Georgia to pick up my son so I found another good excuse to call Johnny because I needed someone to watch my dog. He still didn't have any work to speak of and was staying with friends so he agreed to dog sit at my house for a few days while I was gone.

While in Georgia I was able to attend a couple of awesome church services at Free Chapel. I was feeling full of the spirit when I returned and so desperately hoped Johnny would want to know all about it when I got back. We returned in the very early morning just before dawn and the dog woke him up when we came in the door. I was trying to be very quiet and hoped he would come back to bed once Nick went to bed. I'm not quite sure if he felt uncomfortable with Nick being there or if Satan had just really tormented his mind about our past while I was gone. But he was very anxious to leave as soon as we walked in and all my hopes of happiness walked out the door with him.

That was the last time I got to see him or talk to him until I came up with the money to have a deck built and thought that would be a good excuse to call him. By then Aunt Lorene had just come to stay and I wasn't sure for how long. When I called and ask him if he could build the deck, I heard the hesitation in his voice when he said he could. The price he gave me was only $50.00 less than a price I had already gotten from my sister's ex-husband who was a professional deck builder. Needless to say, I wondered if I had made a mistake by asking Johnny because I really didn't have the money to pay someone else to fix it if he screwed it up. So I decided to pray about it for a few days before I called him back to set up a time.

I was in my car driving to one of my side jobs that was out of town and that is where I most often got time to do my best praying. I had been seeking God's wisdom on this matter ever since the day I called Johnny but hadn't gotten an answer from Him. So that day

I decided to ask God for a specific sign if He wanted me to have Johnny build the deck.

I said, *"God I promised you I would never ask you to bring Johnny back and I want you to know I still won't! But please God, I need your help on this one because I don't want to make a mistake when I barely have the money to have this deck built anyway. I know Johnny needs the work and you know God there is no one in this world I would rather give my money to if it is your will. So please God, if you want Johnny to be the one to build the deck have him call me back today and if you don't please just have him blow me off."*

Within 10 minutes of saying that prayer Johnny called so I got my answer. I was so happy because I thought there could be some slim chance if God wanted to let him build the deck He may be willing to bring us back together. So beaming with joy when he called I set up a time for him to meet me and get started.

I hung up the phone and immediately that spirit of fear began to torment my mind so I asked God if I did the right thing. Was that just a coincidence or did He really want Johnny to build my deck? For the first time since I began to ask, I heard the Lord say **"Yes!"**

Then I decided since He was finally talking to me, I would ask was He sure Johnny knew how to build the deck. I will never forget what He said to me that day.

God said, ***"I'm the great carpenter and I know how to build that deck, let me be his teacher!"***

His words rebuked the spirit of fear that so often got in my head but I had no idea what He expected me to do next!

The first day Johnny came, God told me to go out and ask him to pray with me before he got started. But I didn't listen because the spirit of fear sounded so much louder than God's still small voice when the thought of him thinking I had gone fanatical crossed my mind. So instead of asking him if he would pray with me, I asked if he wanted a glass of tea!

After all, he brought his uncle who was supposed to know how to build decks so I was sure it couldn't have been God telling me to ask him to pray anyway. Shortly after he got started he got frustrated because he hit rock when he was digging the holes for the posts. Then again, I heard that still small voice tell me to ask him to pray and again I ignored it and rented him a machine to get through the rock. The next day God told me to ask him to pray with me before he got started but I was afraid he would think I didn't trust him to do a good job so I ignored that still small voice once again. That day went pretty well until he got to the stairs and I could see him getting frustrated again. The third day God told me again to ask him to pray with me before he got started but again, I ignored that still small voice for fear he would think I didn't think he was doing a good job.

I knew how important it was to Johnny for me to be proud of him and I wanted him to know I was very proud of him! By this time I was afraid he was going to stroke out with frustration so I told him to just calm down and we would think about what to do with those stairs and he could come back later to finish. I paid him most of what I owed him for the job, which wound up being $50.00 more than it was to hire a professional because I had to rent a machine. The next day he came while I was at work and put up a set of stairs that he said would be temporary until I figured out what he was supposed to do with them and I paid him the rest of what I owed him. Shortly after that, he got a new girlfriend and I figured he forgot all about my temporary stairs since I didn't hear from him again.

Each day I walked out my door and had to go down those steep little stairs I was reminded of my disobedience. I didn't have the nerve to try to reach him after I found out from his sister he had a new girlfriend because I figured if he ever cared about me at all he would have wanted to do the right thing and just come back. Besides that, I couldn't stand the thought of him ignoring my phone call or even worse, telling me he couldn't come back to finish the job because of her. Looking back I realize it wasn't that he didn't care, it was that he felt I didn't need him. My stubbornness of wanting him to just do the right thing on his own was the same old song and dance that had gotten me nowhere with him in the past. Johnny wanted to be wanted and needed; but so did I, so we were constantly running from each other for fear of feeling inadequate.

Days turned into weeks, weeks into months and before I knew it a couple of years had gone by since I had seen Johnny other than in passing at the county fair with his new girl. It was right at a year since he had built my deck that the dreams started. At first I just blew it off as a silly dream but then I had the same dream again and again. So after about the 3rd or 4th time I got brave enough to send him a message on Facebook. We weren't friends on Facebook at that time but we had several mutual friends so I had seen many pictures of him and the new girlfriend. I felt like that country song, *"I hate her and I'll think of a reason later"*. Never the less I continued to keep on keeping on with life and pretending I was just fine. Then one night when I was stalking his Facebook page I decided to send him the message below and tell him I had been having some strange dreams and wanted to make sure he was o.k.

March 24, 2010 Hi Johnny, I just wanted to drop you a line and see how you are. I keep having these strange dreams...."about once a month" with you and sometimes your dad in them. I never remember my dreams and am not even really sure I dream very often but I have had several dreams that involved you in the past few months and it is kind of weird. Anyway, it was just on my heart to check on you today and this is the only way I knew how. I hope everything is going good with you; it looks like it is "Praise God" for that. You are still in my prayers and I hope not to offend you by sending this message. Shalom to you and your family!

A little over a year later I got a surprise visit from his daughter who was now old enough to drive. I was working in my yard when she pulled up with a couple of friends and said, **"Mom, what are you doing"?** I knew that voice but was in disbelief it could really be her until I turned around to see her face. I was so shocked that she had come to see me I could barely speak. Here she was all grown up with a boyfriend and a car and she actually took the time to come see me.

We talked about old times for a bit, sharing stories with her friends and then she said, **"When are you going to go back with my dad?"**

My first response was, *"Your dad has a girlfriend!"*

Then she told me he wasn't with her anymore and immediately my heart started racing and I suddenly knew why I was having those dreams.

With my voice shaking searching for something to say, I softly said, *"Sweetie, your dad doesn't love me anymore."*

She immediately said with a smile, **"Yes he does!"**

At that point my head was spinning and I don't really know what else was said. She left shortly thereafter and I immediately began to ask God what was up with the dreams!

Of course God is a man of few words and He rarely answers the first time I ask Him a question. So I was left to wonder if I had become psychic or if it was just a coincidence about the dreams. Now in every one of these dreams the setting was always different as far as the buildings that I saw but the sky always looked the same. It was always a grey overcast sky that looked like it was about to rain and I could smell rain in the air. The ground was always very dry with dead looking grass and mud puddles here and there. The setting of these dreams reminded me of an old black & white western. It always started out that Johnny and I would be in a house or a trailer and I knew we were together. Then suddenly his new girlfriend would walk in and he would walk away without saying a word. I would always see his dad somewhere outside and I knew he knew Johnny wanted to be with me but without putting up a fight, I would let him walk away with her; even though I knew he wanted to stay with me. It felt like he had to be with her to make everyone else happy, but we both knew he was supposed to be with me. The funny part about the dream was that no one really spoke much. I just knew in my heart what everyone was feeling. I felt I had to let Johnny go to make his family happy but I knew he wasn't happy without me and his dad knew it too, but never said a word.

Each time I woke up from having this bazaar dream I told myself it must just be the hurt in my heart from the good things his family had said about the new girlfriend. Johnny's mother, whom I adored, certainly didn't care to spare my feelings when talking about how good she was for Johnny and what a really good girl she was. Maybe it was because I had gotten so good at pretending I was doing just fine without him. Or maybe it was because she never really wanted us together to begin with that she didn't care to spare my feelings. In the early years of our relationship I thought she was my friend and really believed she loved me; but she was always trying to convince me to get away from Johnny. Don't get me wrong, I know she had good reasons for not wanting us together. But I would have given anything if she could have just seen how much we loved each other and how we both needed her to encourage the positive things about our relationship instead of focusing on the bad. She once told Johnny our love was poison that made us toxic together and I won't even try to tell you how damaging that was to both of us! I'm sure the reasons she didn't want me with her son far outweighed anything positive she could see about our love.

She knew my family very well and told Johnny when we first met, **"The apples never fall too far away from the tree."**

You see her mother and my mother were best friends at one time and my mother had an affair with her husband. Her mother being the wonderful woman she is, told my mother she would always love her but she never wanted anything to do with being her friend again. I'm not sure if there was anything my mother ever regretted more than falling in love with her best friend's husband; but sometimes sorry just isn't enough to heal a wound like that! Then of course there were my sisters who had created some bad blood with Johnny's mother back in their younger years. Robin had even dated Johnny's dad when Johnny was about 2 years old. So you see she had good reason for concern that her son had fell in love with someone that came from the same *"bad tree"* like me when she had tried so hard to raise Johnny in the church.

I'm sure she found it hard to believe I was totally innocent in knowing he was married when we met, considering it never seemed to bother my mother or sisters. I'm sure she found it hard to believe I wasn't the one who got her son addicted to alcohol or drugs considering he never seemed to have a problem before he met me. How could I blame her for all the thoughts Satan made sure he put in her head to poison her mind against me, when I had fell prey to his lies so many times myself? I had even been guilty of believing she may be right about our love being toxic by the time those tormenting spirits of fear and confusion got done with my mind. Sure, I wanted her to just know in her heart I loved her son and that I loved Jesus too much to do the things she thought I was capable of doing. Sure it hurt that she was a Christian but she didn't seem to believe I was a good enough Christian for her son because I didn't look like the Christians of her church.

All I ever wanted was for her to look me straight in the eyes and say, *"Do you love my son?"* So I could say, *"Yes, with all of my heart!"* and then have her say, *"Well then, let's pray about the problems you two are having and trust in the Lord to help you find a way to fix them"* like I knew my mom would have.

Even as messed up as my mother may have been at times, if she had been alive when Johnny and I were going through trials she would have loved both of us enough to help pray us through it. My mother may have made a lot of mistakes in her life but she knew there was only one person in this world that could fix any mistake and she was humble enough to look to Jesus in all things. She taught me to praise Him for the good things and the bad things because at the end of every trial was something God wanted to teach us to help others.

Through all those years of trials I never had anyone but Beth to help me pray my way through anything and sometimes I just wanted an elder to lean on. In all honesty Johnny's mother was one of the biggest reasons I never felt good enough to fight for the man I loved more than life. How could I expect God to bless our life and accept our marriage if Johnny's own mother who had been the very core of his walk with God didn't? I knew his dad's side of the family loved and accepted me because they were all rebels like my family; but that wasn't ever going to be enough for me and Johnny.

You see we had both been filled with the Holy Spirit when we were children and the spirit inside us longed to be in the presence of our father in heaven. However, the spirit of religion had tormented both of our minds to believe we weren't good enough for the church because God didn't design us to be happy in their doctrine. I was 6 years older than Johnny and had gone through a whole lot more rejection by the church than he had by the time we met.

Johnny lived two different lives and had gotten really good at playing both sides of the fence. When he was with his dad's family he felt free to be a rebel like them. But when he was with his mom's family he felt he had to walk the walk and talk the talk. When he was living in sin, he rarely went around his mom's side of the family. When he was going to church he rarely went around his dad's side and when he did, he made sure he got out of there before temptation got a hold of him.

Johnny hated being alone but he wanted a woman who could fit in with both sides so he could be happy all the time. I believe that is why he stayed with the new girlfriend so long is because she was loved and accepted by both sides of the family. He met her through her being related to his dad's wife somehow, so she was already golden on that side. Then his mother just fell in love with her at first sight; so by all means it just had to be perfect!

I may never know if Johnny truly fell in love with her or if he talked his self into loving her because she fit the profile of what he wanted. You see Johnny was down on his luck and needed someone to pull him out of the pit again when he met her. He wasn't happy living with his buddies in a trailer park and had managed to go through all of the money he made from selling his trailer when he got arrested for driving while intoxicated a few months before he met her. Of course I was the one he called to go get his money from his mother and drive an hour away to bond him out of jail. But I think he was too ashamed to ask me to help him out of the pit and I was too afraid he would reject me if I offered to help. Then suddenly she comes along, had her own money, a house, a car and didn't expect anything out of him that he wasn't able to give at first. Johnny had the gift of Love so that came easy for him. All you had to do was be in his presence and you could feel love. It was a perfect situation because Johnny was able to slide off into a moment of peace away from the demons that had all but destroyed his life when he found refuge in her shelter.

It didn't take long before he was back in his mother's good graces when he showed up with a girl she found pleasing to be with her son. Shortly thereafter he was back to work at his mom & step dad's company and it appeared he had finally found happiness. It seemed like no time at all and his status on Facebook revealed he was engaged. Since I was trying so hard to do all the right things; I went to the Lord and told Him I was sorry for feeling the way I did and ask Him to please help me to be happy for Johnny. But no matter how much I prayed or how hard I tried, I couldn't be happy for him when I knew in my heart there was no way she loved him the way I did.

Shortly after his daughter showed up at my house and told me he had left the new girlfriend his sister was going to be married. It was the hottest part of July and she was having an outside wedding. She asked Johnny to get ordained so he could marry them and I was praying my heart out that meant he was leaning towards going back to church. However, when the day finally came, I took one look at him and knew he wasn't on the road to church. He was very thin and his eyes didn't have that flicker of light present I was looking for. He seemed very nervous as he performed the ceremony and I knew it was because this was a reminder to him of the times he had stood on a pulpit preaching the word of God; but that day he didn't appear to be feeling very comfortable about being in an ordained position. It was about 115 degrees that day with not a breeze to be found. Johnny immediately changed out of his black pants and long sleeved white short into shorts and a tank top as soon as the service was over. He sat down at a table next to mine and I could feel him staring at me; but the pounding of my heart and the lump in my throat kept me from looking his way.

Within a few minutes he said, ***"Are you too good to come over here and sit with us?"***

I swallowed hard and said, *"I was sitting here first, are you too good to sit down with me?"* then I got up and moved over to his table.

We chatted small talk about the weather and work for a few minutes and then he said he had to go meet a man who wanted to buy his boat. I knew in my heart he was making an excuse to get out of there, but I didn't want to believe what I was thinking was the real reason he was leaving. No one else seemed to think it was odd that he would leave his sister's wedding to go sell a boat so I told myself I was probably jumping to conclusions. After all, he said he was so thin because he had been insulating attics in this heat. He said he barely drank beer at all anymore; so why was it so hard for me to believe he was really doing as well as he said he was? Maybe it was because I knew every curve in his body and every light flicker in his eyes. Maybe it was because I had seen him look just like this before when he was doing a lot of drugs. Or maybe it was because that man shared my soul and I just instinctively knew when something wasn't right with him!

So I stayed until they finished all the important reception stuff and then I drove an hour from there to go to work at the bar. The whole hour in the car all I could think about was Johnny, how he looked and how he must really be completely over me if he left that fast with me there. I wondered if he left because I was there. I wondered if it was because he was really in love with the new girlfriend or if it was because he knew I knew he was back on the drugs. By the time I made it to work I was ready to drive off a cliff!

As soon as I walked in they said they had been trying to call me to tell me not to come to work because we were so dead but my phone kept going to voice mail. The wedding was way out in the boonies so I didn't have any reception to get the call, how perfect was that? Suddenly I felt a very strong urge to have a very strong drink and didn't even think twice about it. One led to two and two led to me drinking myself into a crying, puking mess! The next day I woke up to that old familiar enemy, the tormenting spirit of depression I thought I had kicked to the curb the night before when I opened the door for **"good time Charlie".**

Oh wait a minute, I've been here before! I must have forgotten depression always opens the door for good time Charlie and then when Charlie gets done with you, he lets depression back in. Then depression opens the door for confusion, doubt, anger and anxiety; and that is how the whole mess of torment begins and ends!

Thank God I had figured all these guys out and how they work together to destroy my body and soul a couple of years before. They may have tripped me and caused me to fall down but I was determined to get back up and fight back, through the blood of Jesus!

Shortly after the wedding I sent Johnny a friend request on Facebook and to my surprise he accepted it. He didn't open the lines of communication but I had gotten strong enough to rebuke the spirit of fear that had put all those "what if" thoughts in my head for so many years and eventually got the nerve to send him a message. As long as it was small talk like *"what are you doing up so late?"* he would respond. However, he never responded to any of my serious messages about my concern for what he was doing that had gotten him so thin or all the crazy dreams I had been having. A few months after we had become Facebook friends Robin passed away and Johnny sent me a private message to my inbox telling me how sorry he was to hear the news. He said if I needed anything to let him know and he would do what he could. My heart melted when I got that message and I wanted so badly to send him a message back and ask him if he would just come hold me. But once again fear stepped in and kept me from saying what I really needed. So I sent him a message back and told him out of all the people in the world that could have sent me a message, it meant more to me to hear from him than anyone. Of course I was hoping he would respond back and say, **"Do you need me to come hold you"?** But he didn't! I sent him several messages throughout the next few days to let him know about funeral plans, in hopes he would come and stand by my side; but of course he didn't.

About 3 weeks after Robin passed I went to a local pub to meet some friends for a birthday dinner.

On my way to the birthday dinner the Lord spoke to me and said, **"Johnny will be at the pub".** Foolishly I thought it was my own thought and a stupid thought at that.

Then the thought came to my mind again and I thought to myself, *"Why on earth would I be thinking Johnny is going to be there?"*

You see over the years Johnny and I had been apart I had dated a man that often went to this pub, so in my mind I thought if anyone was going to be there it would be him instead of Johnny. Never the less, every time I tried to push the thought of Johnny being there out of my mind by saying to myself that is silly because if anyone will be there it will be him instead of Johnny, the thought came right back. Now I have to wonder if I had listened to the Lord trying to tell me Johnny would be in there if that night might have turned out different.

If only I had said, *"Lord why are you telling me Johnny is going to be there? Is there something you want me to say to him when I see him?"*

Could it have been the Lord had something He wanted me to say to Johnny? Could it have been I would have been more prepared to handle what Johnny was about to tell me if only I had listened when God tried to speak? Yes, I think so! I think if I had been more in tune with the voice of the Lord and sought Him to tell me what He was asking me to do, that night would have turned out so much different!

As soon as I pulled in the parking lot God spoke to me one last time and said, ***"Johnny will be inside"*** but again I ignored Him for fear I was actually about to run into the man who had left me a few years before for his younger wife. Wondering what I would do if they happened to be inside and keeping my eyes peeled for them as soon as I walked in the door. I totally ignored the thought of Johnny being inside.

Within a few minutes of me sitting down at the large table of friends I heard the first song Johnny and I ever danced to the night we met begin to play on the juke box. The thought crossed my mind, *"That's weird; I kept thinking on the way here Johnny would be here and now this song plays as soon as I walk in!"* As soon as that song stopped playing, another one of our songs began to play. Again I thought, *"This is really getting weird, if I didn't know better I would think there is someone in this place messing with my mind."* As soon as that song finished, another one of our songs began to play; by then I began to look around the room to see who may be in this place playing all of our songs that would actually know they were our songs. I could barely focus on the conversation at the table for thinking there was something weird going on with those songs that kept playing. But still I never dreamed it could really be Johnny playing those songs.

I had gotten to the birthday party late because I had been working all day so I was trying really hard to pay attention to what everyone had to say and kept ignoring the songs. A little while later, I had to go outside to get something out of my car for one of my friends. When I was walking out the door I felt a tug at my coat, when I turned around there was Johnny with a note in his hand.

He said, *"I kept trying to get the waitress to take this note over to you but she wouldn't so I had to bring it to you myself"*.

Then he said, *"It looks like you're busy, I'll let you go"* and he turned to walk back inside after he handed me the note.

My heart was pounding as soon as I saw his face. I immediately wanted to go right back in for fear if I walked to my car he would be gone by the time I got back. So I told him, *"No wait, I'm not leaving, I just have something to get out of my car for a friend who is leaving, I'll be right back!"*

I went to my car and immediately said, *"Lord, was that you warning me Johnny would be inside?"* But I don't recall the Lord answering me soon enough before that spirit of confusion got a hold of me. I just remember a million different thoughts were going through my mind and I felt in a panic to get back in there before he was gone!

I opened the paper place mat Johnny had written the note on and it simply said, *"You my friend.... Yes or No"*.

Immediately I thought of the George Straight song, *"check yes or no"*. I grabbed a pen and circled yes with a big smile on my face!

I raced back in to say my goodbyes to the friends so I could find Johnny; praying the whole time he would still be there when I got through with my goodbyes. It felt like it took me forever to say my goodbyes and make my way around the pub to find him; but praise God my prayer was answered and he was still there. He was sitting on the back side of the bar eating his dinner when I made my way over there. He offered me to sit down beside him and offered to buy me a drink. I told him I wasn't drinking so he bought me a diet coke and then he asked if I was wondering why our songs kept playing

194

on the juke box. He said he was watching me through the lattice on the bar to see what my reaction would be each time he played a song. He said he could see me looking around the room like I was wondering who was playing the songs and he told his friend, **"She must not be drunk or she would be crying."**

I laughed and said, *"No, I don't get drunk and cry over those songs anymore but I did wonder if there was someone in here that knew our history and was trying to mess with my mind".*

We laughed about old times and how I used to be a handful for my friends to deal with every time I heard any of the songs he played. We talked about the night we met and how we had come to that very pub and got so drunk. The more we talked, the more nervous I got until I finally ordered a shot to calm my nerves and then Johnny said, **"So what is this about this letter you sent me on Facebook? There isn't anything wrong with me, I'm just trying to stay fit, eating healthy and working out"!** As he lifted the sleeve of his shirt, flexed his muscle and then pointed to the grilled chicken breast he was eating and said, **"See I'm eating healthy and I rarely ever drink anymore, I'm just having a few beers tonight but I will only be having a few and going home!"**

I took one look at him and said, *"Bull, I'm not buying it; I know you better than that!"*

He laughed and told me I wasn't right but that was what he always said when he didn't want to admit to something. Of course I wondered if it could really be true that he had stopped drinking and started working out but something in my gut said he was lying. So you will understand why he brought up the letter I had sent him just a week before, here it is.....

November 16, 2011

Some food for thought...... A long time ago I asked God why I never stopped loving you no matter what...Why wouldn't He just answer my prayers and take you out of my heart and out of my mind...I'll never forget what He told me that night! Surprised that for once, He finally answered one of my millions of questions about love and confused because I didn't really understand the answer until tonight! His answer was simply "Because you are like minded spirits"...that made no sense to me so of course I asked what that was supposed to mean.... but you know God is a man of few words and never spoke another word about that again...until tonight! I was reading a book tonight; I started a while back and never finished called "Another Man's war" the story of Sam Childers who is known as the Machine Gun preacher for his mission work in Sudan. I know, me reading a book, NO WAY Right? Well, I guess God has been working on me ;-) Anyway, I started feeling sleepy on chapter 7 and almost closed the book for the night when I felt compelled to rub my eyes and read another chapter. When I got to the last page of chapter 8 I knew why God wanted me to read on...Sam had quoted a scripture...Romans 8: 27-28 on that page...As soon as I read it, God said to me..."like minded Spirits"...Needless to say, that is all He had to say for me to remember what He had told me before. I won't give you the scripture because I feel God wants you to read it yourself. I just want you to know, I was praying for you before I got the idea to go read that book...I feel like God put the desire in my heart to read that book tonight because I was praying for you and He has been trying to get your attention! ! I was praying for you because I saw the photo you posted today...You are looking mighty thin to me Johnny and well as the George Straight's song goes..."you know me better than that" and I know YOU better than that!! And you aren't made to be that thin!!! So, I was praying and asking God if there was anything He wanted me to do...I got my answer when He led me to the book. I knew when I read that, He had something He wanted to tell you in that scripture...so now it is up to you to find out what He has to say ;-)

God knows I wished I had asked if he ever read that scripture but I didn't! Until that night I wasn't even sure if Johnny had read the message at all or the one I sent him about the dreams back in March when he was still with the girlfriend. When he brought up the message I had written the week before I was so shocked he had actually read it I didn't know what to say! Then he decided to change the subject to why he had broken up with the girlfriend and how his mother had disowned him after he gave me a good reason for why he had gotten so thin. He began to spill his guts and tell me all the bad things he had been doing the last 6 months he was with her, which was about the time my dreams started back up again. He told me of how he had hurt his daughter and his mother because he had gotten back on the drugs and made bad decisions and yet all the while he couldn't admit any of it was his fault. Sure he admitted things went bad when he got back on drugs; but he kept justifying his actions by blaming others for why he had done wrong.

To be honest, my head was spinning while he was telling me what all he had done and I was practically speechless. I just sat there listening to him, chiming in every now and again with a *"Now Johnny, I'm sure you don't mean that!"* Looking back I can't help but wonder if only I had listened when the Lord was trying to tell me he would be there, could I have come up with something better to say? Could I have been prepared to look him in the eyes and tell him he was giving in to the lies of the enemy and he needed to say no to all those thoughts in his mind? Was it meant for me to ask him to come home with me that night and love away all of his fears and confusion? Did I allow the enemy to attack me with spirits of confusion, fear, and doubt that Johnny didn't still love me enough to let me love him through it? Yes, I think I am guilty of doing just that! Now I know Johnny still loved me enough to let me love away his problems and I believe that is the very reason he came after me that night; in hopes I still loved him enough to do so!

Deep down I think we both knew our love was still there but we were both so used to hearing those familiar spirits of fear, confusion and doubt tell us it couldn't work we both gave up at the first sign of rejection from the other. Looking back I realize Johnny must have felt rejected when I sat there just listening when he really wanted me to still love him enough to say, *"You are coming home with me and together we are going to get your life back on track!"* I think he remembered how much I had loved him before and how I held him in my arms for two weeks while he went through withdraw from the needle. My guess is he so desperately wanted to believe I still loved him that much and he was looking for a sign I did. However, the letters I had sent him made room for the enemy to torment his mind with thoughts that I didn't love him in that way anymore and now that I had gotten my life on track with God I wouldn't understand his addiction.

You see when I was broken it was easier for him to believe I needed him and therefore more believable that I could actually love him. The stronger I got over the years the more distant Johnny's love got from me. Looking back I realize it wasn't that he ever stopped loving me but that he stopped believing he could ever be good enough for me. As I got stronger in the Lord I stopped chasing after him and begging him to come back. I stopped crying in public and he stopped getting reports of how much I loved him. It is easy to fall into the arms of someone you know still wants you but not so easy to get over your pride and ask for help if you doubt they still do! Johnny and I had battled the same demons for years and no matter how good I thought I had gotten at the fight, I later realized I had lost yet another battle that night!

As soon as I got in my car to leave I began to think of all the things I should have said and done. I wanted to call him and ask him to come over and talk some more but I doubted he still loved me enough to do so. The whole problem was that I still wanted Johnny to want me. I still loved him so much I couldn't stand the thought of being second best in his life. When Johnny poured his heart out to me that night, the only thing I could focus on was what he said about her. The pain he was going through over his mother and daughter never penetrated my heart until almost a year later! I was so jealous over the feelings he had for that girl, nothing else was sinking in. Yet I had so much pride I couldn't admit he still had that much control over my heart and soul; so I pretended to listen and tried my best to give him good advice. How selfish could I be? After all, I knew how easy it was to have feelings for another and still have him consume the biggest part of my heart and soul! Still to this day I can't help but be angry with myself for not asking him to go somewhere alone with me and talk that night! I'm angry at myself for going home and writing him yet another letter that left room for the enemy to get in his head and make him feel I didn't love him in that way anymore! In all of my letters to Johnny, I had no problem of admitting my love in past tense; but never once did I admit my love was still that strong in the same way it was then.

Before I could get home Johnny sent me a text saying he was sorry for laying all that on me but he wanted me to know the truth. I don't really remember exactly what I text back but I know the message I sent back was not what I wanted to send back. I wanted to beg him to come over! I wanted to ask him if he still loved me enough to come home and try to have a good life but I was too scared, stubborn and prideful to take a chance on him rejecting me!

So the rest of the night I sat in my bed asking God why but too anxious to wait on Him to answer. I can't say for sure if I knew God was telling me to send Johnny a letter that night or if I just knew how bad I had screwed up by not listening to the voice of the Lord telling me he would be there and was trying to redeem myself. Never the less, I sent Johnny this letter that I have no idea if he read or not because he never responded to it.

November 23, 2011

Well I thought if I drank those 2 shots it would calm me down so I could go home and go to sleep, but all it managed to do was give me a headache! Thank God for Alka-Seltzer Plus!! Anyway, there are a few things I wanted you to know...First of all, I know you are still in Love with your ex and my guess is she must be a pretty good person or you wouldn't have fell in love with her to begin with. Although I don't know her at all my bet is she probably loves you too! My guess is your reasons for not caring if you live or die is because you feel like you can't keep from screwing things up with the people you love and you feel like everyone would be better off if you weren't here to hurt them anymore...Am I right?

Well, just let me remind you of the reasons you have to live and all the reasons you have to make things right! First of all, there was once a girl who was dead inside and God used you to bring her back to life! Yes, it was a slow process but God's time and our time are a thousand years to a day apart! So in God's time it probably only took you a few seconds to bring ME back to life. Just like the words in the song that used to be one of our songs "It was your Love" that brought me back to life!! Then of course it was the seed of your Love that gave your children life and no matter how bad things may seem with them right now... that is a Love that will never die!!! Just as the Love your Mom and Dad have for you "and you for them" will never die either!!! Not to mention your 3 sisters and nieces and nephews who would all be left with an empty hole if they didn't have you..."Just like the empty hole that eats at all of us without Robin" You know Robin wasn't perfect Johnny...She battled the same demons you do and maybe even some you don't.. But it is very hard to remember her faults now that she is gone! My point is, you are very important to a lot of people and you need to start telling the enemy he is a liar every time you feel rejected or unappreciated!! Many are *called but few are chosen Johnny and I happen to know you are chosen to do a job you keep putting off!!! Why do you think you have been so tormented with addiction, seduction, depression and confusion "just to name a few dark spirits"? Why? Because Satan knows when God put's his mark on someone and he always puts a target on those who are chosen of God to try his best to keep them out of God's will!!! How do I know this? 'Because the dirty liar put a target on my head too!!! It is called a generational curse that was supposed to end with us! The bible says the curse will carry through to the third or the fourth generation....we both come from families that are cursed with spirits of Pharmacia "addiction" and spirits of depression; and when there is one dark spirit in control they will open the door for many others!!! The way I see it, we have 2 choices...We can either be the warriors God created us to be and fight the good fight or we can surrender to our enemy and let him keep us in bondage for as long as we may live!! My guess is, the longer we stay in bondage the longer we are going to be stuck here because God won't take us out until we have either loosed the chains that keep us here and complete our mission or until He finds someone else to break the curse! Trust me Johnny, just because you would rather be dead doesn't mean you're going to get out that easy, I tried my best for years to get out of here and guess what, I'm still stuck here!!! Trust me Johnny, I know I'm far from being perfect...I screw up about a million times a day and fall short of the Glory of God but I have learned enough to know if God had to find a perfect person to do His work, He would have lost it all to Satan a long time ago! Look at what God had to work with in the Bible...a bunch of murderers, adulterers and drunks!! I heard a preacher say once..."The miracle wasn't that Peter walked on the water but that he had the faith to step out of the boat to get to Jesus"...Step out of the boat Johnny, it is sinking!!!! I'm not saying it is going to be easy but I promise you there is still a light that can lead you through the tunnel;-) If you ever want to get that girl or your family back "and make things right" you will have to surrender! Otherwise, any happiness you may find will only be temporary! I'll be praying you will come to your senses, sooner rather than later.. Tell the family I said Hi and a Happy Thanksgiving to you all...*

Love Always ;-)

As you can see I was trying very hard to get the message across to Johnny what he was going to have to do to get *that girl* back in hopes *"that girl"* would be me! Needless to say, I hoped he would be able to read between the lines. Never the less, I managed to find a way to save face just in case *that girl* was really her, like I feared. Looking back on that letter I can see God must have had a big part in what I had to say. However, I still can't help but wonder if my foolish pride as well as the spirits of fear and confusion had not gotten in the way, if maybe He would have inspired me to write something more.

Never the less, I know God is an all knowing God who must have known I wouldn't listen when He tried to talk to me earlier that night. He must have known I would be blindsided by what Johnny had to tell me that night. He must have known those old familiar spirits were going to get a hold of me at that pub and keep me from speaking the words He wanted me to speak. Therefore, I have to believe God had to have known He wouldn't get my attention until much later in the night and He must have been in control of what He wanted me to say in that letter. I can remember asking God to give me wisdom and use my hands to write what He wanted me to say to Johnny. I just can't remember if I waited until I knew for sure I was acting in the will of God.

So time went on and each day I checked my messages to see if there was a response from Johnny. I would check his status on Facebook to see if he had checked in each day for fear one day he wouldn't. When he did, I felt a sigh of relief; but most of the time he didn't and I would always ask God to watch over him and do whatever he had to do to draw Johnny closer to Him. I loved Johnny so much I would often tell God if Johnny had to be with someone besides me to get back in church and be happy I could handle it even though I knew in my heart that wasn't what I wanted. Sure I would have had no choice but to handle it but the thought of him being back in church with anyone besides me just didn't seem fair after all the years I had prayed for him. Never the less, I was convinced God must not want us together or he would have changed both of us so it could work out. Now I realize how foolish I was to think God would take control of our free will so we could be together. But at the time I needed an excuse for something to make sense! So often people make the mistake of putting everything in the hands of God without stopping to think if He controlled our every move like we expect Him to, He would be going against His own rules of giving us free will. God doesn't choose to make us do anything, not even love! Although people may not have any control over whom they fall in love with; they certainly have a choice to engage in that love or suppress it. Johnny and I both chose to suppress our love for one another.

Over the next few months I found myself praying for Johnny more and more. The urge to pray for him would hit me randomly and I often wondered what must be going on that I felt such urgency from the Lord to pray for him. I had put the place mat Johnny wrote the note on in my bible and would often hold it up to heaven as I prayed.

I can remember trying to pray for other people several times *"especially Nick"* when God would say, **"I got this! I want you to pray for Johnny"**. Still not 100% certain if I was actually hearing the voice of the Lord or if it was my hidden desire to be with Johnny that had him constantly on my mind and in my heart, I often told myself there wasn't any reason for concern. Although I couldn't stand the thoughts of him rejecting my phone calls or messages I would sometimes lower my foolish pride and try to reach him. He never responded to my calls or messages but twice. Once I called him after I had a bad dream that I don't even remember now but I remember he actually answered my call for once and simply said, **"I'm fine".**

Another time I had sent him a text and he sent a message back asking me to pray for him. I sent a message back and told him, *"I always do!"*

Looking back I wonder why I didn't say more. Why didn't I ask him if I could come to him and talk? Why didn't I lower my foolish pride and ask him to come home? I have to believe it wasn't meant for me to do anything but alert him to listen to what God was trying to tell him or I wouldn't be able to live with myself!

In January of 2012 I sent Johnnie a message about an issue that had burdened my heart for years. You may recall I had mentioned earlier that Johnnie didn't tell me he was married when we first met. For the first few years of our relationship I had a hard time forgiving him for putting me in a situation that made me feel I was choosing him over the will of God when we were together. In my mind there was no way our relationship could ever survive the wrath of God until we confessed our sins before God and made things right. One day I was walking into a room after I had been listening to a teaching about curses when God began to reveal to me some things I felt Johnnie needed to know; so I sent him another letter.

I've been doing some learning about generational curses and blessings. Trying to educate myself on how to get rid of the generational curses of addiction and poverty on my family and implement blessings for my future generations.. "Just in case the Lord tarry's a bit longer"... Anyway, I feel it is very possible that my children's father put a curse on me to be alone the rest of my life....as a matter of fact; I remember him doing so but didn't put much stock in it at the time. So of course when I remembered him doing so, I took the bull by the horns and denounced that curse in the name of Jesus! For some reason I was just walking in my room and the thought came to my mind that your ex-wife may have cursed us both for what we did to her. Not that I think she knowingly did that but there is power in the words we speak out loud and I can only imagine the things she may have said out of anger!!! To be honest, I wasn't even thinking anything at all about curses, you, her or anything that would have made that thought come to my mind...I don't know maybe a song may have come on that put you in the back of my mind or something...never the less, I feel it is important you know what I have found out about this stuff because I know you have the same generational curses of poverty and addiction in your family. I don't claim to know the source of these curses in either one of our families but I know they exist and I know there is a way to break them! For some reason I just felt like you needed to know that. I know you probably think it is weird that I keep telling you all this stuff but I just know I am supposed to! I hope you don't think this is some ploy to try and get you back because I swear I haven't begged God to bring you back since I promised Him I wouldn't if we didn't work the last time...it really isn't about that at all Johnnie but for some crazy reason I have you on my heart to pray for you all the time and I feel like I'm supposed to tell you stuff when it pops in my head! Too many times in my life I have ignored those thoughts that pop in my head as just my own silly thoughts and then the next thing I know that person I thought about calling or stopping by to see is gone forever and I wonder if what I had thought about telling them would have made a difference. Now that I know God communicates with us through our thoughts and dreams I try my best to not just blow things off when I have reoccurring thoughts, dreams or overwhelming desires to speak up! In the past few years I have learned so many things that helped me to understand things I didn't understand before and get through this hard life that I think would help you too. I just feel I need to share this information with you. I'm not gonna promise to quit bugging you until God either takes you out of my heart or I know you are where you need to be to fight this battle on your own! But I do promise with all of my heart, I'm not doing this just to get to talk to you if that is what you are thinking. You rarely ever respond to me so I always wonder if you think that and don't respond because you're afraid I will try to get you back. So please don't think that and at least let me know you read this message. If you don't want to hear any more about what I have found out about this stuff that is fine... and I will leave you alone until the next time I feel an overwhelming nudge to let you know something or just check on you;-) If that is the case just send me a message back and say I got your message but I really don't want your help right now. But know if you ever feel like you want a change in your life and need someone to talk to, I will always be here for you! Oh and just one more thing...every time you cross my mind I see you in a boat that is rocking in a wicked storm and the same thought always comes to my mind...."Tell Him to get out of the boat"....I assume that must be God telling me to tell you that because I can't imagine why I would have that same thought almost every day!!!! In my heart I feel like God is telling you to get out of the boat because it is like you are hanging on to a sinking ship in dangerous waters and He wants you to get out of the boat because He has a solid rock waiting for you to stand on and get to safety! I know it is probably hard to believe that God would use a rebel child like me to speak through but you know if God had to wait on perfect people to get anything done He wouldn't have had to use Noah "the drunk" to build an arch...Moses "the hot headed murderer" to deliver the children of Israel out of bondage or The Apostle Paul "Saul the man who was determined to destroy Christianity" to write most of the New Testament! As crazy as it seems Johnny, I'm convinced this may have been the very reason why God never allowed me to hate you even though I tried....heck, He wouldn't even let me completely stop loving you even though I begged Him to make me forget you exist;-) The bible says He will use ALL THINGS for the GOOD of those who Love Him...I was a screwed up mess for a lot of years Johnny..."you probably know that better than anyone" but I always loved and trusted Him so I'm thinking He will use the mistakes we made by hurting your ex "as well as each other" for our good somehow if we let Him;-) I know you're probably wishing I would shut up by now so I'll say goodbye for now..... But PLEASE remember this....you can run but you can't hide my Dear;-)

Until recently I didn't even realize what a curse really is or how a curse can be put on someone's life. A curse comes in when God's hedge of safety is lifted in an area due to a non-repented and repetitive sin. Without God's hedge of safety in every area of our life, Satan has the power to use his dark spirits to speak into our thoughts and tempt us to go against the will of God. It isn't that we no longer have any thoughts of our own, it is just that the spirits of darkness know the hedge of protection against them has been lifted so we are more likely to give in to their tempting suggestions. For instance, when a person knowingly goes against the word of God to commit an act of adultery, they have lifted the ceremonial hedge of blessings and safety from destruction off of their marriage. Unless that person repents before the Lord and the spouse whom they have wronged by asking for forgiveness and turning away from the desires of their flesh; the spirits of darkness will continue to torment their life and the life of their children. When people speak negative words against someone who does not have a hedge of safety on them, they are feeding the forces of darkness with power to rule and rein in that person's life. On the other hand, if someone tries to speak negative words over someone who is righteous with God and lives in the shelter of His hedge of safety, their words will turn back on them. Remember what the bible says, "Thou shalt not curse what I have blessed." The blessings of God and His hedge of safety can and will only be taken away by God Himself because of our willingness to sin.

CHAPTER 12

Johnny's Journey

In February of 2012 my sister Lynn and I went to Florida to pick up Beth. On the way down we stopped at a friend's house in Georgia where Lynn stayed for a few days while I went on to pick up Beth. Beth and I went back to Georgia to get Lynn on our way home and stayed with them another night. My friend was going through some trials and had asked me to send her a prayer she and her husband could say every day to help get them through their trials. I promised I would pray and ask God to give me something to send her so on the way home I prayed about what He wanted me to send her. We got home late but I had gotten my second wind and knew I wasn't ready to go to sleep so I sat down at the computer and asked God to help me send her what he wanted her to have.

When I began to type the message I thought God had for her, He spoke to me and said, ***"This is for Johnny."***

Of course I questioned the thought I just had and said, *"God, I just thought I heard you say this is for Johnny but that doesn't make any sense, why would you say that"?*

He said, ***"Because I want this message to go to Johnny."***

Me being certain I must be imagining God putting these thoughts in my head, continued to question Him. Finally I felt confident it must be the voice of the Lord and surrendered my hands to write the message he wanted me to give to Johnny. As soon as I totally surrendered to the Lord the most amazing thing happened that I don't even know how to explain. I was sitting there typing a message when all of the sudden I could clearly see a situation as if I was looking down from heaven upon it. My heart was so vexed and I could hear the spirit inside me screaming out to Johnny as if I was yelling from a million miles away. I could feel my spirit pleading with him to wake up and get out of the boat I saw him sleeping in. I could see a dangerous storm off in the distance. I could see Johnny sleeping in a sail boat that looked like a mini arc with white sails. I could see the rope to the anchor pulled very tight in the water and the boat gently swaying in the very calm lake. The moon was shining bright down on the boat and the sky above the boat looked clear but I could see the danger off in the distance. By the time I finished the message to Johnny I was physically exhausted! I felt like I couldn't even move but I was so scared I wanted to run to my car and go find Johnny. If I had been physically able to get to my car I'm sure I would have; but I felt like I was waking up from a surgery. I cried out to the Lord in panic begging Him to tell me what to do! Begging Him to tell me why I had just seen a vision while I was wide awake! In a desperate attempt to get someone to help Johnny, I typed a letter to his mother telling her what I had just seen in the vision and begging her to do something to save Johnny for what I feared was about to happen. The whole time I was typing the letter to Johnny's mother God kept telling me **NO!** Very firmly I could hear His voice telling me to not send the letter but I kept typing.

Finally I finished what I wanted to say and stopped for a moment to ask Him, *"God is this really you telling me to not send this letter"*?

I knew He was telling me not to send it and I questioned why. He then told me it wouldn't do any good because she would never believe someone like me could have a vision from God and she would ignore me. Crying, begging and pleading for Him to just tell me what I was supposed to do, I went ahead and deleted the message to Johnny's mother like the Lord had instructed me to do.

Nothing like this had ever happened to me in my life; I didn't know what to think or what to do! All I knew to do was cry out to the Lord until I fell sound asleep. When I woke up the next day I wondered if I had dreamed about the vision and sending the letter to Johnny. I immediately ran to my computer to see if I had indeed sent such a message. When I got to my messages, I found this letter that had been sent at 2:25 a.m.

February 04, 2012   *2:25 a.m.*

Hi Johnny, how have you been? I just got home from picking Beth up in Florida and trying to wind down from the long drive. I had a lot of time to think and of course I'm always trying to figure stuff out. Well I got on FB because my friend in Georgia asked me to send a prayer to her inbox and I was intending to send her some things that might help her with some things she is going through. So I was sitting here asking God to help me with this and I began to remember a teaching I once heard about the verse that says "A 3 fold cord is not easily broken" so of course I thought I should tell her about that and send her a prayer but then God told me no, He wanted me to send it to you so here I go bugging you again;-) Anyway, here is what I think He has for you today....Imagine a nylon rope...much like a rope that you would see tied onto an anchor......after many years of being pulled in and out of the water the rope will begin to fray. As the rope frays one strand will separate from the other 2 and it will become weak but you can still use it...each time you pull the rope out of the water you check to see if you still have 2 strands hanging on to one another because you know as long as there are still 2 strands the rope will hold on to the anchor and you won't lose it. Eventually the 2 strands will also start to fray and you know it won't be long until one of them will break loose and the one cord will not be strong enough to hold on to the anchor. Once the rope is severed from the anchor your boat could get lost at sea.

We are a 3 part being...body, soul and spirit. Our spirit "which is our breathe of life" has already been in the company of our Father "Jesus" and longs to be forever in His presence! Our body. Otherwise referred to as our "flesh" is carnal, it is born into this sinful world and desires sin...our soul, "our mind" is the follower of the 3 and it always makes an alliance with the stronger of the other 2. When we have 2 form an alliance against 1 the 1 is going to suffer until it joins the alliance with the other 2...just the same as 2 countries being at war against 1 will most often be surrender or certain destruction for the lone country! As it is the same as that one strand of that rope that breaks away from the other 2 will surely fray away! The Apostle Paul said, "My Flesh dies daily". Meaning, his soul and spirit had formed an alliance against his flesh that was so powerful it killed the desires of his flesh on a daily basis! Because our spirit will never stop crying out to be in the presence of the Lord and our Flesh will never stop crying out for sin, it is up to our soul to whom it will form the alliance with. If we CHOOSE "because it is our soul that has the choice" to form an alliance between our soul and spirit our flesh will eventually get tired of fighting and surrender and we will get a brand new rope "otherwise known as a celestial body" to hold on to our anchor "otherwise known as JESUS". However, if we choose to allow our soul to form an alliance with our body or "FLESH" we will surely fray away until our rope is so broken it floats away into the bottomless pit, never to take hold of the anchor again! I had an absolutely wonderful week spending time in the presence of the Lord Johnny, but I sit here tonight with an aching back and a gnawing in my gut as I see this image in my mind of your rope! My heart breaks as I hear the Lord calling out your name in the midst of the darkness. I can see the light of the moon shining down on a boat and the boat keeps drifting further and further out to sea. I see clouds in the sky as a storm approaches that will very soon cover the light of the moon. I see you asleep in this boat and you don't even know that the rope has broken loose from the anchor. You don't even know the storm is approaching, you can't even hear the voices telling you to get out of the boat! I can feel my spirit screaming wake up!...wake up while the moon light is still shining on the water! Wake up, while you can still see the light! Wake up before the darkness carries you away forever!!! That's all I have to tell you and Dear God I hope you can hear Him calling you in your spirit...If I knew where to find you I would be pounding on your door myself! I pray this is just a bad dream that I will soon wake up from or just my own mental torment and this isn't real!!! All I know to do right now is pray but my body feels so weak and my spirit feels so wounded from the vision I just had in my mind that I don't know if I have the strength! Please call me as soon as you get this message and let me know your o.k.!!! Laugh at me if there is no truth to what I just saw in my mind but Please Johnny, CALL ME!!!!!

When I look back on that letter it totally amazes me I was able to continue writing once the vision started. Not that it was my own will that kept writing, because I still remember feeling unable to function during the vision; but that the spirit of God used a wretch like me to deliver a message when I felt so helpless. I never asked Johnny if he read the message but I know in my heart if God wanted me to write it, He must have made sure Johnny read it!

That was the last important message I sent to Johnnie personally. It seemed several months went by that I had fallen into a place of peace about Johnny. I don't recall God impressing on me to pray for him or having any dreams about him at all. I don't remember if it was during that time I called and he answered or sent the text he responded to, or if we had no communication at all. All I remember is from time to time I would walk by that place mat he wrote the message on that was sticking up out of the bible and think to myself, "I haven't been praying for Johnny like I should." I remember during that time when I tried to pray for him I felt I was praying out of my own will to pray, not the will of God. I remember asking God what had happened and why He stopped impressing upon me to pray for Johnny the way He had in the past year. I wondered if I had fallen back into a state of depression over Robin's death and questioned God if I was failing to hear His voice. I kept telling myself if it was in fact God who had impressed upon me the urge to pray for Johnny, it must be that Johnny got the messages God wanted him to get and he was simply doing fine without me.

One night in May of 2012 I got an invitation from Johnny's roommate to come to a surprise birthday party he was having for Johnny the next day. With very little notice I had no time to go shopping for a gift because the party was to start as soon as I got off work. I was so excited to get to see him again but scared to death he would be with a girl when he showed up at his house not expecting there to be a surprise birthday party. I had seen a post he had put on Facebook in April regarding being back together with the ex-girlfriend he appeared to be in-love with, so I feared I would have to see her face to face. In his post, He mentioned she had saved him and I felt like a dagger went through my heart when I read it. Never the less I wanted to see him so bad I figured I would just have to choke it up if he showed up with her or another girl. The next day I rushed to get all my work done so I could leave the office in time for the surprise. I rushed into a convenience store looking for anything I could grab to take him for a gift and drove as fast as I could to get there on time. When I arrived I saw Johnnie standing in the yard surrounded by a bunch of guys. My eyes scanned the yard quickly to see if there were any girls that could have been there with Johnny. I wasn't sure what he was doing there because one of his friends was supposed to have had him out running around until it was time for everyone to be there. Never the less he was there and didn't seem to be too surprised to see me.

It was a beautiful day and I had worn a pair of shorts and a tank under my dress at work so I could just take off the dress when I went to the party. We sat outside and talked for a while and I felt I had the most of Johnny's attention. He somehow managed to keep a conversation going with me despite all the interruptions from his friends. At one point in our conversation he brought up the ex-girlfriend I really didn't care to hear about. I'm not sure if Johnny could tell by the look on my face that I was holding back what I really felt or if he just instinctively knew my heart was breaking to hear him mention her.

He asked if it bothered me when he talked about her and I said, *"No Johnny, its o.k. I know you love her."*

He looked me straight in the eyes and said, ***"Yes but it isn't like I love you, it isn't that kindred kind of love if you know what I mean."***

Once again, I lied and told him I knew what he meant but I didn't! Then of course one of his friends started talking to him and at that point I wanted to go over and grab him by the hand and say, *"Can we get out of here for a while and go somewhere to talk?"*

I wanted so desperately bad to ask him what exactly he meant by that statement! Was he trying to tell me he got my message about the ***"Like minded spirits?"***

Was he trying to tell me he loved me like kin now? Was he trying to tell me he still wanted to work things out? Did I want to read more into his actions or was he feeling the same way I was? His body language said he felt the same way I did. But every time we got into a serious conversation about anything we got interrupted; so it was easy for that old familiar spirit of confusion to get in my head and my bet is it was getting in Johnny's head too!

Not long before dusk a couple of girls showed up to the party and the temperature started to drop along with the mood. I could tell Johnny had some interest in one of them and he felt a little nervous when she showed up because he kept walking in and out of the trailer and he started drinking more. He had mentioned to me earlier he had been hanging out with one of my friends and asked me if it would upset me if she showed up at the party. Of course I lied and told him it wouldn't bother me but I knew if Johnny was asking me how I would feel there had to be something more to their friendship than what he was telling me.

As dusk began to fall I was getting really cold but all I had to put on was the dress I had worn to work that day and it didn't keep me warm for long. I sat outside and talked to the girls for what seemed to be forever as people came and went. Finally I decided it would be best if I left before the urge I had to start drinking got any stronger. I knew if I gave into that urge to drink, I would wind up trying to pull Johnny away from his party to make him talk to me and I wasn't 100% certain that is what he wanted. So I finally got up the nerve to walk inside and see if I could feel him out before I told him goodbye. I told him I needed to use the restroom and he showed me to it. As we walked down the hall I felt like he wanted to talk to me too but neither one of us said a word. A million different thoughts went through my mind when he walked away from that bathroom door but I convinced myself I would have to be a fool to think he would want to leave that pretty young girl and all of his buddy's to talk to me. Not to mention the friend he told me about was so much prettier than me, I thought there was no way he would want me back if he had a chance to be with her. So I went in the kitchen where he was talking to some friends and told him I was cold and thought I would go home and get in my bed. He offered me a sweat shirt if I wanted to stay but I told him that wouldn't do me any good because I didn't have any long pants or socks for my feet. He said he could hook me up if I wanted to stay but he understood if I wanted to leave. I gave him the flashlight I had bought him at the convenience store; he said he loved it and then he hugged me tight and told me he loved me before I left.

All the way home that night all I could think about was *"what if's"*. As soon as I walked out his door my heart felt empty and once again I was left with a troubled soul. Looking back I have to wonder why I never even thought to ask him if he had read the message I sent him the night I had the vision. It was almost as if God had wiped the vision and all the other messages I had felt led to send him completely out of my mind both times I got a chance to ask. Maybe it wasn't meant for me to ask or maybe I just failed to do what I was supposed to do again for getting wrapped up in my own emotions.

When I got home that night I got on Facebook to try and get my mind off of Johnny. Someone had posted a picture that caught my eye and when I read the message that was attached to it I felt like God had put that message up just for me to read. So I shared the message and wrote my own little message that Johnny read and commented for the very first time on any of my posts.

My Comment: *This post hit home for me today....what a wonderful feeling to be thankful for those you love; even if you lost the love as you once knew it. True love should not be judged on how long you lasted at being "In Love" but how long you loved without being together.*

The post I commented on: ***"If you have ever loved someone ..even for a moment ..That love never dies because it was felt from the heart and soul...from deep within ...for that moment which was very special...No matter later where you land up in your life that special moment remains in your heart till eternity...It is not necessary that everyone in this world gets to spend their lives with the one they love...but it is necessary to respect that very moment when you felt love..and respect the person who made you feel that love"..***

- Aarti Khurana

Johnny simply commented: ***"Very well said "love"...... elegantly put!!"***

That was enough to let me know there was a great chance he had indeed read my many messages and it gave me hope there could still be a chance for us some day when the time was right!

In a short time it would be Memorial Day weekend and I was supposed to go camping with some friends. Johnny was all I could think about since the night I left his house and I wondered if he would be camping somewhere for the holiday weekend too. So I sent him a message asking if he was camping and hoping he would invite me to come along. He actually responded to that message but he usually did respond to the messages I sent that had no spiritual meaning. He said he was camping at the time I sent the message but didn't know for how long. I told him I was supposed to camp with friends but wasn't sure I would. I was trying to leave a door opened for him to say, ***"You should stop by and see me"*** at whatever camp ground he was at; but he didn't.

The weekend finally came and I had to work late so all of my friends were really drunk by the time I got to the camp ground. My head was already spinning over Johnny so it didn't take long before I decided I was going to have to start drinking if I wanted to hang out with my friends because there was no way I could handle it sober. After a few glasses of wine, I decided I couldn't take it any longer and called Johnny. He actually answered the phone and I told him I was camping right down the road from his house but I didn't want to be there because I was hot & sweaty and needed a shower or I wouldn't be able to sleep. He said he wasn't home but I was welcome to go to his house and shower anyway if I wanted to. Of course I didn't want to go there if he wasn't there; the whole purpose in going was so I could tell him how I felt and beg him to come home! Looking back I can't help but wonder if he would have come home if he knew I was going to be there.

I had a lot going on at work during the summer and it didn't take long before the days turned into weeks and the weeks turned into months since I had seen or heard from Johnny. It was easy to divert my thoughts away from him during that time because there was so much going on and it was summer so I had a lot of work to do in my garden each night after work. It seemed I went through phases where I couldn't think of anything but Johnny and then there were times I seemed to get along just fine until I heard one of our songs or drove down a certain road. I had a routine going that I went straight to my garden as soon as I got home and worked until it was too dark to see every day of the week. Then on July 21, 2012 I got home about 4:30 and was so tired I couldn't hold my eyes open. As soon as I walked in the door I thought there is no way I can go to that garden without a nap! So I went to my room and immediately fell right to sleep. I'm not sure how long I was asleep but I know the sun was still shining very bright when I woke up. As soon as I woke, fear surrounded me and the thought came to my mind. *"You just saw Johnny surrounded by dead people and this can't be good!"*

I jumped out of my bed, grabbed my cell phone and took off running outside, praying every step of the way! When I got outside I immediately called Johnny but he didn't answer. In a panic, I left him a voice mail and then ran inside and grabbed my laptop to get on Facebook and send him a message to see if he would respond that way. As soon as I got on Facebook I saw his status had changed from single to in a relationship. I knew that was why he wasn't answering my phone call because Johnny never answered my calls when he was with someone; so I didn't even bother to send him a text or try to call him again. My heart and soul were so vexed I didn't know what to do. So in desperation I sent a message to his roommate begging for answers.

Hi Fess, how are you doing? I had this really strange dream earlier and woke up scared to death for Johnny. I tried to call and see if he is doing o.k. but he didn't answer so I got on here to send him a message but I see he has a girlfriend now and figured that is why he didn't answer. L.O.L. he tends to not want to talk to me much when he has a girlfriend..."I can't imagine why"! Anyway, I don't want to send him a message and cause any problems "besides, he probably wouldn't answer me anyway" and I'm pretty worried about him. He told me about the crap he had been doing a while back and I've been praying he has stopped that stuff but haven't really talked to him at all since his birthday so I don't know what is going on with him. One of my friends told me she had a strange dream about him a few days ago and said she felt like he needed prayer. To be honest, I've been pretty busy lately and hadn't been praying for him like I should and didn't really think much about it when she told me about her dream until I had that dream today that freaked me all the way out! I know this puts you in a bad position because he is your best friend and you wouldn't want to say anything he would get mad over so please just tell me if I need to pray harder for him or not! Not that I won't be praying for him every time he crosses my mind but if I thought he were in danger I would be up all night praying my heart out! Although I know Johnny and I have had our ups and downs, I will love that man until the day I die and all I want is to see him happy, healthy and back in church where he belongs! I would give anything if I understood his torment when we were together the way I understand it now; but I was in too much torment myself to understand or help anyone else! I pray he has found a good girl that will help him get back to the loving arms of the Lord because I know that is the only way Johnny will ever find any peace on this earth. He is a child of God that was chosen for a job that he will have to submit to one day or he will perish. I'm sorry to lay all this on you but I don't know anyone else to ask and my heart is breaking right now, I'm so worried about him. I saw him in my dream surrounded by dead people Fess and he was upset, trying to tell me something. I never got to find out what he was trying to tell me because I started crying and woke up. I know it sounds crazy to be so disturbed over a dream but I have had dreams about Johnny before and then found out something was going on that was relevant to my dream. It is some kind of weird connection we have I guess like "soul mates" or something. I.D.K. but the thought of anything bad happening to him has got me crazy right now. I almost got in my car and drove to your house when he didn't answer! I have lost more people than I care to think about to drugs and 2 of them "my 2 sisters that died of drug over dose" were in the dream I just had about Johnny. Please don't tell Johnny I sent you this message, I don't want to freak him out...On the other hand, maybe he needs to be freaked out if he is still doing drugs! I.D.K. Fess, I'm a mess right now! I need to go pray some more but please, let me know something! If he has got clean and it was just a crazy dream, Great, Please let me know that! But if he is still even dabbling in drugs even just a little, I want to know that too! My sister that died on Halloween last year was just dabbling a little here and there..."for God's sake she was in drug court" but she is in her grave right now and I know the crap Johnny said he was doing is turning people into Zombies! Please just call and talk to me when you get a chance!

Fess didn't respond to my message for over a month and when he did, he didn't say much about what was going on with Johnny. By the time he finally got back with me, I had calmed down and decided I was completely over reacting to a bad dream. After all, it didn't make any sense why Johnny would be telling me how much he loved me in the dream when he obviously didn't or we would be together. It didn't make any sense to me that he kept saying, *"You don't understand how much I love you and you don't understand why we aren't together."* In the dream I didn't even realize all the people in the dream were already dead. I kept walking past each one of them not even realizing they were all dead and I hadn't seen them in years. I remember right before I woke up, I could see the whole room as if I was looking down on the room from high above watching everything that was going on. I could see Johnny, both my mom & dad and both of my dead sisters watching me sob in my dead Aunt's lap and that didn't make any sense at all. So I prayed for days for answers and got nothing! As usual, I managed to convince myself it was just a crazy dream and there was no need for concern since I had been praying and still hadn't gotten an explanation from God if there was even a need for concern. From time to time a thought would cross my mind about the dream and I would pray it didn't mean anything but for the most part I just continued to go on about my life and chose not to dwell on it.

It was September 11, 2012 and I was very busy at work trying to get an apartment remodeled so we could get it rented for the 2012/2013 school year. I was on my way to meet Kline to show him the tile I had picked out for him to lay in the kitchen and bath of the apartment. We had both just pulled in the parking lot and my sister called. We were both pressed for time so I decided to reject the call and figured I would call her back when we were finished. Before we could get in the door a friend of ours called and I rejected that call too. Then my sister called again as soon as we walked in the door and I thought, *"What in the world is so important that it can't wait"* so I answered that time.

When I answered she said, ***"Are you in Menard's?"***

I said, *"Yes, why?"*

She said, ***"I need you to come outside."***

I laughed and said, ***"Why? Are you out there?"***

She said, ***"You need to go outside."***

I said, *"Can't this wait? I'm busy!"* but at that point I got a really bad feeling and turned around to walk back towards the door. I could sense there was something going on but Lynn didn't let on until she knew I was outside. When I got outside I said, *"Where are you?"*

She said, ***"Are you outside?"***

I said, *"Yes, what is going on?"*

She softly said, ***"Johnny is dead!"***

I thought my knees were going to buckle as I said, *"What? My Johnny?"*

She said, ***"Yes"*** and I lost it!

Kline could see me through the glass doors of the store walking toward my car so he followed me outside. In no time Lynn was in the parking lot and they were both standing at the window of my car. All I could think of was the dream and how I had failed to take head to God's warning. How ironic that the very man Johnny thought he had to worry about me leaving him for was standing beside me when I got that call! All the past 16 years of memories were flooding my heart & soul and I felt I couldn't breathe. So many regrets, so many lost chances, with no way to turn back time!

Somehow I convinced Lynn and Kline I would be o.k. and drove myself home but I never felt so broken in all of my life. I honestly believe God must have driven me home that day because I don't know how I would have made it otherwise. By now I thought I had suffered through so much pain that nothing would ever break me again; but I was wrong! This was a different kind of pain that I had never felt before. The one and only man on this earth I could see myself growing old with had been ripped away from me more times than I could remember; but this time it was forever! All I could think about was the way he held me in the dream telling me, ***"You just don't understand how much I love you.... You just don't understand why we can't be together."*** Suddenly everything in the dream made perfect sense but I still didn't understand why.

I was angry that God had allowed me to see something was about to happen but He didn't allow me to stop it! How could He leave me to think it was just a dream when it clearly wasn't? How could He watch me pray for days after the first vision and then after the last dream and still not lead me to stop this from happening? What kind of sick joke was He playing on me? How did He expect me to live with myself knowing I saw this coming and did nothing but leave a voice mail, write some letters and then give up when I didn't get a response? He is the maker of the Universe and He has the power to get my attention when He wants to! How could He let me think it was just a silly dream and allow me to give up?

I didn't know who to blame. A big part of me blamed myself for not tracking Johnny down "girlfriend or not" and finding a way to get him out of the boat! Even still there was a part of me that didn't understand how God could allow this to happen. Johnny didn't die of a drug overdose like I expected, he was ran over by a car! He was riding a motorcycle down a street that has a speed limit of 30m.p.h. and was hit from behind by a drunken, drug addict in a car around 8:00 in the morning. How ironic that I was expecting him to be the one who was drunk or drugged up when he died but instead it was the man who took his life! His head was so badly flattened his parents weren't even allowed to see his body. The man who hit him then backed up and ran over his head after he knocked him off his bike. He then turned around with Johnny under his car and dragged him down the road in the opposite direction of what they were traveling upon impact. Some nice lady was at a stop sign in front of the scene and got a good look at the car that hit Johnny and left his body mutilated in the road. She called 911 and stayed with Johnny until the E.R. team arrived. She asked to remain anonymous and kept out of the paper. My guess is the poor woman was so devastated at the sight of the scene she couldn't bear the thought of being questioned and having to re-live that nightmare.

Still to this day, I have not driven down that road. I was told there was so much blood the road had remained stained for several months. The man who hit my Johnny took off to his parent's house and tried to get the blood off the car before he turned himself in several hours later. He was seen at a convenience store getting cigarettes and spraying off his car before he went to his parent's house. My guess is, he had no intentions of turning himself in until he heard on the radio an eye witness gave details of the car that had left the scene and the man driving the car had been seen buying cigarettes and washing his car. The car was registered to his parents so I'm sure they made him turn his self in before the cops showed up to arrest them for Johnny's death. The man bonded out soon after he was arrested and I have been told He still to this day continues to drive the murder weapon around town under the influence of drugs and alcohol.

The first week after Johnny was killed I went through one emotional mood swing after another. I think my constant crying the first 2 days took its toll on Nick and drove him to drinking. When I realized he had left the house I thought about trying to find him but decided it would probably be best if he wasn't there to hear me cry any more than he had to. I tried my best to not cry in front of him but sometimes I broke down and I knew he saw me before I got into my room. The first day I went in to work, I had only been there for an hour when my brother called. I was talking to a carpenter about some things I needed him to do on the apartment so I didn't answer. I know it must have been the Lord that alerted me to listen to his voice mail as soon as I walked back to my office because typically I would have waited until I got off work to listen to what I thought was just a personal call. As soon as I heard his message my heart sunk into my feet. He told me he needed me to call because there was something wrong with Nick. I called him immediately to find out Nick had drank himself into alcohol poison the night before and had been throwing up for hours at my brother's apartment. I hung up with my brother and called Lynn because she lived in the same complex and I thought she could get there faster than me.

Lynn wasn't home at the time but said she would be there as soon as she could. She was with the same friend that called me the day Johnny died and they both feared this would be enough to push me over the edge if something happened to Nick. So they called the E.R. before I made it to my brothers to see how bad things were with Nick. As soon as Nick saw me, he tried to get up off the bathroom floor where he had been laying for hours; because he didn't want me to see him like that and worry. He was so weak he could barely walk and only made it to the hall before he almost fell in the floor. He was very upset with my brother for calling me but I think he may have been a little glad I was there all at the same time. When I told him the ambulance was on its way he got very upset and said he wasn't going with them because he didn't have the money to pay the bill. So I tried to call and cancel the ambulance but it was too late, they were already there. I told them he was refusing to go before they went in but they said they needed to check him out and offer to take him just in case.

Nick was so sick when they got in the apartment he didn't put up a fight and willingly went to the hospital. It didn't take too long after he got some I.V. fluids and nausea medicine he started feeling like he was going to live again. However, he had drunk so much vodka the night before his labs kept showing he had drank anti-freeze. At first he said there was no way he would drink anti-freeze when they asked him. So they took a second lab and came back to ask him if he was sure he didn't drink anti-freeze the second time. Nick was so drunk the night before he didn't remember what he had done so he told them he didn't think so but couldn't say for sure if he did or not. They took another lab and we waited in fear for what the next result might be. It turned out that vodka and anti-freeze both contain ethyl alcohol and he had consumed so much vodka the night before his ethyl alcohol level was as high as it would be in anti-freeze. Shortly after the 3rd lab result Nick was released to go home. Suddenly I began to realize the importance of embracing life among the living. As bad as I was still hurting over the loss of Johnny, I was equally as joyed over taking my son home.

It is so like God to take the worst possible situation and use it to teach me a lesson. Just a few hours before, I was unable to see how things could get any worse or any better. I felt like a rat trapped in a maze with no way out but somehow I knew all along Nick was going to be o.k. Maybe it was all the times God had told me, ***"I got this!"*** when I was praying for Nick. Maybe it was because I knew God had told me Nick would be a counselor one day and help people with his same problems. Maybe it was because God had told me many times

He had to allow Nick to go down this road so Nick would be able to understand the people he was sent here to help. All the while the enemy kept tormenting my mind with thoughts of how God had not protected Johnny and what if He let me down with my son the way he let Johnny's parents down. The enemy kept reminding me how much more faithful Johnny's mother had been to the church than I had been. He continued putting the thought in my head if God could let Johnny die after all the years she had been faithful to the church, why wouldn't He let Nick die too?

As soon as I got Nick home from the hospital I went in my room and told the Lord how sorry I was for letting the enemy get in my head. I told Him how thankful I was that He had spared Nick's life again because I knew the enemy was out to destroy him just like he was Johnny. I told him how sorry I was for wishing I would die so I could be with Johnny and all my other loved ones who had gone on before me when Nick clearly still needed me here. The more I repented and praised the Lord for all of his goodness and mercy, the more He told me about Johnny. He told me to stop blaming myself for Johnny's death because it wasn't His will I save Johnny or He would have instructed me how to keep this from happening. He said it was His will that Johnny would choose life over death and that is why He used me to warn him of what was coming. God reminded me of the scripture about the ***"like- minded spirits"*** and told me I was used as the mediator between Him and Johnny because Johnny knew in his heart he could trust what I had to say. God began to give me a revelation of how like-minded spirits are connected in heaven before they come to a body here on earth. He explained it is fate for the like-minded spirits to find each other on earth because they were never apart in heaven. Therefore their spirits are never at rest until they find one another and once they do there is no doubt they will be joined together. However, the enemy is privy to this spiritual connection and will use the misunderstood power to feel one another's emotions and the shared ability to get into each other's thoughts to destroy the relationship of the like-minded spirits. The enemy will attack the like -minded spirits with false emotions and tempting thoughts that will make the other feel inadequate and hopeless. He backs off long enough to keep their love alive because their love is his greatest weapon he has against them. As soon as one or the other starts to move on, the enemy will create a situation for them to come in contact with one another long enough to rekindle both of their desires to be together. During the rekindling process he allows their love to be free of tormenting spirits that will later come along and tear them apart yet again.

As I sat there that night being enlightened by the Lord as to why, when and how things had gone wrong; I felt I had revisited spiritual boot-camp. Sometimes knowing the answers to your questions can be harder to handle than not knowing at all. The enemy is always right there waiting to sneak in with the spirits of doubt and confusion; in hopes to destroy every revelation. Needless to say, as soon as my visitation from the Lord was through; the tormenting spirits of darkness came in two's!

Please understand when I speak of a revelation or a visitation from the Lord, I do not wish you to think I can see Him in body or hear Him speak audibly. A visitation is simply a feeling of God's presence and a revelation is an understanding received through thought. You have to understand it had taken me years of trial and error before I even believed the Lord would possibly communicate with a wretch like me. Still to this day I struggle to believe some of the things I feel the Lord is trying to tell me could be anything more than my own passing thoughts. However, I have pushed off more thoughts than I care to mention and then later found out those thoughts were not my own at all. It wasn't just some meaningless psychic ability that told me Johnny would be in the pub that night in November. God told me he would be there because He wanted me to seek Him and be a willing vessel to allow Him to speak through me to Johnny. However, I didn't listen in time so I had to write Johnny a letter that night so he could hear what God had to say. It wasn't just a coincidence that I had a dream Johnny was surrounded by dead people less than 7 weeks before he was killed. I'm not 100% certain I did all I was supposed to do when I had the dream. But I do know I begged God to tell me what to do and I have to believe if a person is willing to be used, God will make sure they know what He needs them to do. The hardest part was wondering if I did enough to make him know the death angel was after him and not knowing if Johnny read any of the letters; but I have to believe he did.

God spoke to me in my darkest hour of grief and simply said, **"Ye of little faith! Do you think if I wanted him to know what was coming I wouldn't have the power to make sure he read the letters?"**

Even though I knew God had the power to make sure Johnny read the letter and I was told by one of his friends he did; I still struggled to let go of the guilt of not going after him. Guilt is one of Satan's most powerful weapons against us and yet knowing that doesn't seem to help.

The bible says**, *"My people will perish for lack of knowledge"*** but I'm not sure if the knowledge does us any good if we're not willing to use it!

I have the knowledge to know how to fight off those tormenting spirits of guilt, condemnation, doubt and confusion but sometimes it takes me a while to work up the strength to fight them off. God had led me to send Johnny messages that were meant to give him the knowledge he needed to escape the death angel, but I'm not sure he had the strength to use what he had been given. Therefore, it is very hard to not feel there may have been something more I could have done when I know in my heart it was not God's will for Johnny to perish like that. If it had been, He wouldn't have tried so hard to warn him of what was coming and He wouldn't have had me on my knees praying for Johnny so many times in the last year of his life.

The bible tells us it is appointed to a man once to die; but it also says our days can be shortened by sin. There is no doubt in my mind that Johnny's days were shortened because he continued to follow the desires of his flesh instead of taking head to God's warnings. Satan was out to take Johnny's life but all Johnny had to do to escape the death angel was repent and turn from the things he was doing that kept him outside of God's hedge of safety. I think Johnny was so tired of fighting the battle he just gave up and was counting on the grace of God to save him from hell. I don't think God wanted it to be this way or He wouldn't have tried so hard to get Johnny to change the course he was on. However, I do think He finally decided Johnny had suffered enough and let him come home.

The next day after Nick's experience with alcohol poison was the showing which was more like a gathering because Johnny could not be seen. A part of me was glad I couldn't see him but another part of me felt I would never believe he was gone without seeing him dead. I took my own sweet time to get to the funeral home because I wasn't looking forward to seeing the family suffer. Besides that, I had anxiety about what I might find out and how many new girlfriends I may have to meet. Johnny had a pretty big family but I never expected so see the amount of cars that I did when I pulled in that parking lot. My heart began to race 100 miles per hour as I stepped out of the car to go inside. This was a man who had always told me no one loved him but there were more people at the funeral parlor than I imagined he even knew. Everywhere I looked there were sobbing women that I couldn't help but wonder if he had dated. Several people I never expected made their way over to tell me how much Johnny loved me which only deepened my pain. I wondered how in the world he could have loved me so much and not respond to any of my messages if he read them. Suddenly I found myself fighting a whole new sea of emotions and struggling to find a way to cope. It was clear to me the knowledge I had received the night before was only there to enhance my ability to overcome my emotions rather than keeping them at bay. It seemed no matter how much knowledge and wisdom I may have received over the years I was still a human that was subject to an ever changing sea of emotions that would forever keep me searching for yet more answers from God.

Johnny's roommate had invited several people over to their trailer after the viewing but there were only a few people there when I arrived. Johnny's newest girlfriend was sitting in a lawn chair outside when I walked up on the porch where I had last spent time with Johnny. I had expected to meet her at the funeral home but found out once I arrived she wasn't welcomed by his family, so she wasn't there. She was very cordial and began to speak freely with me as soon as I arrived.

She said, *"Johnny told me I would really like you if I ever met you"* and that made me feel really good to know he still spoke of me to his girlfriend's after all these years.

She also said he spoke of me often and once told her she reminded him of me and that wasn't good because he would wind up falling in love with her and stalk her like he did me. We shared Johnny stories, laughed and cried together for several hours and my heart broke for that young girl when I left that night. She was in her early 20's and had just lost her father a few months before and I could relate to her pain because I was about her same age when I lost my own daddy to cancer. Although Johnny was friends with her dad and that was basically how they wound up together; he had gotten her through the grief of losing her dad the same way he got me through my grief. Even though we didn't meet until 4 ½ years after I lost my dad and a year and 3 months after I lost my mom; it seemed Johnny had once again played the role of savior to a broken rebel child. She told me of how he was always telling her she needed to take vitamins and I laughed inside without saying a word to her because he was always making fun of me for all the vitamins I took. She asked Fess for a Nutter Butter and again I laughed inside without

231

saying a word to her that Nutter Butters were always my favorite cookie. I went home that night wondering if Johnny had finally found a girl he felt he could mold into me and found myself seeking God for yet more answers.

The next day was the funeral and I had great expectations of how wonderful this service would be. The funeral was going to be held in the Pentecostal church Johnny's mother attended. I sat up half the night pondering how great the anointing would be on Johnny's special day. Johnny would have one last chance to be on a pulpit and there would be a large sanctuary full of people I knew he wanted to see saved. I prayed all night the spirit of God would fall on that church and turn Johnny's loved ones inside out. I prayed the word of God would be manifest that day as He used ***"All things"*** for the glory of God and the good of that child called Johnny who loved Him. I prayed Johnny's death would have purpose and he would bring more people to the Lord at his funeral than he ever did in his life. I prayed broken hearts would be mended and empty vessels would be filled with the spirit of God but I didn't see any of my prayers answered that day. Don't get me wrong, the spirit of God was alive and well that day but for every spirit of light present in that church I think there may have been 2 spirits of darkness. For those who were there in search of the light, it was ready to be found. However I didn't see the anointing fall on the prodigal and the lost like I hoped. Never the less, I got exactly what I was expecting for me, More Answers!

During the service the preacher began to speak of an anchor and a rope; which sent me walking down memory lane to the night of the vision I had of Johnny in the boat. As he spoke I could see the vision in my mind all over again and I received another revelation to the vision. The preacher talked about Jesus being an anchor to the believer and when a believer is anchored in the love of Jesus they are at peace and have no fears.

God spoke to me and said, *"**That is why Johnny wouldn't wake up is because the spirit inside him was resting in my love.**"* I nearly jumped out of my seat when I got that message! Suddenly it was clear to me why the rope was pulled so tight in my vision. Johnny had been anchored to Jesus since he was a child. He feared not death because the spirit inside him longed to be with his father. When he was asleep in the boat his flesh had no control over his soul so his mind could be at rest and be in peace with the spirit. Although I'm sure it was not the will of God for Johnny to die because he had a special job for him to do, God still has rules and He can't go against his own rules. Johnny had a chance to turn from the sin that controlled his flesh and get back in a hedge of safety so he could live. All he had to do was repent and walk away from the life he was living to get back in the safety of the Lord but it had to be his choice to do so. Johnny chose to take the easy way out because he knew how hard it would be for him to take the high road. During the service I sat there looking around the room at all those people that loved Johnny, wondering how could a man who was so loved, feel so alone.

Then God spoke to me again and said, *"**Because Johnny had the gift of my love.**"*

Suddenly it was like the sky opened up and I received another revelation of love. The bible tells us that love is one of the fruits of the spirit and there is no greater gift than the gift of love. Since God is love we know love can only come from God. Therefore, if you know not God, you know not true love. However, the bible also says that gifts are without repentance meaning once you are given a gift it is never taken away, no matter what you may do. Therefore if God sees fit to give a person the gift of love when they are born, "even though he knows they will never turn to him in their life", He has the power to do so; and He just might to benefit someone else who loves Him back.

Have you ever wondered why there are certain people that are so easy to love and you just loved them from the moment you met them? I believe some people are just anointed with the love of God. I believe when a person is anointed with the love of God there is no greater feeling in this world "outside of being in the presence of God himself" than being in the presence of someone who is anointed with love. Some people will never be in the presence of the Lord because they have to be willing to welcome Him to be in their presence and some people won't. However, those same people will most likely come in contact with someone who is anointed with the gift of love at some point in time in their life and they will forever be drawn to that person. Without even knowing why, the people who come in contact with the person who has the gift; will feel a sense of security while in their presence. Most often people will find themselves doing anything the recipient of the gift wants just to be in their presence, even if they know it is wrong.

I believe Satan knows those who have been anointed with this gift and will stop at nothing to destroy their mind so the gift will not serve its intended purpose. Since God is love, Satan knows this is His greatest gift and fears when non-believers get in the presence of a believer who is on fire for the Lord with this gift; it would be a powerful weapon against him. When a non-believer is in the presence of this gift they are closer to the Love of God as they have ever been. If the recipient of the gift is living in sin the people they come in contact with will never make the connection of the gift to God. However, if the recipient of the gift is walking the path of righteousness and living a Godly life, the gift will give them power to draw others closer to God.

Johnny had tried his best many times to walk the path of righteousness and live a Godly life; but that tormenting spirit of religion had him bound to shame and insecurity. When Johnny opened the door to addiction to drown out the voice of religion, he lost all hope in fulfilling his dream of preaching the gospel. Johnny had received the gift of love before he was old enough to understand the gift. I believe Johnny loved so deeply because of his gift that it hurt. I believe he was anchored to the love of God in such a way that no other love would suffice. I believe the reason Johnny and I loved each other so deeply is because we both loved the Lord and had been filled with the spirit of God, so we recognized the feeling of God's love. I believe this because the greatest feeling of peace and security I have ever felt in my life outside of the presence of God was the way I felt in Johnny's arms. After all I have heard from others since Johnny's death, now I truly believe Johnny felt the same way in my arms as well.

I remember Johnny told me once his dad had asked him what it was that he loved about me and he said, ***"Have you ever had someone who knew just how and where to touch you at all times?, that's how I feel with her. She doesn't have to say or do anything, it is just the way she touches me that melts me."***

I remember so many times Johnny would lay in my arms and beg me to promise him our love would never end. He would beg me to promise we would never be apart again and it would always be the way it was right then. I never understood why he didn't just know in his heart I would love him forever because I felt in my heart he would love me forever every time he held me in his arms. Now I know he was so afflicted with spirits of insecurity and doubt where I was concerned because Satan wanted to make sure he used our love against us. Looking back I would give anything if I had only known then what I know now because I would have cast those spirits out of our home in the name of Jesus and held him in my arms until the Lord comes!

I can't say for sure how many days it had been since Johnny's death when I first felt his presence, because the first few weeks after that dreadful 9-11 were such a blur. It seemed to be within the first week when I first felt him lying next to me one night. I felt him touch my hair and then I heard him tell me he needed to talk to me. This wasn't an audible voice that I heard, it was a loud thought; much like those we get from the Lord. At first I became very scared because I wasn't sure if I could trust it was really Johnny so I tried to ignore it. However, the voice wouldn't stop and I could feel a presence holding me just like the way Johnny used to hold me. Eventually I would start crying and I could hear him begging me to not cry. The whole time this was going on I would be praying silently in my mind begging God to tell me what to do because I was scared.

I could hear Johnny saying, *"I know you're scared red but please listen to me, I have something I have to tell you."*

This went on for almost 3 days before I finally decided to listen to what Johnny had to tell me.

The bible tells us the half has never been told so I thought there could be a chance this presence I felt could indeed be Johnny. Never the less, the whole time I kept praying for God to let me know if I could trust this spirit because I had never read anything in the bible that would indicate it was o.k. to speak with the dead. As a matter of fact, the bible speaks quite the contrary so there is no way I was going to take that kind of chance again. I had made that mistake when my dad died and didn't even realize what I had done until many years later. I saw the dark spirit that came in my room and tried to attach itself to me but I was in so much grief I didn't even realize it wasn't my dad because I wanted it to be him so bad. Years later God revealed to me that I had opened a door for a dark spirit to come in and try to seduce me into thinking it was my dad so it could get a strong hold on me.

You see I had been going to my dad's grave crying and screaming for God to please let him come back. Satan can't read our minds but he can sure hear the things we speak out loud so we must be very careful as to what we say. He heard my cry for my dad so he sent a dark spirit in my room one night while I was asleep. I could feel a presence on my back like a hand was touching my back and it woke me up. When I looked back to see what was touching me, I saw a dark image in the moon light quickly leaving my room and I heard a voice that said, *"I brought your dad to comfort you but you*

mustn't look at him." I immediately closed my eyes and begged God to bring him back and I promised I wouldn't look again if He did. So the presence came back and I could feel it touching my back but as hard as I tried, I couldn't keep from looking. Each time I tried to sneak a peek at my dad I could see the dark spirit leaving the room and each time I heard the voice saying you mustn't look! This happened several times until the presence finally left. I believe God had mercy on me that night because He knew I had no idea what I had done and kept that thing from getting a strong hold on me. Once I found out what I had done years later, I begged God to forgive me, thanked Him for mercy and vowed I would never be so stupid again!

Never the less, I'm a person who believes God can do anything He wants to do and if He wanted Johnny to tell me something, He is perfectly capable of letting him come back and say what he needed to say. Besides that, I'm 100% positive I can trust God to protect me when I ask Him to and I had been praying for 2 days about this presence I felt was Johnny.

I prayed silently each time I felt the presence so Satan couldn't hear my prayers and deceive me; *"Lord, I know your word speaks against conjuring up the dead but you know I did not ask for this presence to come. Lord, if this is Satan trying to trick me, please cast him out of my presence in the name of Jesus I pray! But Lord, if it be your will that Johnny tell me something; Please Lord, let me know it is o.k. to listen."*

It was on the third day when I heard that still small voice say, **"It is o.k. my child, you need to listen to what he has to say."**

I was standing in my shower which is where the Lord most often speaks to me when I heard his still small voice. I began to cry so hard I could barely breathe, then all of the sudden, I felt Johnny's presence holding me and heard him say, **"Please don't cry red, I can't stay long and I need you to listen to me."**

237

That only made me cry harder when I heard him say he couldn't stay long. The truth is, even though I was scared at first because I was afraid Satan was trying to trick me so I would embrace his touch, I still loved the feeling of the presence and missed it when it left me for a while. Now that I felt sure it was Johnny and knew he would leave me again once he said what he needed to say; I didn't want to listen because I didn't want him to go!

I can't say for sure how long I stood in that shower crying my eyes out but eventually Johnny asked if I was listening and I nodded my head because I dared not let the enemy find out I was listening to the dead. Once he knew I was listening he began to tell me how sorry he was for ever leaving me. He told me if he had known everything then that he knows now he would have never left. He said he was sorry for hurting me and ever doubting my love. He told me Jesus told him everything I went through and how much I truly loved him.

Johnny said, **"You were right about the like-minded spirits and that is why I'm here."**

He told me we would never really be apart because we were connected in heaven. He told me he was wrong about a certain man I had dated off and on over the years since we had been apart and that man really does love me. He told me he wanted me to let him have a chance to make me happy and to not judge the book by its cover like he did.

He said, **"Things aren't always how they appear to be. Just as you thought I didn't love you anymore and I thought you didn't love me anymore, this man really does love you; he is just guarding his heart!"**

He told me he wanted me to be happy and he knew I could be happy with him some day if I would stop being stubborn and acting like I didn't care. He begged me over and over to please listen to him because he couldn't stay long and I needed to get this through my thick head! He told me I had to stop acting like I didn't care when I did because he didn't want me to live my life alone.

Then Johnny told me firmly, ***"Red, you have got to stop comparing everyone to me! You have got to let someone else in and learn how to love again! I know now you will always love me but you have got to keep it to yourself if you don't want to be alone the rest of your life!"***

He told me to remember all the things he had told me about how important it was to tell others how you feel about them and then he said, ***"You don't have to be so brutally honest about how much you love me, it will only breed jealousy!"***

At one point I remember I was crying so hard I almost fell to my knees in the shower and it felt like he grabbed me around my waist and held me up! His presence was so strong I could almost see him! He told me over and over how sorry he was that he wasn't there to hold me in real life and how sorry he was that I had to hurt like this over him. He told me I had to start writing again because it was time to finish the book. He kept telling me over and over to please listen because he couldn't stay long and then just like that, he was gone!

Words can't even describe how bad it hurt when he left me in the shower that day; it felt as if I had lost him all over again. I feared he would never be back but I dared not to think I could beg him back because I knew that would open the door for Satan to try and trick me again. I was so cautious I never even spoke out loud to Johnny because I didn't want to take a chance on Satan using our communication against me. Johnny had told me in the shower we were able to communicate through our thoughts in the same way I communicate with God because we were soul mates. I knew if God were willing Johnny would be back and he was. One day when I got upset over something I heard him say, ***"Red, remember what I told you!"*** and I just had to smile to let him know I knew he was there.

There have even been a few times when I was slacking off he has showed up to tell me I really needed to get back to my book because there was no need in putting it off if I had nothing else to do. I can't say it happens as often as I would like; but from time to time, I believe he stops in to check on me and sometimes I know he is there.

One night I was sound asleep and I woke up needing to relieve my bladder. I started to get out of my bed and I felt Johnny pull me close to him and say, **"Where are you going?"** At first it didn't even hit me that he was dead, it just felt like it always did when he felt me try to get out of bed and pulled me closer to him.

So I said, "I'm going to the bathroom" out loud because I really thought he was there.

Then he said, **"No don't, stay here and let me hold you."** So I melted back in his arms and went back to sleep for a while longer.

The next time I woke up it happened again; so I laid there until I was about to bust and then I said, *"I'll be back, I really have to go to the bathroom!"*

I got up and went to the bathroom and then it finally hit me he was dead and his spirit must be there holding me at night while I sleep; so I tried to hurry for fear he would leave while I was gone.

When I got back in bed I thought to myself, *"Is he gone?"*

Of course I couldn't see him so he waited until I got situated in the bed and then I felt him wrap his arms around me again. I went right back to sleep and slept like a baby! When I woke in the morning, he was gone and I couldn't help but wonder how often he came to hold me at night when I didn't even know he was there.

Over the next few months I struggled to deal with my emotions. Although I had been through the pain of losing many loved ones in my life, this was a different kind of love that seemed to take me to a different level of pain. Maybe it was with each loss I was at a different chapter in my book of life or maybe it was simply that I loved each one I had lost in a different way. Never the less, I was thankful for the increased level of strength I now had through my higher level of faith in the Lord. Although there were days when I thought about going to my room and giving up; in hopes the good Lord would have mercy and finally take me home, I still managed to look for a bright side.

When I saw others hurting the way I was, it gave me the strength to fight the grief for their sake. I think it must be that warrior spirit in me that stirs up my inner strength when I see others in need. Somehow I managed to pull myself out of grief long enough to write the letter below to someone else who was still hurting over losing Johnny. I don't remember why I wrote this letter or who I wrote it to.

I found this letter and thought to myself *"Thank God for the power of the Holy Spirit that is able to work through a willing vessel even though the vessel isn't able to work."*

During that time I tried my best to find an inspiration to work on this book but thought I just couldn't write at that time. When I found this letter I thought *"maybe I was writing after all, even though I didn't know I was."*

Could it have been that God was using my hands to bring forth a message that I myself needed to hear? Could it be that I myself somehow found comfort and strength from simply being a willing vessel? I'll let you decide!

After 4 long weeks of trying to figure things out...Trying to accept the things I cannot change and seeking answers that won't change things anyway. I suddenly remember the definition of insanity! I still don't have the answers I want but I do know why it hurts so bad to lose someone you love. The answer to that question has always been clear... Love is God's greatest gift to us, without it there would be no happiness. On the flip side of that, Satan knows Love is God's greatest and most powerful weapon against him; therefore, it is his most powerful weapon against us! If there were no love in this world, there would be no heartache because people don't miss something they have never had. If we didn't have love it would be hard for Satan to attack us with tormenting spirits of anger, confusion, control, depression, doubt, insecurity or jealousy. Even the spirit of addiction often gets control of our life because we fear being alone or living without a loved one. I knew years ago, Satan used the love Johnny and I shared against us! If *we hadn't loved each other so much, Satan wouldn't have bothered to tear us apart. Glory be to God, we found a way to escape the torment by loving each other from a distance. Satan hates love and the joy it brings to our life; so he is determined to destroy that joy in any way he can. Most of us aren't strong enough to endure the torment so we just give up! Because I know Love can only come from God, I know Love still lives when all else is gone! We have all spent the last 4 weeks giving in to the torment Satan so gladly brings to our mind each day; "that the Love Johnny brought to our life is gone forever". This is nothing but a lie from the pits of hell! Yes that gorgeous man that carried that love will only be seen on this earth in our memories and photos "thankfully we have plenty of them"! However, the love Johnny brought to each of our lives is very much alive; but the only way we can feel it, is if we start saying NO to that tormenting spirit of grief! We may not be able to change the fact the enemy robbed us of a life we held so dear to our hearts 4 weeks ago; but we can certainly stop him from robbing us of another day of joy! I pray God will give us all strength to say NO to the heartache and grief! I pray we will all remember to seek the Love God gave us through Johnny among our living loved ones. Remembering Johnny's love through smiles and hugs instead of heartache tears and mental torment is what has got me through all these years without him by my side. Living with the hope of seeing him again one day in a world without end; is far better than reliving the day that his life here on earth had to end. May the emptiness in our hearts be filled with as much love & laughter, as we felt on our happiest day with the man we all love so dear<3*

As it turned out I had been doing a lot of writing during the first few months after Johnny's death. It seems I find answers to questions when I write or at least I find clarity to what God has already told me. Maybe it helps me to write it down so I will remember it later. I'm not sure what the purpose is but I'm sure there must be a reason I have found yet another letter I wrote during that very hard time in my life. This one is a letter I wrote to Johnny even though he wasn't here to read it. Maybe it made me feel better to talk to him or maybe it was something God needed me to see on paper. Whatever the reason I wrote it is not important. However, I think it is important enough for me to share if it was important enough for God to lead me to find a letter I don't even remember writing to a dead man.

Remember all those scriptures I sent you in the past year? I've been looking back on those a lot lately because I'm still searching for answers and trying to make sense of this whole thing. Sometimes I start feeling weak and neglect to call on the Lord before my mind starts going in a million different directions. Before I know it, I start hoping for things that don't make any sense. Things that won't make anything better or bring any peace to those who love you. Then I remember what the word says and how God promises to shine a light on the darkness if we trust Him to do so. I remember that His word says He will use all things for the good of those who Love Him. I remember how much you loved Him and I'm sure you Love him even more now that you're in His presence. I told you not long ago that you had a purpose and I knew Satan had put a target on your head to keep you from fulfilling that purpose. It is hard for me to not get angry that he succeeded in destroying your life so you wouldn't fulfill the purpose you had. But I know God is perfectly able to use what Satan meant for harm for His Glory and I promise you I'm going to do everything in my power to make sure that happens! I pray God will grant me the serenity to accept the things I cannot change, the courage to change the things I can and the wisdom to know the difference! I pray He will continue to shine His magnificent light on this darkness and bring an appropriate justice for the life you were robbed of! I pray He will chastise all of those whom you loved for our wrong doings so that we may be found worthy to see you again one day! Most of all, I pray He will put a desire in the heart of each and every person who Loved you to want to pay the devil back for stealing your life; by turning to He who has given your spirit a glorious life that will never end! As I say goodnight to you I think of a song that has always reminded me of *you...."if you get there before I do, don't give up on me. I'll meet you when my chores are through, I don't know how long I'll be. But I'm not gonna let you down, Darling wait and see..... Between now and then, until I see you again, I'll be loving you....Love Me<3*

CHAPTER 13

The motive behind the madness

All throughout this book I have told you stories of people that some may look at as an insignificant part of society; but they were all people who meant the world to me. Sure I know none of them did anything great like finding a cure for polio or saving a village in Dar 4; but each and every one of them played a significant role in molding me into the woman God created me to be. If you can remember in the beginning of my life when God called me Molly "the sea of great sorrow" most of my life was consumed by what I now believe to be spirits of darkness. That is not to say there were never any good times or that the power of God's love was never present during those years of great sorrow. It would take me several more years to tell you of all the wonderful memories I have of each and every person I have mentioned in this book. My mother for example, had a radiant inner light that was still able to shine in her darkest of days! I find myself speaking the same words of wisdom she often spoke to us over the years quite often. During my years in great sorrow I wasn't always able to see the beauty in the breaking as I see it now. Just recently I found a poem I had written in a card I gave to my mother on June 13, 1992. I'm not sure why I gave her that card because it was no special occasion and that was one of the darkest times in my life as I suffered to function with my own depression. Never the less, I see in that poem a need for my own inner light to shine bright amongst the darkness and realize it was then He carried me like the footprints in the sand. Maybe it was His way of getting me to see my wrong doings. Looking back I have often regretted my lack of understanding and compassion for the demons my mother battled each day of her life to survive. Now that I have an understanding of what she went through; I hang my head in shame as I thank God for the gift of His precious Love that was able to shine through her world of darkness. How beautiful my mother truly was in every way, like a love bird that is trapped in a barbed wire cage. Although I do not claim to be a poet, I would like to share the poem I found in that card so you can see how truly wonderful my mother was to all those who knew her.

I called the poem *"A prayer for my Mother"*

She is a woman I love; she is a woman I admire.
She is someone I depend upon to lead me from the fire.
She is loved by so many because so many she has loved.
She gave us joy, we gave her pain; she brought us sunshine; we brought her rain.
Her doors are always open; she is waiting with open arms.
To take us in and comfort us, and keep us safe from harm.
She listens to our troubles with an open ear.
She feels our pain and sorrows as she wipes away our tears.
She is always forgiving when she is treated bad; and when I think of all she has gone through it makes me feel so sad.
My prayer is Dear Lord you will continue to love and guide her.
When the joy turns to pain and the sunshine turns to rain; when the doors are no longer open in your home, she will rule & rein.
Then you'll take her in your arms and remind her of why she is there; is because she was always so loving, to everyone down here.

I'm sure some will think **"isn't that what a mother is supposed to do?"** Yes, but my mother did that for everyone. She loved everyone so much her door was always open even when I'm certain there were many times it should have been shut. My mother was the youngest of 6 children but I can only think of one other person in her family that would have opened her door to anyone in need and her husband wouldn't allow it. My aunt Mary also had a heart filled with love and compassion for others even though she had been treated badly by so many people in her life. I watched my grandparents and 3 of the other children lock their doors to their own family on numerous occasions but my mother never did and my aunt Mary wouldn't have either! When I was a child I can remember thinking how horrible it was that my grandparents and my aunt Lorene would lock their doors and pretend they weren't at home when people came to visit. Although there were several people I wished my parents would have locked the door on, I can't bring myself to do it either. Now I realize not everyone is willing to keep their door open all the time because not everyone is made to deal with the torment of what may be on the other side.

Now that I understand the spirit realm the way I do, I realize my parents must have been blessed with the gift of love. As I've mentioned before, Satan knows those whom God has given special gifts and he will stop at nothing to use their gift against them. I truly believe that is why my parents made it through all those years until death did them part. I think they were *"Like-minded spirits"* that carried the gift of God's love to others. I think the enemy often sent people who were afflicted with tormenting spirits to our home because he knew my parent's door would always be open to let the spirits of darkness in. The bible says *"Perfect Love casts out all fear"* and I know perfect love can only come from God Himself. Therefore it makes sense to me now that the only fear I ever really had as a child was losing my parents to death. Although I remember feeling angry and disappointed most of the time about the people my parents allowed to stay in our home, I do not recall ever feeling I was in danger. Looking back I can remember so many people who came to stay in our home over the years often seemed to have that same sense of peace and security in the shelter of our home until they all started drinking. I truly believe that is why the bible tells us *"not to drink the wine that moves"* and *"all drunkards will have their part in the lake of fire."* I believe alcohol and drugs hinders our natural ability to bring forth the fruits of our spirit. I'm sure most people have known at least one person in their life that they considered to be one of the sweetest people they had ever met when they were sober but didn't want to be within 100 miles of that person when they were drunk or on drugs.

Now I'm a deep thinker and I have always tried my best to understand the word of God but there was a time it made no sense to me and seemed to contradict itself. My mother used to tell me *"Marci, there are some things it isn't meant for us to know and you have got to stop thinking about this or it is going to drive you crazy."* My mother just accepted there were things in the bible she would never understand and told me we can ask God if we make it to heaven and if He wants us to know, He will tell us then. I can't help but wonder if that is why my mother became an addict. Could it be there was a burning desire in her soul to know the answers to why she was the way she was because God wanted her to seek out the answers? Could it be she used drugs and alcohol to drown out that still small voice of God that summonsed her to seek Him because religion had taught her to not question God? It has been my experience that some questions will just not go away unless you either impair your mind in such a way you are unable to think clearly or you seek God until He answers. I believe it must be the will of God for us to seek Him for the answers to our questions because His word says, *"Seek and Ye shall find."* So why is it that we teach our children to just live on faith that God knows all things and we don't have to? I believe it is because we don't know the answers to their questions and most of us have a hard time believing God will truly give us the answers if we seek Him. I believe the reason we have such a hard time believing we will ever get our answer is because we find it hard to trust our own thoughts to be the voice of God. As humans we are programmed to depend on our 4 senses. If we cannot hear, see, taste or feel something we find it hard to believe it. Even the most faithful of humans still struggle to believe God could have given them an answer to a question no one else has ever known.

For example, it is hard for some to believe Daniel was thrown in a Lion's den and not eaten alive because they weren't there to see it. Or that Noah built an arch big enough for 2 of everything and Moses parted the red sea. Or that Abraham was willing to sacrifice his own son and God so loved the world He gave His only begotten son Jesus Christ for the ultimate sacrifice. However, there are some who are willing to believe because they heard the story spoken audibly by someone they trust and they saw the evidence of the story written in the Holy Bible. But what if I told you I truly believe with all of my heart God gave me some answers to questions I had been seeking Him for? No, I did not hear Him audibly nor did I see His face when He revealed to me what I believe to be truth. I did not have an out of body experience or an incredible dream I believe God gave me to reveal any kind of truth. This is just a sense of peace I received when this thought came to my mind. But I ask you to search inside your heart and ask yourself if you can come to the same peace when you read what I believe God told me.

For many years I was disturbed about the scripture that says all homosexuals will have their part in the lake of fire because my sister Robin spent many years of her life in prison and always had a girlfriend when she got out. Although Robin dared not admit she was a lesbian or even a bi-sexual when she was in her right mind she was certainly bold enough to admit it when she was high and that bothered me greatly. Please understand the reason I was so disturbed about her being bi-sexual is because I had always been taught homosexuality was an abomination unto God. Therefore I pondered that scripture allot and wondered why some Christians could forgive the drunkard or the adulterer whom are also mentioned to have their part in the lake of fire so much easier than they could the homosexual "including myself". It made no sense to me how I could talk to my sister about her addiction problems with love and understanding but I couldn't stand the thought of acknowledging she was actually gay. The embarrassment of her being high got much worse when she decided to display signs of affection towards the girls I already knew she was in an intimate relationship with. As long as they didn't talk about it or make it obvious in any way, I was o.k.; but as soon as it became evident, I suddenly wanted to get away from them. Back then I knew I was nowhere close to being where I needed to be in my relationship with God but still I called on Him to help me to understand and to be able to deal with this situation in the way that I should. It wasn't until years later after I had gone through spiritual boot camp that I got my answers and was able to talk to Robin about what I believed God had told me.

One night I was taking a bath and talking to the Lord as I most often did in the bath or shower. At that time I had some clients who were gay and I could tell they were really good people whom I felt had a love for the Lord that they suppressed because their lifestyle wasn't accepted.

As I was praying for my clients God spoke to me in that still small voice "meaning I had a thought that was backed up by a feeling of His presence" and said, ***"Is the sin of their love any different than the love you felt for a married man?"***

I immediately bowed my head in shame because I knew I had just been chastised by the Lord for falling in love with Johnny. But the Lord quickly spoke again and said, ***"You cannot help who you love my child so I warn you to not commit acts of homosexuality, adultery or fornication for the same reasons I warn you to not kill, lie or drink the wine that moves; to protect you from the strong holds of Satan!"***

He began to tell me how He gave humans sexual desires so we would be willing to go through the pain and hard work of having children. The Lord told me Satan knew how special a covenant of marriage is to Him so he does anything in his power to destroy that covenant or keep it from taking place. He said Satan sends seductive spirits to torment humans with thoughts in their mind to commit homosexual acts so he can convince them they are gay and therefore stop them from procreating. He said Satan never misses an opportunity to put temptation in the path of a married person because he knows nothing will destroy the covenant of marriage faster than adultery. He said Satan has used his unclean spirits of seduction to get people to commit acts of fornication because he knows how easy it will be to torment the minds of people who fall in love with someone that will not love them back once they have consummated their soul tie.

You see when we have a sexual relationship with someone we are creating a bond that is meant to be forever. However, most people these days only think of the moment they are in right now and rarely think of what the consequences could be if they develop feelings for someone that aren't reciprocated or that person develops feelings for them they aren't willing or capable of feeling back. Therefore, when God tells us *"fornicators"* will have their part in the lake of fire, He is warning us that having an unpleasant soul tie to someone could be as painful as spending time in hell. The same as the drunkard, the adulterer, the murderer and the homosexual will surely face a mental and sometimes physical torment much like that of hell even if they are forgiven and escape going to an eternal hell.

God is usually a man of few words but sometimes He floods my mind with information that makes me glad I have the guts to keep asking questions; even though I've been told it isn't His will for me to know some things. It never made sense to me why we are taught Jesus came to die for our sins and there was nothing we couldn't be forgiven of but the bible clearly says there will be certain people who will have their part in the lake of fire. Then it also says the lake of fire was created for Satan and his Angels. So how could it be that we will all have our part if we have ever committed the sins that are mentioned even though we have been forgiven when we repent? I truly believe the part we will take in the lake of fire is a part most of us will take while we still live in our human bodies because it is our soul and spirit that suffers the torment of hell anyway. Our natural bodies are left in the ground when we die unless we take on a celestial body. It is our soul and spirit that will be sent to hell with Satan and his Angels of darkness if we choose to not receive the gift of salvation while we are still on this earth. Therefore, it makes sense to me that our soul and spirit could have a part in torment here on this earth when we choose to go against the warnings of God to stay away from things that will put us in that horrible place.

The word says in Revelations 21:8 **"But the fearful, and unbelieving, and the abominable, and murderers, and whoremongers, and sorcerers, and idolaters, and all liars, shall have their part in the lake which burneth with fire and brimstone: which is the second death."** It does not say, *"All of these who have not repented before they died"* It said all those that were listed **shall** have their part. For many years I looked at that verse as yet another contradiction. However, it is not another contradiction because there really are no contradictions in God's word at all. There are simply scriptures we do not yet understand because we have not yet sought the face of the Lord to give us a revelation of their meaning. Therefore, we all need to understand God only warns us not to do these things because He loves us so much He doesn't want to see us suffer one moment of torment. He knows those of us who will accept His gift of pardon and those who won't; but *it is NOT His will that any should perish,* not even for one moment!

That night was one of those nights where I felt completely content with the answers I had been given and couldn't wait to share the revelation I had received with Robin. You see I knew how condemned Robin felt about the years she spent in homosexual relationships;

because we had always been taught it was an abomination to God and I knew Satan used that to torment her mind. Now I'm not saying God told me this type of relationship is pleasing to Him at all. I'm just saying it was one of those *"He who is without sin should cast the first stone"* kind of things. Nor do I want you to think all preachers give a message to their congregations that bisexuals and homosexuals are any less important to God than anyone else; because that is not the case! However, I do want you to understand what I believe God was trying to tell me is anything that is outside of the will of God comes from a willingness in our flesh to open the door for that dark spirit to enter and separate us from the peace that comes from being in God's will.

You see our flesh knows no boundaries and has a desire to indulge in that which is pleasing to its carnal nature. Some say it isn't fair that God would judge us for our human desires when He is the one who created us to be this way; but I tell you today there is more to it than that! Yes, God gave us a sense of sight, smell, hearing and touch to enjoy the good things on this earth and to have an ability to get rid of the bad things. He also gave us a desire to love and be loved because He is love. He also gave us a desire for sex so we would reproduce and replenish the earth. He knew no one would go through the pain of child bearing if there was no desire in the pleasure that is involved in the making of human life. However, Satan managed to find a way to screw up all the rewards of God's master plan by adding more pain to our pleasure. As I have mentioned several times in this book Love is the greatest weapon God has against Satan and Satan knows it. Therefore, He will stop at nothing to destroy God's *"Perfect love"* by trying his best to counterfeit it.

We have all heard the old saying, *"It is better to have loved and lost than to never have loved at all."* That is another one of those things that never really settled right in my gut even though I have been known to say it many of times and I'll tell you why. First I would like to say if you have ever known the Love of God you will never lose it. His love is always present and is only a desire away if you dare to believe He exists. Second, Satan has a counterfeit for everything and since most people don't know the difference between fact or fiction it is easy for them to desire that which is not truly the love of God or misuse God's gift of love to benefit their carnal desires. I have heard people often misquote the scripture that speaks of money by saying, *"Money is the root of all evil."* However, the scripture actually says, *"The Love of money is the root of all evil."* Now if God is love why is it wrong to love money? How can love in any form be wrong if God is love? I believe Satan has counterfeited the desire to love and the feeling of joy it brings to receive that love in something or someone you so desire.

Most crimes are committed in the name of love for something or someone. Wars break out in the name of Love for Religion. People kill other people in crimes of passion and claim love to be their defense. Serial killers and rapist often claim they committed such violent acts for the love of power and control they felt while committing the act of violence. Pedi-files will most always claim they loved their victims and meant them no harm! People steal things that don't belong to them because of their love for money and things they can't afford. People lie and try to hide the truth because they are afraid no one will love them if they know how bad they have been. Alcoholics and drug addicts love their fix so much they are willing to lose everyone and everything to get it and the list goes on and on.

So I ask you, if God is love, how can all this love cause so much turmoil and chaos in the world? You must have questioned God on this matter at least once in your life. You must have wondered why being in a homosexual relationship or being involved in adultery is wrong when it feels so right to your flesh. You must have wondered why it is wrong to get drunk or high when it feels so good at the time. I believe this to be a matter of fact or fiction. The fact is God is love and there is no greater feeling in the world than a feeling of a love God is a part of. However, it is sometimes hard to see a counterfeit. Therefore, we find ourselves being caught up in the fiction of love because it isn't something that is easily detected by our senses.

Please understand although we all have a choice to do right or wrong; not all of us have a choice on what we desire to do. I believe a desire is something that can be controlled if you are equipped with the power to control it. However, when you are born into something and that is all you have really ever known, it is hard to break free of a desire that seems to be a part of who you are. This is why I think it is so important we live our life according to God's word so we will stay under His hedge of protection and not be cursed. If we open a door for sin to enter our life, it will also enter the lives of our children and that is how a generational curse is formed. Take Gene for an example; do you think Gene had the power to overcome his desire to drink when he had been given beer in his baby bottle? Sure, Gene could have been given the power through the Holy Spirit to overcome his desire to drink and do drugs if someone had given him the knowledge to seek that power. Even still, the desire was so strong it would have taken many years of people praying to break down those strong holds to set Gene completely free of that unclean spirit unless God wanted to miraculously deliver him.

I do not have the answers as to why God delivers some but not others. I wish I could tell you why he spared me from being consumed by addiction when almost everyone I ever loved was not so lucky, but I can't. I wish I could tell you why I was born loving Jesus but not everyone else in this world is. I wish I could tell you why I never doubted His existence and why others do but I can't tell you that either. I wish I could tell you why the good Lord gives some gifts at birth but yet others may not see their first spiritual gift until they are 50 or more and some never will at all. All I know is God chooses the gifts He wants to give people and the bible says, "***gifts are without repentance***." I thank God they are because there were times in my life if I had to repent for all the things I did wrong to keep my spiritual gifts, I would have either lost them or I would have spent most of my time in repentance! There are still a lot of things I do not know for sure; but there are some things I know for sure God has told me and no one will ever change my mind.

The things I have told you would be considered controversial at best. I'm sure there will be some that think I'm crazy or confused. Some will question my ability to tell the difference between fact or fiction myself and some will criticize my points of view. Never the less, I feel there could be at least one person in this world that needs to look at their life in a different light that could make more sense to them than it all being black or white.

Several years ago I kept having the same thought when I was praying at night. I kept thinking God was calling me John Paul Jones and eventually I told my best friend Beth I thought God was calling me John Paul Jones when I was praying. Beth asked me if I knew who John Paul Jones was. I told her I knew he was some guy we learned about in elementary school history but I couldn't remember exactly what he did. Beth told me she suggests I look it up because God may be trying to tell me something important. Of course I just blew it off because I doubted God would be trying to tell me anything about John Paul Jones. Beth couldn't let it go because she had already learned how to communicate with God and knew He often said things that didn't make any sense so we would seek Him. She got up in the middle of the night that night and went to the computer to look up the history on John Paul Jones. When she called me the next day, she was so excited to tell me all the things she had found out because what she found out about John Paul Jones reminded her so much of me.

Beth said, ***"Marci, I think God is trying to tell you something important. John Paul Jones was a writer and God has been telling you to write a book. John Paul Jones was the one who made the quote "I have not yet begun to fight" which you are notorious for saying and I think you need to pray about this!"***

So Beth intrigued me to dig a little deeper and talk to God about the John Paul Jones thing and to my surprise there was quite a few more similarities between me and John. John Paul Jones mother shared my middle name which also has the same meaning as the name John, "God's gracious". John Paul Jones was a warrior and my first name Marcella means "warrior of God". Now God had already told me why I have the name Marcella Jean was because I had to fight my way into this world and it was His grace that I be born. He had told me of how the enemy set out to destroy me before I was born because he knew I was going to be a warrior for God. He told me of how my mother had prayed and why he sent me here to help her fight the good fight. There were certainly too many coincidences to ignore the thoughts I had any longer and that was enough inspiration for me to start this book.

Although I was learning to hear the voice of the Lord I still struggled to believe He would actually take time to talk to a wretch like me. Time and time again I would go to Him whining over a certain situation and I would hear Him say, *"It isn't easy to be king."*

This made absolutely no sense to me and I wondered why on earth God would say it isn't easy to be king when I couldn't possibly be a king because I'm a female. I thought I must be losing my mind! He wasn't saying, *"It isn't easy to be Queen"*, He was clearly saying King and that just made me mad! Was I supposed to be a man? I had been accused of acting like one several times in my life so I had to wonder what did this mean? Once again I went to Beth with this because she was the only person I had to talk to that wouldn't think I was crazy. Beth told me to pray about it and seek God to help me find out why He would say this.

Beth said, *"Marci maybe God is trying to tell you something, maybe you are supposed to be a leader, maybe you are supposed to get in to politics."*

Although I know Beth is a visionary, I also know she can sometimes have a wild imagination and that just seemed crazy to me. Never the less, I took her advice and humbly went to the Lord asking Him to help me understand.

Then one night I was watching the story of King David on TBN and God softly spoke to me in that still small voice and said, ***"It isn't easy to be king."***

I knew right away He was trying to tell me something so I called Beth and told her what had happened. Beth knew right away what the Lord was trying to tell me. King David was also a great warrior like John Paul Jones. King David was a writer and He dearly loved the Lord. King David was anointed as a child to be King and Beth thought God may be telling me why He had filled me with the Holy Spirit as a child was because He had big plans for me some day.

Beth said, ***"Marci, I don't think God is referring to you as a man, I think He is letting you know you have been given a warrior spirit and because of this you will face a great opposition and things aren't going to be easy for you."***

That made perfect sense to me! All of my life all I could remember was fighting for what I thought was right. Even in my drunkest and darkest of days, I still remember fighting for what I knew was right; even if it was against my own self! King David had battled against his enemies as well as himself. King David had been anointed by God to be a righteous man as a young child and yet he had failed miserably at being righteous when he fell in love with a married woman. King David had to suffer through a pretty severe punishment from God for his wrong doings and yet he never doubted God's love. Now I'm not saying I think God was trying to tell me I will someday be the leader of a great Nation here on this earth; although I have always wanted to be the President of the United States and feel quite certain I could do a much better job than our current administration! Never the less, I do feel God is preparing me to ***"Fight the Good Fight"*** like King David did.

For as long as I can remember I have had a fantasy of riding along side of Jesus in the battle of Armageddon. Almost every day since I was about 10 years old I have said the scripture, "**Also I heard the voice of the Lord saying, whom shall I send and whom shall go for us? Then said I, Here am I Lord; send me!**" Isaiah 6: 8

Now I will have to tell you I can see myself in this battle when I say that scripture. I can see myself riding on a chocolate brown horse alongside our Lord Jesus with a giant sword in my right hand and I can see myself wearing a crown. I know some may think that sounds boastful but I know what the word of God says and I believe we should look forward to the plans He has for us. We each have our own place in this world and we all have a job to do that will prepare us for our place in heaven. Some of you may have a more glamorous job in heaven like singing praises unto the Lord; and some of you may have the job I wanted of planting His flowers. Never the less, one job is no more important than the other and no matter what our job is, we should do our very best at it and be proud to be chosen for that job. I told God I really want to plant some things in heaven one day and I know if it is important to me, it will be important to Him; so I plan on doing some planting as soon as I get back from the great battle.

Now if you have made it to the end of this book, the fact is you have a choice to make. You are no longer clueless to the spirit realm so the way you have always looked at things will forever be changed. No matter how crazy you may think it would be to believe in some or all of the things I have told you, the fact is you will forever wonder if what I have told you is indeed *"Fact or Fiction."* You can either choose to believe in the God of salvation that holds the keys to unlock any of the chains that bind you and your loved ones, and get to know Him on an intimate level; or you can take your chances this is all fiction. If what I have told you in this book is fiction, it will not matter whether you choose to believe or not believe. However, if what I have told you in this book is fact and you choose to believe it is fiction; it will have a major effect on not only your afterlife but also your quality of life here on this earth.

Not that it is important for you to believe the stories I have told you; but it could be very important to believe in the savior who has helped me to make it through all the things I have told you about. I would like you to ask yourself this one question. If you knew for a fact there was a wonder drug out there that would help you to be set free of addiction, poverty, illness or feeling alone would you take a chance and take the drug? If you knew someone who had taken this drug and you saw with your own eyes they had been healed of an illness would you take it if you were sick? If you knew an addict that took the wonder drug and is now clean of any alcohol or drugs would you recommend it to other addicts? If you knew someone who had struggled financially and found out they suddenly had enough money to pay all of their bills after they took this wonder drug, would you consider taking it if you were broke? If you were lonely and found out someone you knew took this wonder drug and then found their soul mate and had been living happily ever after for several years, then would you take the drug? If your answer is yes to any of these questions, I challenge you to give the Father, Son and the Holy Spirit a try. If this is all just fiction, what do you have to lose other than a little time? There are no side effects involved in this experiment. There is absolutely no way any situation or problem you or your loved ones have could get worse by giving faith a chance. Don't be afraid to ask Him for a specific sign to prove He is real. He made you and He understands how hard it is for humans to believe in something they can't see, hear or touch. This is why He depends on us humans who do believe, to be His voice and share His love.

Fact or Fiction Conclusion

In the beginning God created the heavens and the earth. The earth was without form, and void; and darkness was on the face of the deep. And the Spirit of God was hovering over the face of the waters. Have you ever wondered what the passage meant when it said "and darkness was on the face of the deep?' Could it have meant that this was the place where Satan was cast into? Could it be that God hovering over the very place where he cast his most beloved in hopes Satan would come to his senses? I've often wondered how it must have hurt the heart of God to be forced into casting out His most beloved Angel into the deep. Have you ever wondered why God allowed Satan to enter into the garden to begin with? Have you ever wondered why God gave Satan the power to rule & rein on the earth? I'm sure we have all wondered this at least once in our life and most often felt it to be unfair that evil is allowed to be among us. I ask you to consider one thing, could it be that God is love and He knows not hate? Could it be that even those who hate Him "such as Satan does" He is still unable to hate?

When I think of the crucifixion and how Jesus being hated, beaten, tortured and put to death for taking on the sins of this world, still knew not hate. I hang my head in shame as I know I couldn't do the same. Then I think of the love I have for my own children and how there is nothing I can imagine them to do that would stop my love for them. However, I still have to question, how much I could take before I would take their life to get rid of the evil that led them. I believe this is why we will never fully understand the love of God. As humans we cannot imagine suffering in the way that Jesus suffered through the hands of His own loved ones without fighting back. Therefore, for some it makes the story of the crucifixion a little hard to believe. As humans we find it hard to continue to love someone who doesn't show us love in return for everything we do. We often turn our back on love or at best love from a distance when things aren't going the way we want them to. So how can it be Jesus could continue to love without any reward at all?

All throughout this book I have told you stories of my own loved ones whom I fell short of loving in the way of the Lord. I've told you many stories of those who have gone on before me that I know in my heart were forgiven through the love and grace of Jesus Christ despite their short comings. And yet I know what I believe in my heart to be Fact may sound a whole lot like Fiction to a religious mind. A fact is something we have proof of and yet the stories in the bible that have proven to be a fact time and time again still seem so hard to believe for some. Some will argue the laws of God in the Old Testament do not line up with the Grace of God in the New Testament and I must admit, this is true! However by understanding the love I have for my own children is without limits and knowing God's love for us "His children" is far greater than that; I now understand His grace. God has rules that even He must abide by. Therefore, why is it so hard to believe that God could love His own children enough to make a way for forgiveness after watching them break his rules for thousands of years?

We as parents know how bad it hurts us to punish our own children when they break our rules; but yet we know if they are not punished they will never learn. Over the life of our children we often try to find ways to get out of punishing them because our love for them is so great we can't stand to see them suffer. So why then is it so hard to believe that God himself had to find a way to forgive us

'His Children" to stop the pain in His own heart when we can't seem to refrain from breaking His rules?

My purpose in telling you these things is to get you to think of unconditional love. Think of someone you love so unconditionally that you can't imagine not loving them no matter what they do. Then imagine that person whom you love with all of your heart beating you with a piece of leather that had fish hooks on the end of it that ripped the flesh from your body with every stroke. Imagine that person accusing you of being a liar when you never spoke a lie in your life. Imagine that person spitting on you and laughing at your pain and suffering. Imagine that person driving nails through your hands and feet and hanging you on a cross to be mocked until your death. Then I ask you to imagine crying out to your natural Father to forgive that person whom you love because you know your father has the power and the wrath at that very moment to take that person's life with your own? Could you love anyone that much; to forgive such an outrageous act of hatred and violence against you? As a parent could you love anyone enough to forgive them for doing such an evil thing to your own child; even if it was another one of your children who did it? As much as I hate to admit this is an area I feel I would most likely fall short in, I'm pretty sure I would. Although I would like to believe I could forgive in time, my human mind isn't sure I could.

By now you may be wondering what forgiveness has to do with the stories in this book being Fact or Fiction. You may even be wondering what any of this has to do with the crucifixion; but isn't that one of the most questioned events in all of history? Some of us find it easier to believe the crucifixion to be a fact than others; but most of us find it hard to believe the crucifixion could have anything at all to do with our own personal sins. Most of us feel the whole idea of something that happened over 2000 years ago could have anything to do with the life we live today as being a little farfetched. To imagine God could manifest himself in flesh because He actually loved someone who wouldn't even be born for another 2000 years; sounds so much like a fantasy it is hard to wrap our mind around it being an everlasting reality. It is far easier to believe the crucifixion to have purpose for the people of that time than of our time. We rarely give it much thought and when we do, we rarely compare it to a level of human love.

With that being said I hope to take you back to a time of your own pain. We have all had at least one day of sorrow in our life. I can't imagine there could be a person on this earth, that hasn't felt their own personal pain or the pain of watching at least one person they love suffer from a disease, an addiction, a divorce, or the loss of a loved one. Even if you couldn't relate to any of the stories I have told you in this book, you must have known at least one person who can and felt their pain when you witnessed their struggle. I realize there are actually people in this world that do not understand the pain of addiction as I do. I know there are people who are much older than me who have never suffered the loss of a loved one or struggled to escape the curse of poverty in the depths I have endured. However, I also know there are many people in this world who have endured this same kind of pain and can't imagine there is any way of escaping the ever haunting memories of their past. Addiction is an unclean spirit that torments the body and soul and will never go away completely. Poverty is a curse that is accompanied by the tormenting spirits of fear and depression that tends to follow a person forever, even if they have escaped the grip of poverty. Grief is a tormenting spirit that will often use its strong hold on a person to open the doors for addiction, fear, anger, doubt in God and most commonly depression. The good news is, there is a way to overcome, or even escape if you will.

The struggles I've mentioned in this book are not things that can be fixed by the Government or going to a doctor. Sure our Government can ease the pain of poverty through entitlements and increasing growth in our economy. Sure a doctor can give us drugs to help with the pain of a disease, addiction, depression, anxiety and even grief. But at the end of the day we are still left with being dependent on someone or something to ease our pain. It would have been much easier for me to give up and go on Welfare when my Dad passed away. I was only 22 and had a 2 year old child that would have been my free ticket to entitlements. Who would have blamed me for taking some time to grieve and get my life together? I could have received free housing, food stamps, medical assistance that would have paid for all of the anti-anxiety and anti-depressants I ever needed. I could have gone back to school and enjoyed watching my children's father being forced into paying the Government for our welfare. Don't think the thought didn't cross my mind a million times as I struggled to take care of my children and watched other mothers on welfare get help from the judicial system in getting their child support. Our system is so inept that most women feel they have no choice but to depend on the Government because they will never get any support from the absent father if they aren't in the system. Working women have to make enough money to hire Attorneys to help them get the child support they need because the judicial system is too busy going after the dead beat dads of welfare moms to help those who are trying to make it on their own. Why would anyone in their right mind struggle to take care of 2 children and work 3 jobs most of the time to get by when they didn't have to?

The only answer I can come up with is because I knew *"I could do all things through Christ who strengthens me."* I knew if I gave into fear I would be stuck in poverty forever. I knew if I gave into depression I would be destined to be an alcoholic and a drug addict. I knew if I gave into anxiety I would have to take the medication my mother and my aunts called "nerve pills" the rest of my life. But the biggest reason of all; was because I loved my children more than myself. It was the love I had for my own children that eventually made me understand the Love God has for us. If I could love them so much that I would be willing to go through most of their life alone and suffer through the things I had to go through; I then knew how much more that He loved us.

If you think about the things a parent is willing to endure for their child it is easy to understand how Jesus could endure such suffering for us. Imagine if you were a child of God that had actually seen Him face to face and knew all of His power was given unto you. Imagine if God told you all you had to do was go through 24 hours of the most horrific torture and death known to man but you would rise again and have defeated Satan and his evil plan to destroy all of your children. You knew you would be hated by half of your children but the other half would love you forever and would be saved from an eternal life of torment with Satan in hell. On the other hand if you didn't suffer this horrific death all of your children would spend eternity burning in hell with Satan. Even if you were only able to pull just one child out of the fire, would it not be worth it?

I knew if I didn't fight for my children to be free of these demons that had controlled the lives of so many of my loved ones; the curse would continue to carry on. For many years of my life I fought to overcome forces of darkness I didn't even know existed. Although I had been taught of the existence of demons in my youth, I never gave it much thought that there could actually be forces of darkness controlling my own life. When I asked God to fill me with His Holy Spirit as a child, I had no idea how much I would need it in my teens and as an adult. *"Ask and it shall be given unto you, seek and ye shall find."* Thank God, I had a desire to ask and to seek!

Believe me I know this all sounds a little crazy! I wish I could say this is normal but I know it isn't! I'm not sure if I stepped into a spiritual realm at some point in time of my life that gave me an ability to feel things an average person can't feel or if I have just discovered something we all are capable of if we are willing to believe the half has never been told. Never the less, in my mind I believe I'm supposed to share my story because God wants those who read this book to seek His face and see where He might take them. If there is anything on this earth I am certain of, it is that God told me to write this book. It has been a long process for me to get to the point that I absolutely knew God communicated with me through my thoughts. It took me a very long time to surrender to write this book because it made no sense to me why God would tell me to write a book when I'm not a writer. Why would He tell a girl who has never taken a writing class in her life and never read a book all the way through until a few years ago to write a book? This I still do not know! But I do know He did; and I prayed each time I sat down to write for him to use my hands to write what He wanted; because all I am, is a willing vessel! May the power of our all mighty God anoint the doubtful reader with an insight to see a revelation, the confused to find clarity, the broken to find hope and the tormented to find faith in the blood of the lamb! May each reader be graced with God's presence in such a way there is no room for doubt or confusion; so you will forever more be able to see the difference between fact and fiction!

Scripture Reference

Romans 8:27-29 And we know that in all things God works for the good of those who love him, who have been called according to his purpose. (NKJV)

Philippians 4:13 I can do all things through Christ who strengthens me. (NKJV)

2 Timothy 3:13 But evil men and impostors will grow worse and worse, deceiving and being deceived. (NKJV)

Romans 3:10 As it is written: "There is none righteous, no, not one; (NKJV)

Genesis 8:21 And the Lord smelled a soothing aroma. Then the Lord said in His heart, "I will never again curse the ground for man's sake, although the imagination of man's heart is evil from his youth; nor will I again destroy every living thing as I have done." (NKJV)

1 John 1:8 (NKJV) If we say that we have no sin, we deceive ourselves, and the truth is not in us.

Matthew 7:6-8 Keep Asking, Seeking, Knocking "Ask, and it will be given to you; seek, and you will find; knock, and it will be opened to you". (NKJV)

Matthew 18:8 If your hand or your foot causes your downfall, cut it off and throw it away. It is better for you to enter life maimed or lame, than to have two hands or two feet and be thrown into the eternal fire.

Romans 11:29 For the gifts and calling of God are without repentance.

Job 36:12 But if they obey not, they shall perish by the sword, and they shall die without knowledge.

John 15:12 Jesus said, This is my commandment, That ye love one another, as I have loved you.

I John 5:3 For this is the love of God, that we keep his commandments: and his commandments are not grievous.

Isaiah 6:8 Also I heard the voice of the Lord, saying, Whom shall I send, and who will go for us? Then said I, Here am I; send me.

I Timothy 6:10 For the love of money is a root of all kinds of evil.

Revelations 21:8 But the fearful, and unbelieving, and the abominable, and murderers, and whoremongers, and sorcerers, and idolaters, and all liars, shall have their part in the lake which burneth with fire and brimstone: which is the second death.

John 8:7 So when they continued asking him, he lifted up himself, and said unto them, He that is without sin among you, let him first cast a stone at her.

Printed in the United States
By Bookmasters